IMAGES
of America

TUPPER LAKE

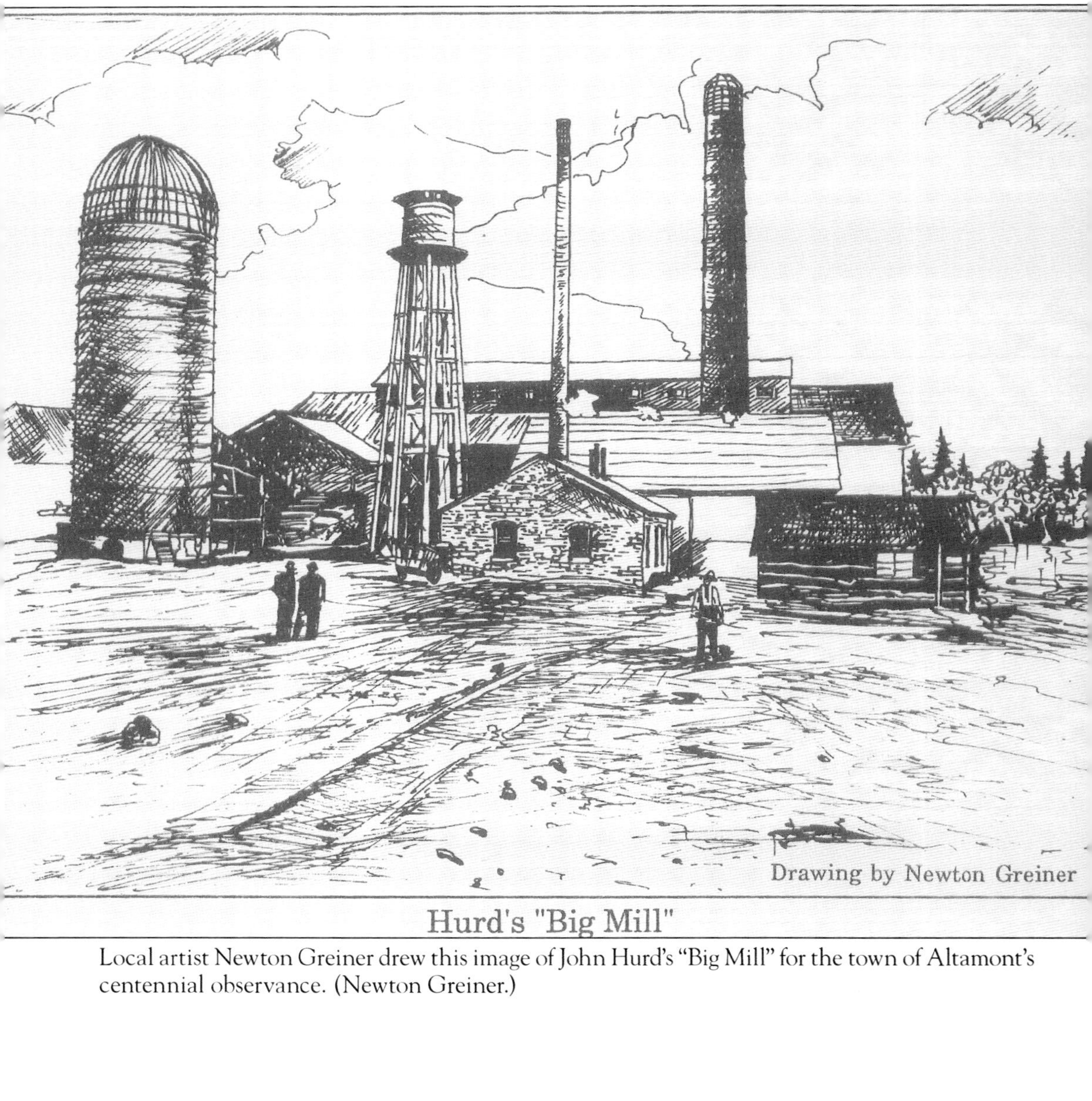

Hurd's "Big Mill"

Local artist Newton Greiner drew this image of John Hurd's "Big Mill" for the town of Altamont's centennial observance. (Newton Greiner.)

On the Cover: This lumber mill, built by John Hurd on the shore of Raquette Pond in old William McLaughlin's cow pasture, grew the village of Tupper Lake to such proportions as to admit only one rival in the Adirondacks in point of population and none in point of trade. (Goff Nelson Library Collection.)

IMAGES
of America

TUPPER LAKE

Jon Kopp

ARCADIA
PUBLISHING

ISBN 978-0-7385-7558-2

Published by Arcadia Publishing
Charleston, South Carolina

Printed in the United States of America

Library of Congress Control Number: 2010943006

For all general information, please contact Arcadia Publishing:
Telephone 843-853-2070
Fax 843-853-0044
E-mail sales@arcadiapublishing.com
For customer service and orders:
Toll-Free 1-888-313-2665

Visit us on the Internet at www.arcadiapublishing.com

I wish to dedicate this book to my family, especially my grandkids Tamika, Jon, and Garrett, who are just beginning their life, and to the amazing people of Tupper Lake, whose work ethic and sheer tenacity to find solutions will keep them in good stead for the future.

Contents

Acknowledgments

I would like to thank the Tupper Lake Library Board and their helpful staff for providing the time and space to procure many of the photographs in the book. Joy Vincent Moody and Camil and Ellen Maroun also provided photographs from their family albums.

Special thanks must go to the late historians William Frenette and Louis J. Simmons for their tireless work to tell the story of this unique logging town.

Introduction

The town of Tupper Lake comprises 76,168 acres of rolling upland, originally covered with a magnificent forest of mixed softwood sprinkled liberally with palatial lakes, winding rivers, and sparkling brooks. Before the settlement of the village, one of the more literate early visitors to Tupper Lake was S.H. Hammond, editor of the *Albany State Register.* He talked about the beauty of the lake and the plentiful wildlife when describing the area known as Moody Marsh as he saw it in the summer of 1849: "A beautiful prairie stretching away, skirted by tall trees. As you look upon it you can hardly believe that it is not a pleasant meadow and you wonder where the farmhouse and all the cattle are."

The first scatterings of white men were hunters, anglers, and trappers. These hardy souls penetrated the Tupper Lake area soon after the end of the American Revolution. In 1850, Maine outfit Pomeroy Lumber Company conducted the first logging of record. They began logging off the virgin pine and left the clearing that overlooked Raquette Pond as a souvenir. They also left behind their foreman, William McLaughlin, who did very well selling building lots in the same clearing during the boom years of the 1890s.

Around midnight on July 29, 1899, the most devastating fire to ever sweep through an Adirondack community burnt 169 buildings to the ground. Undaunted by the loss, the spirited pioneers rebuilt the village. Within a few years, the village was restored and back to business as usual.

The first logging ventures brought a rush of settlers. Sawmills were erected, and dams were built along the Raquette River. Soon, Tupper Lake logs were feeding hungry mills as far away as Potsdam. For the next century, logging would be the signature industry of Tupper Lake. The most famous mill was the Hurd Mill, which once sawed over a million board feet of lumber in one day, a world record at the time.

As the logging industry grew, the railroad arrived. As the junction point for two railroads, downtown Tupper Lake became the leading rail center in the Adirondacks, with a sprawling freight shed, offices, extensive yard facilities, water towers, and a coal chute. It also featured a roundhouse where upwards of 40 men were kept busy maintaining the locomotives operating on the Utica-Montreal and Tupper-Ottawa line. Today, efforts are being made to bring the railroad back to Tupper Lake.

The wealthy discovered the wilderness and built great camps and estates on surrounding lakes such as Litchfield Castle on Lake Marion and Nahasane Lodge on Lake Lila. Along the shores of Tupper Lake, Colonel Barber erected his great camp and outbuildings, which would eventually become the American Legion Veteran Mountain Camp.

The Sunmount Veterans Hospital has contributed greatly to the growth and economic stability of Tupper Lake. In the 1920s, in an amazing display of community spirit, the growing village raised $20,000 to purchase the 160-acre Hosley farm and then offered it to the federal government for $1. The offer was accepted on June 26, 1922, and ground was broken that summer. On August 15, 1924, a crowd of 2,500 people celebrated the new hospital's dedication with a fitting ceremony. Today, Sunmount exists as a development center and is still the lifeblood for the community.

One

The Wilderness Years

Pomeroy Lumber Company centered Tupper Lake's first logging operation near the east shore of Raquette Pond in the 1850s. Some 40 years later, the clearing that was left after the virgin pine was cut off became Tupper Lake Village.

In 1871, the state built a reservoir below Raquette Pond, which backed up the river for miles and killed hundreds of thousands of growing trees. It was an ugly scar to the wilderness and was written about by many early visitors to the region.

Up until the last half of the 19th century, Tupper Lake was unknown wilderness to all except a few hardy pioneer settlers who eked out a living working for lumber camps or living off the land through subsistence farming and seasonal market hunting. In those days, very few people lived in the neighborhood of Tupper Lake, just the families of William McLaughlin, Sim Moody, Mart Moody, Sim Ratty, George McBride, and Ernest Johnson, living at intervals of a mile or so.

It was not until William Henry Harrison Murray, or "Adirondack Murray," a charismatic clergyman and author originally from Connecticut, wrote an influential series of articles that the area became popular. Murray promoted the north woods as health-giving, claiming that the rustic nobility typical of Adirondack woodsmen came from their intimacy with wilderness. Eventually, his articles were published as a book, *Adventures in the Wilderness; or, Camp-Life in the Adirondacks*, in 1869. The encouraging spirituality of the book made it extremely successful, and it went through eight printings in its first year. The author's followers, "Murray's Fools," started pouring into the Adirondacks wilderness. Small cabins located on strategic locations along lakes and portages were expanded into small lodges and, by the end of the century, major hotels.

By 1890, John Hurd pushed his Northern Adirondack Railroad to Tupper Lake, the first line to reach here. A short time later, Dr. Seward Webb's Malone and Mohawk Railroad was built. Dr. Webb's rail line was the first to traverse the Adirondacks and crossed the Hurd line in Tupper Lake in 1891. The intersection, known as "the junction," with its roundhouse, shops, and large railroad yard, developed into the most important rail junction point between Utica and Malone.

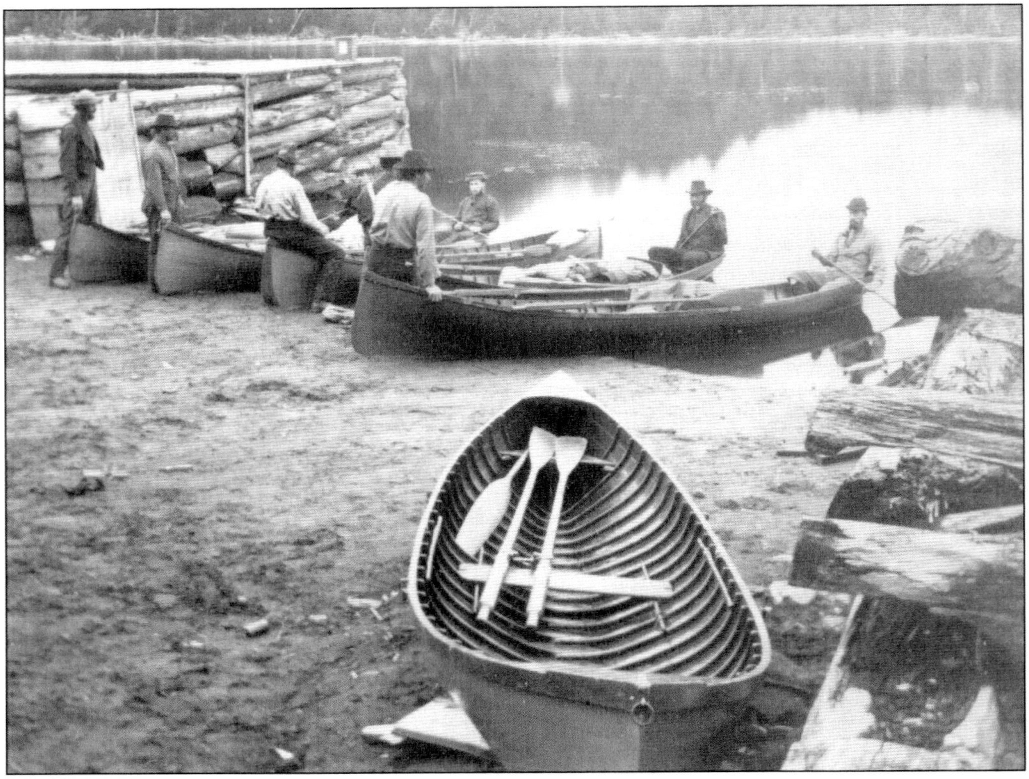

If one wanted to trek to Tupper Lake in the second half of the 19th century, the journey would start here, on the northern shore of Lower Saranac Lake at Martin's launch, where a hired guide would lead the traveler by boat. Only after crossing three wilderness lakes and an ancient Indian carry to the Raquette River could one reach Tupper Lake. (Author's collection.)

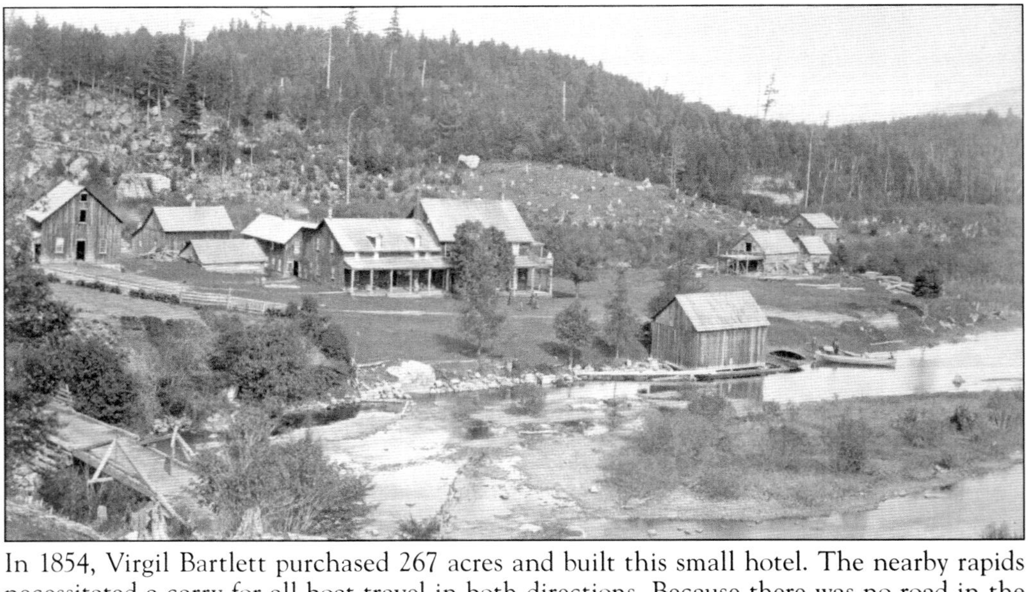

In 1854, Virgil Bartlett purchased 267 acres and built this small hotel. The nearby rapids necessitated a carry for all boat travel in both directions. Because there was no road in the vicinity, all transportation was funneled through this bottleneck, much to Bartlett's advantage. (Author's collection.)

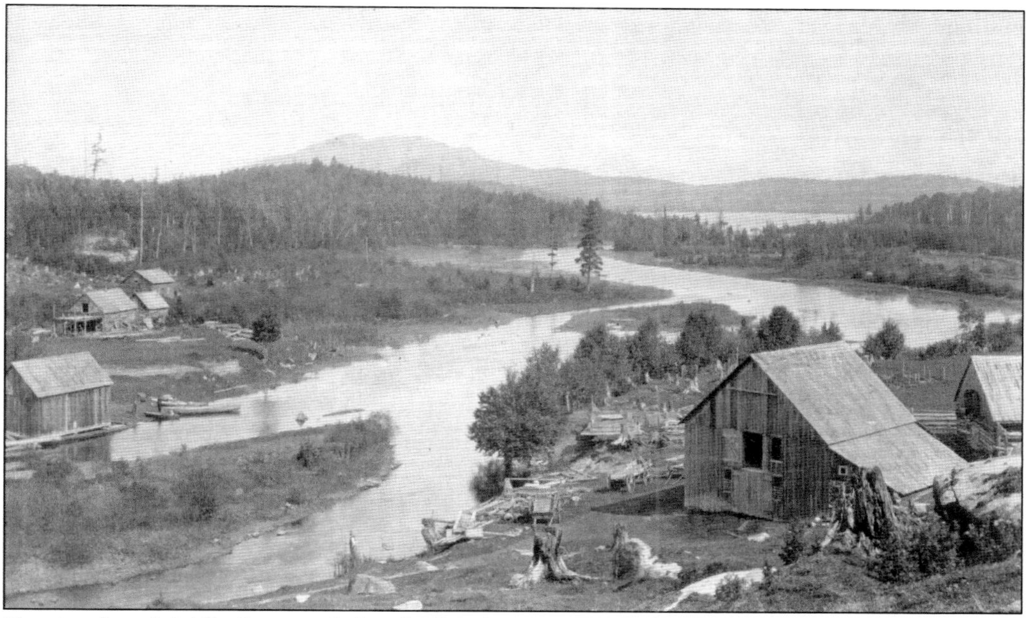

Coming from Middle Saranac Lake, the Bartlett House was the first stop. From there, boats had to be carried to Upper Saranac Lake. The Saranac River drops 30 feet in two tenths of a mile, which makes for a fast, rough current, providing fishermen with some of the best trout fishing in the area. (Author's collection.)

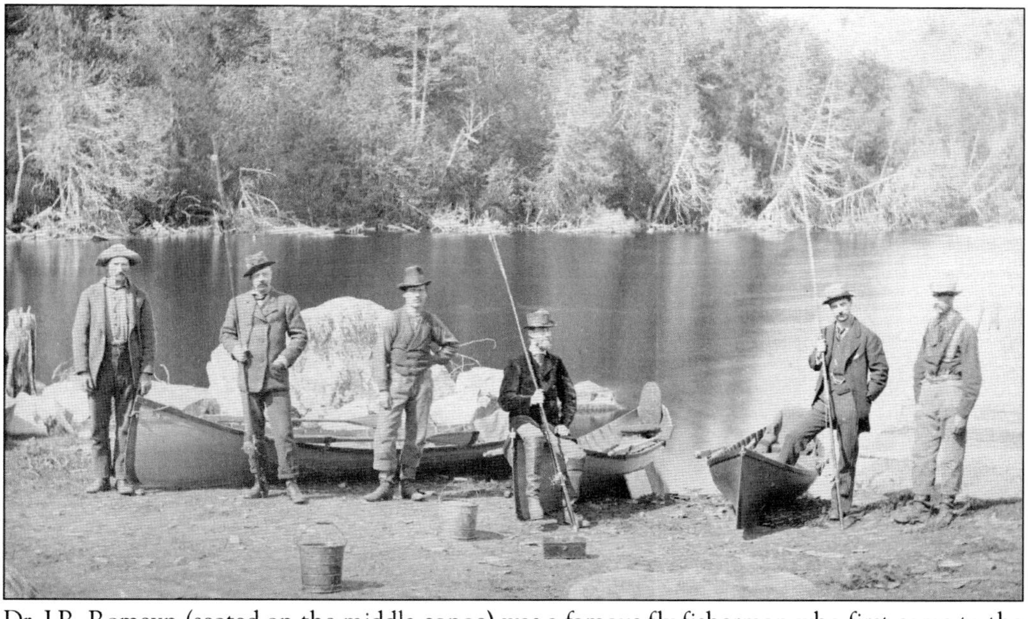

Dr. J.R. Romeyn (seated on the middle canoe) was a famous fly-fisherman who first came to the Bartlett House from Keeseville in 1855. He returned each spring to fish trout at the rapids. An ardent fly-fisher, he was influential in promoting the art, and he believed that the best fly-fishing was found in the rapids between Middle and Upper Saranac Lake. (Author's collection.)

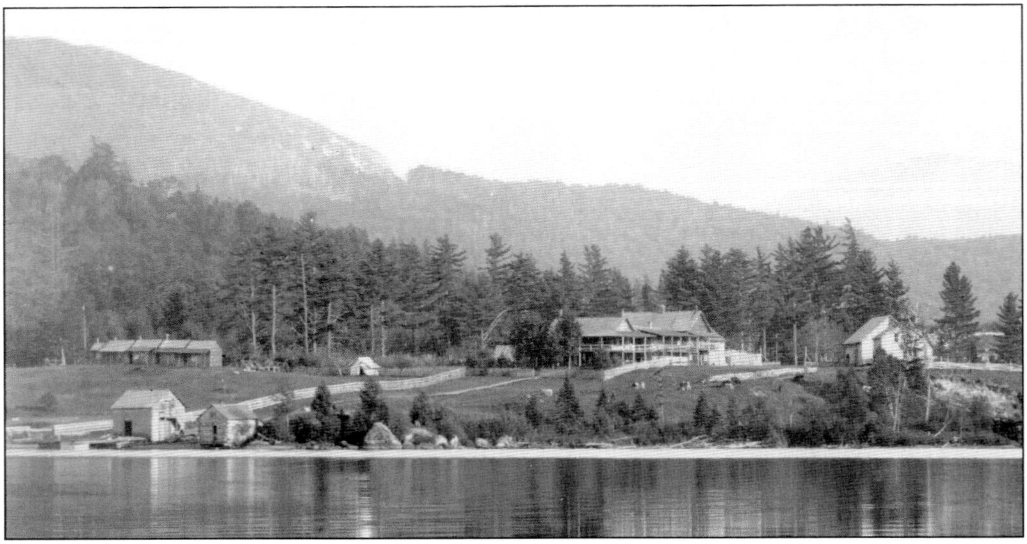

Jesse Corey was the first white settler on Upper Saranac Lake, building his first home at Sweeney Carry in 1830, before moving out west. But in 1850, he returned to build Rustic Lodge here at Indian Carry. (Author's collection.)

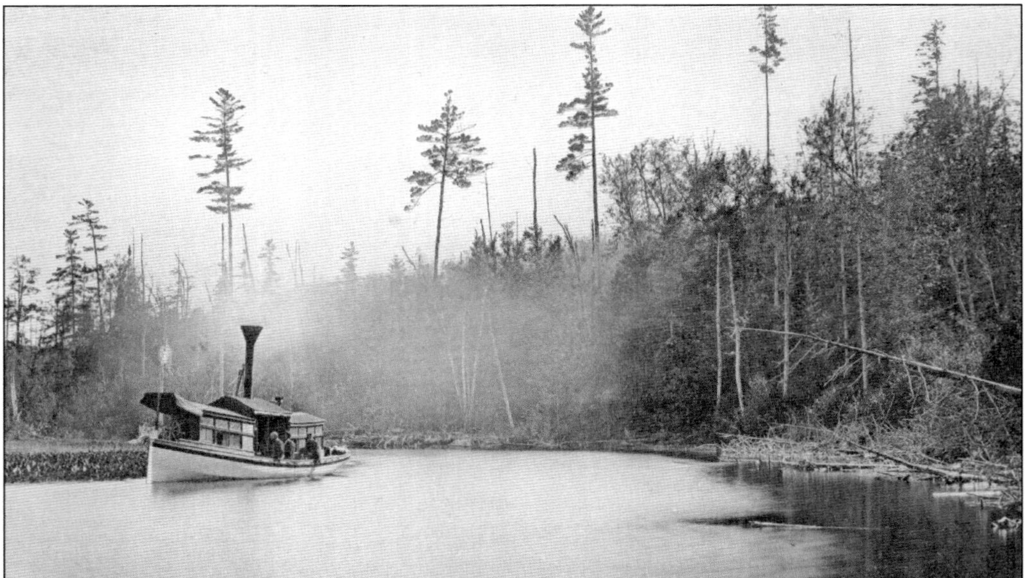

Early steamships delivered mail and supplies up the Saranac River's complex of large lakes and portages. The need for the steamers grew as the hotels grew in size, accommodating the expanding group of people who answered the call of the Adirondacks. (Author's collection.)

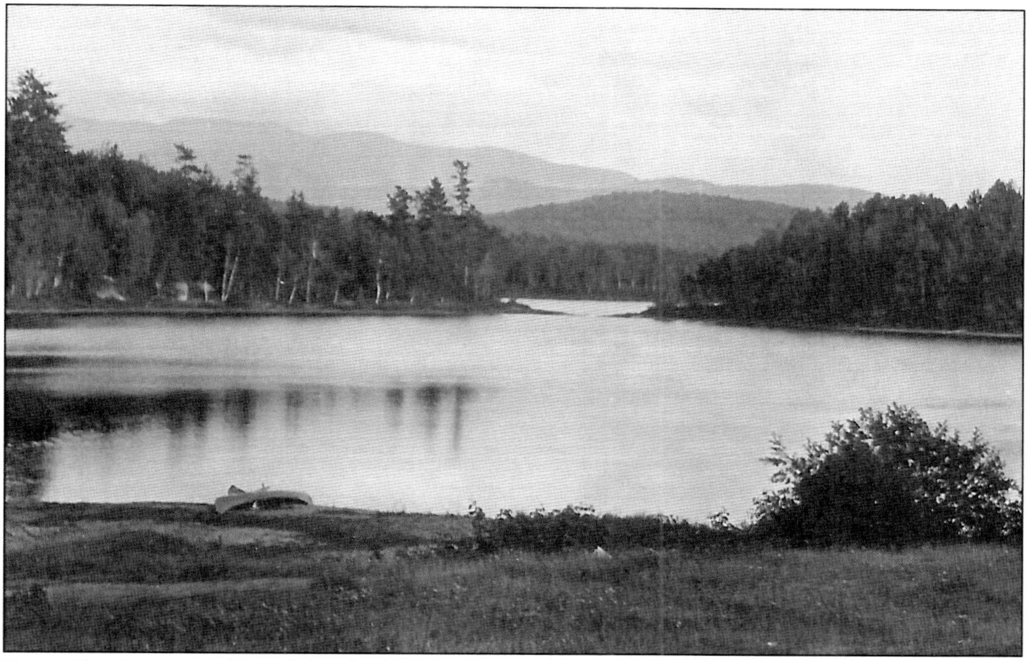

Stony Creek is a winding, sluggish three miles of flat water whose marshy shores were lined with tall grass and the ragged, sprawling silver maples that still flourish today. Traveling to Tupper Lake in the second half of the 19th century required one to glide through a series of three ponds, the Stony Creek Ponds. From the other end of the creek, where it spills into the Raquette River, it was 20 miles to Big Tupper Lake. (Author's collection.)

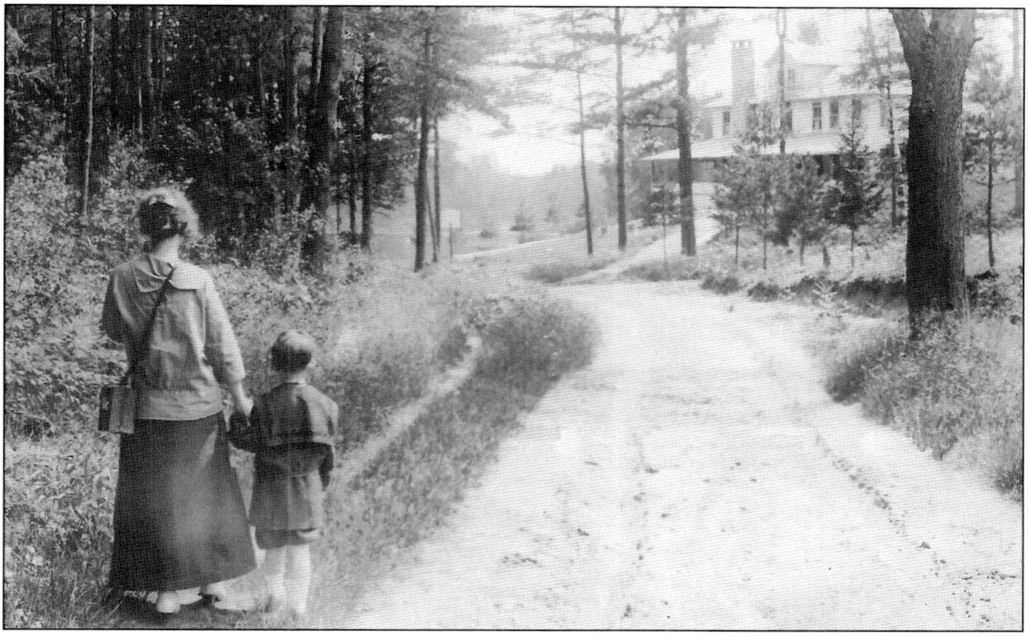

The Hiawatha House was located at the south end of Indian Carry, among the trees on the north side of the first of the Stony Creek Ponds. The house, with its picturesque surroundings, was a popular sporting center, with game and fish aplenty. Conveyance across the Indian Carry to this point cost 75¢ for boat and luggage. (Author's collection.)

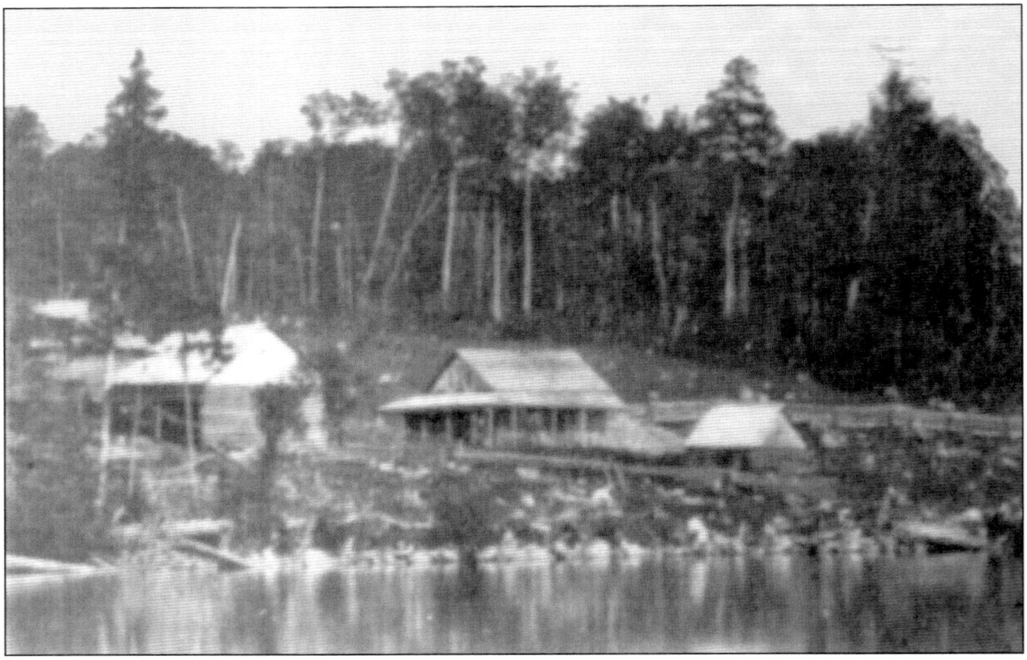

This is a rare photograph of the old Daniel's Cabin, erected by the aggressive lumber king of the Saranacs, Col. Christopher Norton, near Sweeney Carry on Upper Saranac Lake. It controlled the lake end of the carry leading directly to the Raquette River and Tupper Lake, the main river route through the region going north to the Potsdam mills. (Author's collection.)

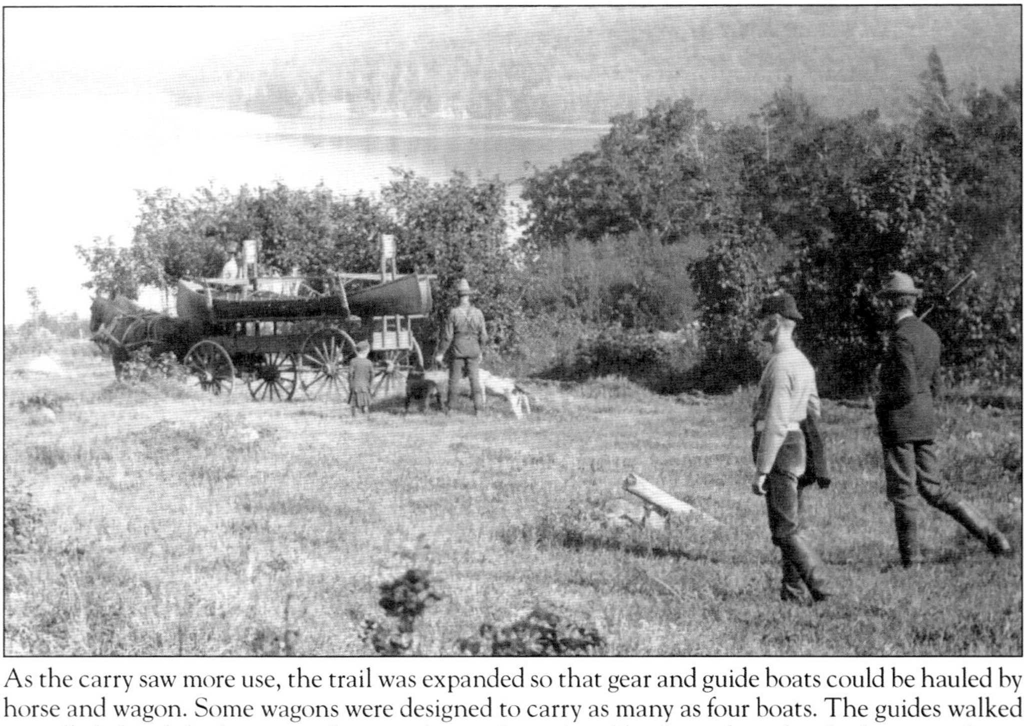

As the carry saw more use, the trail was expanded so that gear and guide boats could be hauled by horse and wagon. Some wagons were designed to carry as many as four boats. The guides walked casually behind the horses, a pleasant change from the older days when they had to carry boats and gear themselves. (Author's collection.)

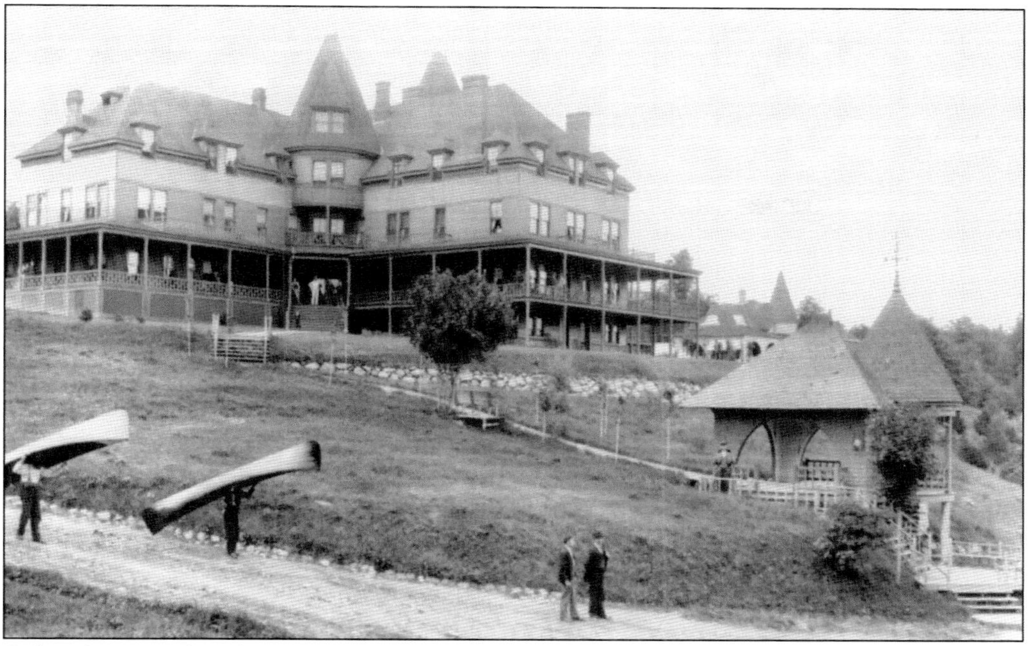

Colonel Norton hired Oatman C. Coville to settle at the lake end of Sweeney Carry. Coville purchased 40 acres from Norton and built a rough halfway house to accommodate the increasing flow of seasonal visitors. After Coville's death, T. Edmund Krumholz and a man named Smith bought out Mrs. Coville and built Wawbeek Hotel, one of the finest in the mountains. (Author's collection.)

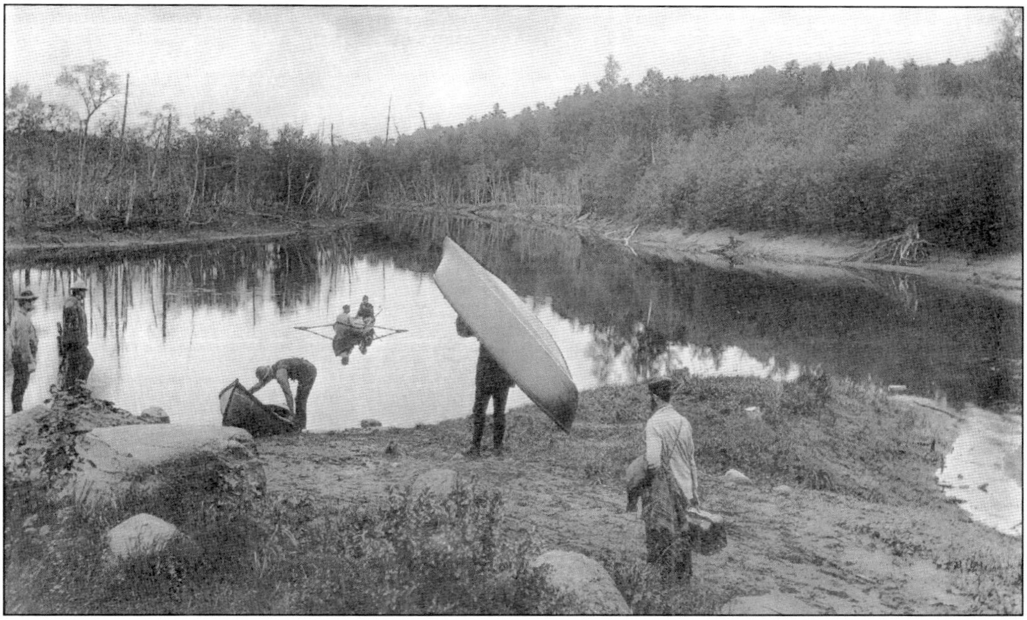

Colonel Norton also hired Oliver Tromblee to settle at the Raquette River end of the carry, giving him control of the land between Upper Saranac Lake and the river, an important piece of river real estate. Tromblee built a small cabin, and it is here, at Tromblee's landing, where Seneca Ray Stoddard (foreground), the famous Adirondack photographer, carries his camera and tripod to the guide boat that will take him the rest of the way to Tupper Lake in the mid- to late 1800s. (Author's collection.)

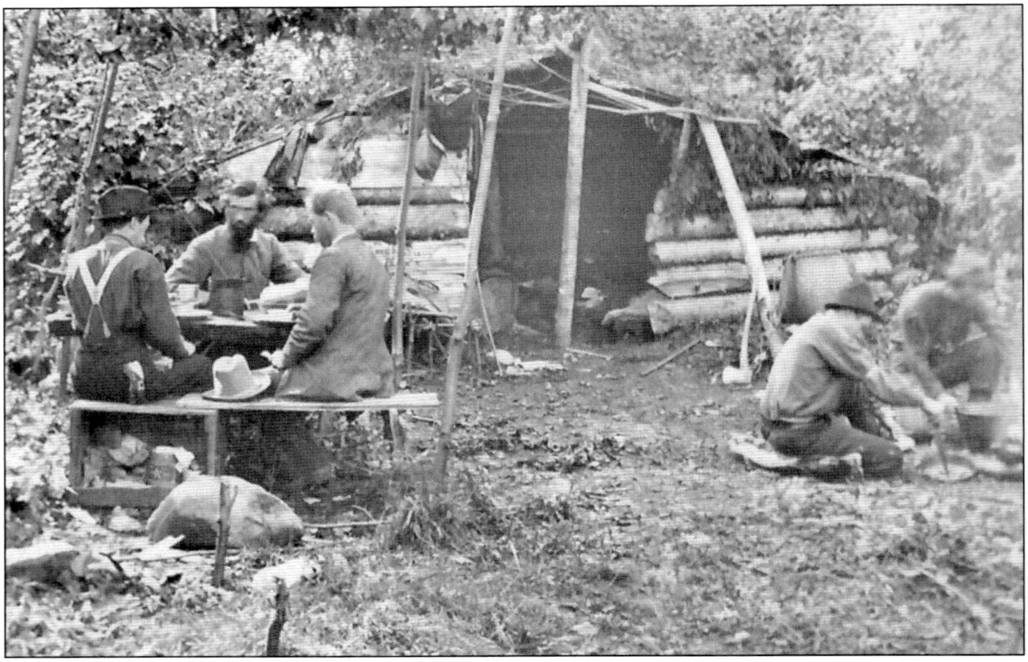

Seneca Ray Stoddard, with the beard, was an American landscape photographer from Glens Falls whose writings and photographs helped popularize the Adirondacks. He was also a naturalist, writer, poet, artist, and cartographer. In this photograph of him and his traveling party, notice the string attached to the unseen camera. (Author's collection.)

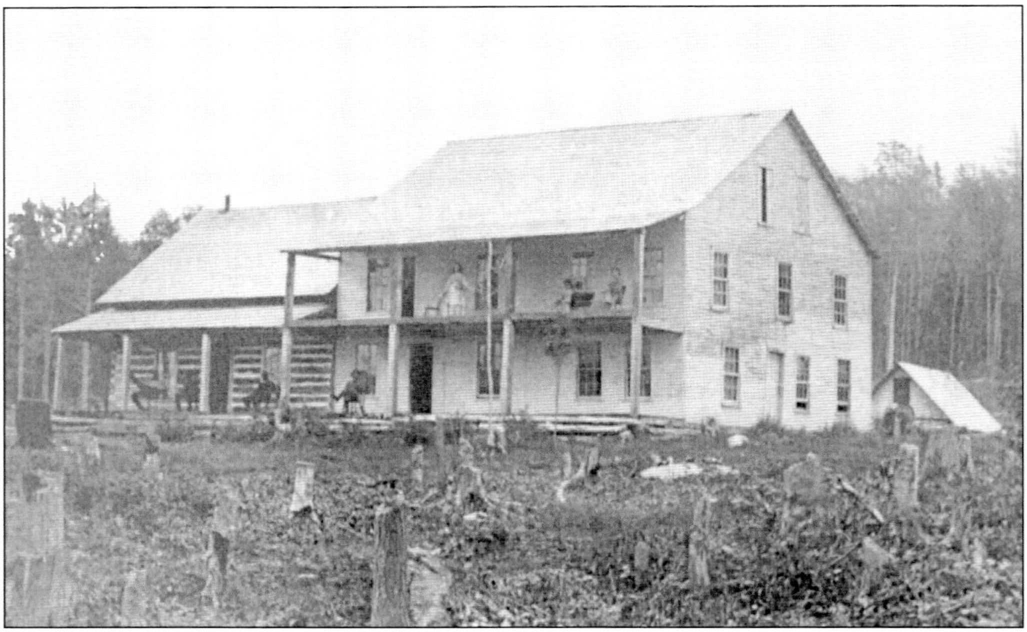

Upon one's eventual arrival at Tupper Lake, their first stop would be at "Uncle Mart's," the first hotel on Tupper Lake, built by Mart Moody and seen here in its primitive early stages. Stumps are still in the front yard from the recent clearing for the new addition on the original log cabin. It was later named Mount Morris House for the mountain that loomed behind it, and it eventually became the Prince Albert Hotel. (Author's collection.)

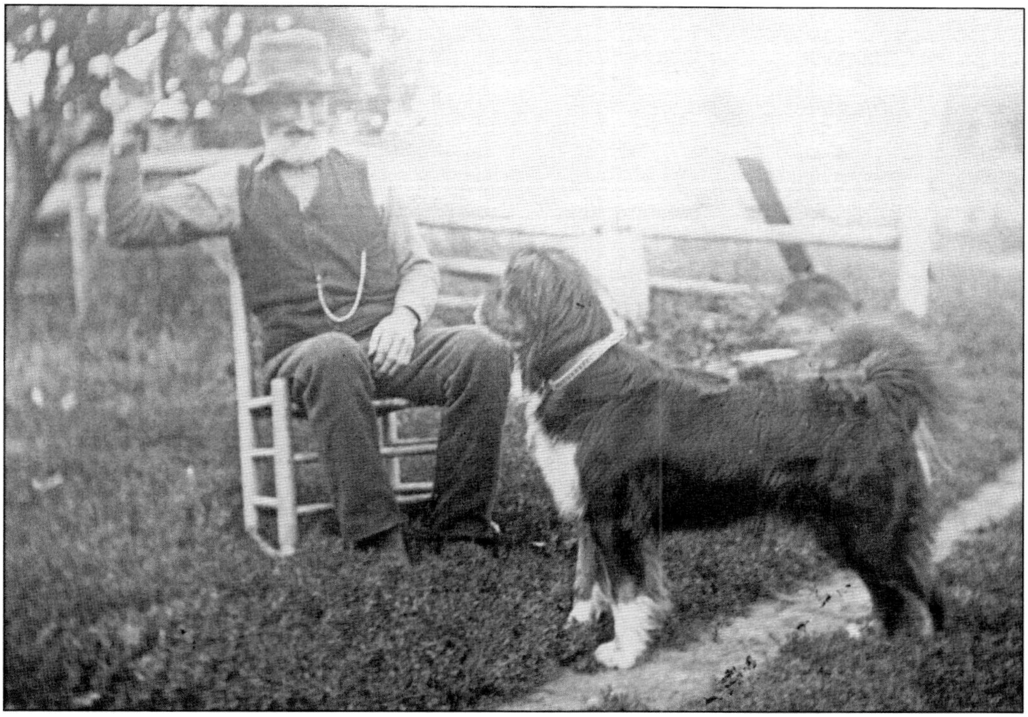

Mart Moody's front yard was an arm of Big Tupper Lake. Behind the house, a garden plot spread from the little ravine up to the edge of the forest. Moody raised vegetables there and sold them to summer campers. Those who found him at work with his hoe noted that he always tucked the bottom of his trouser leg into his heavy woolen socks. (Author's collection.)

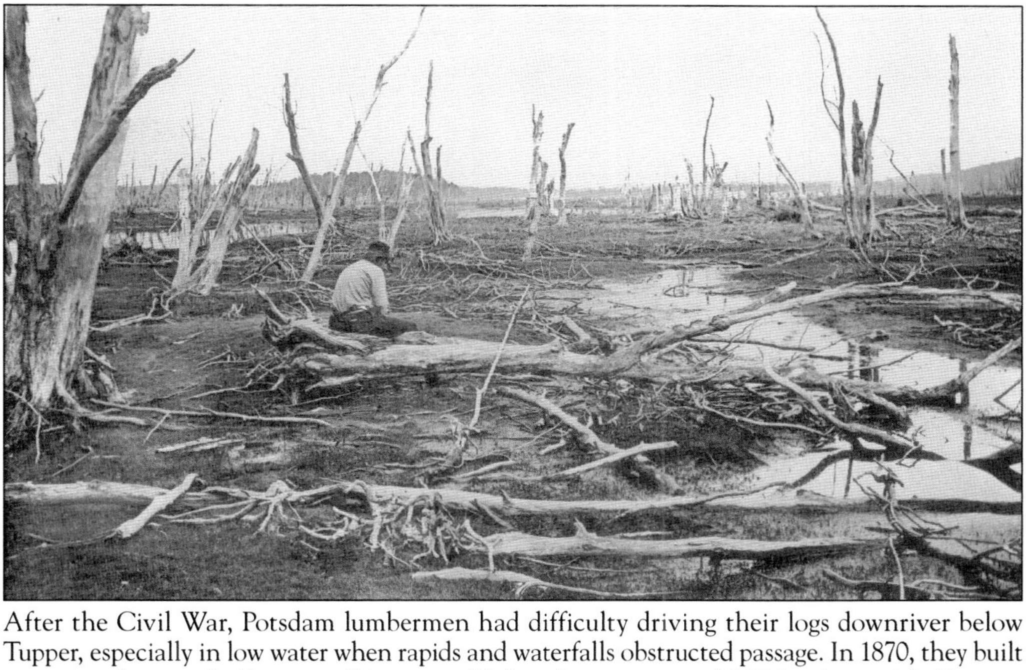

After the Civil War, Potsdam lumbermen had difficulty driving their logs downriver below Tupper, especially in low water when rapids and waterfalls obstructed passage. In 1870, they built a massive dam on the Raquette River, over 10 feet above water and 300 feet long with 10 gates, resulting in 30 miles of upstream flooding. (Author's collection.)

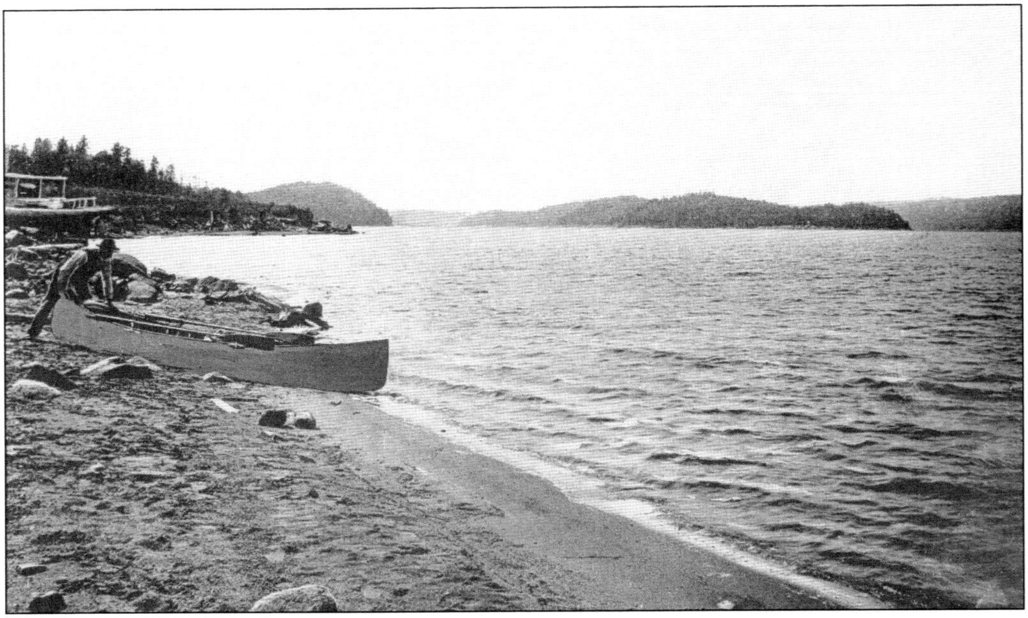

Seneca Ray Stoddard snapped this photograph near the foot of Tupper Lake in 1889. One of the two steamboats then plying area waters is visible to the left, "high and dry" on the bank. (Author's collection.)

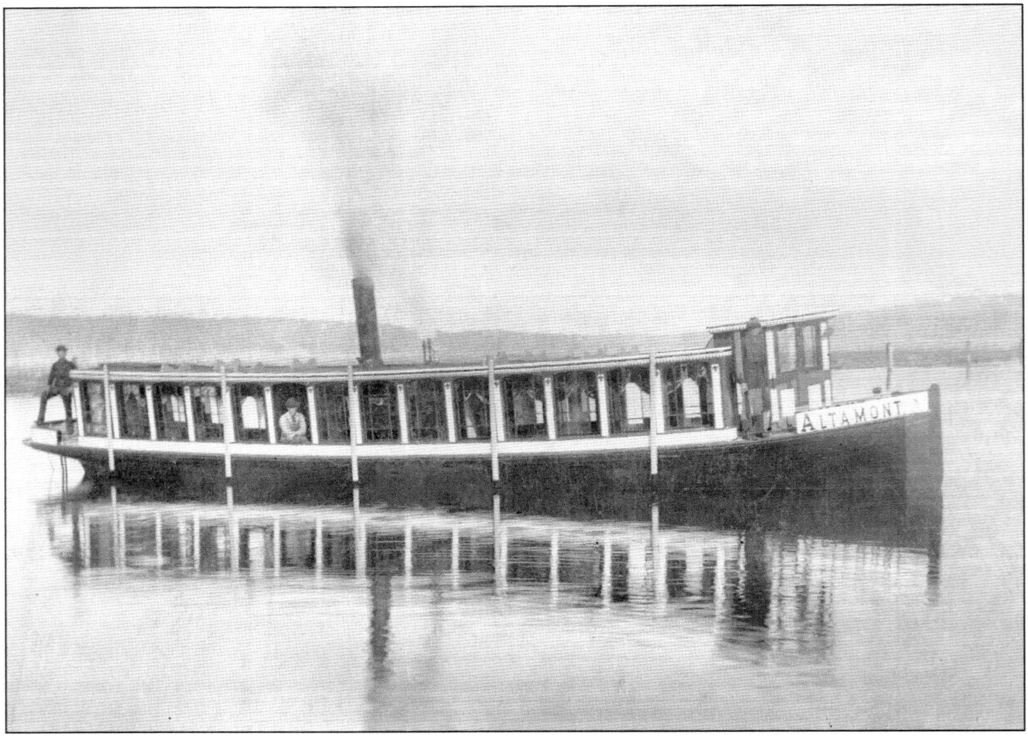

As the wilderness years waned in the late 1800s, larger steamers like the *Altamont* arrived on the lake, much to the chagrin of local guides who lost business to them. Holding as many as 30 passengers, the *Altamont* made daily trips from Owen's Dock to Bog River Falls and Tromblee's Landing on the Raquette River. (Goff Nelson Library Collection.)

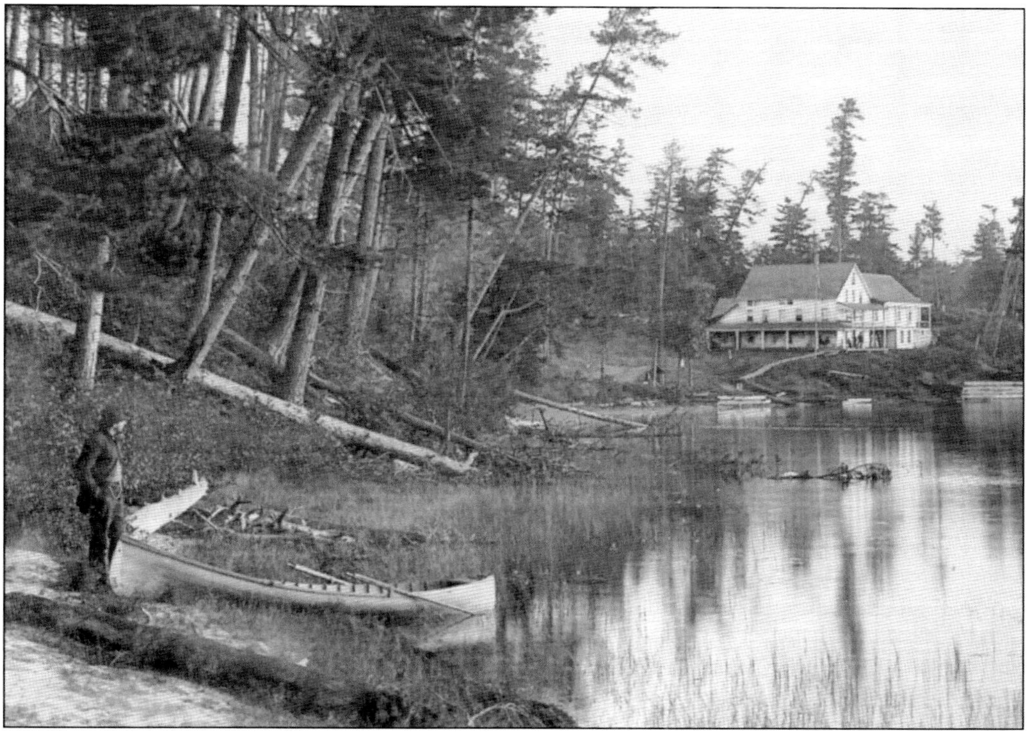

Pliny Robbins was one of the most active steamship operators on Tupper Lake. For many years, he and his wife, Anne, ran the Hamilton House on Little Tupper Lake and the local steamer *Forrester*. (Author's collection.)

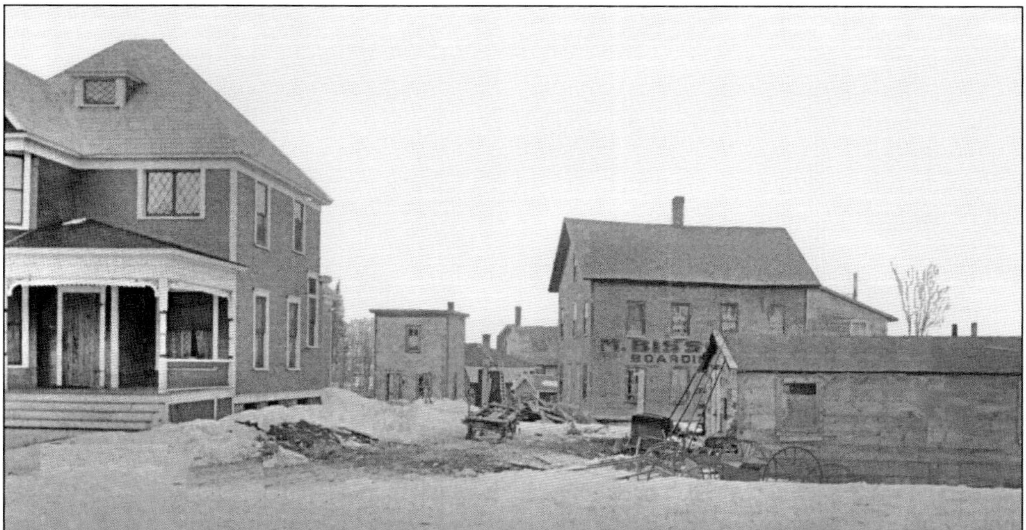

This rare photograph shows the Bissonette boardinghouse and the home of Ben J. Fountain, who operated a livery there. Fountain stayed in town and eventually established one of Tupper Lake's earliest auto concerns, Fountain's Garage, which he operated until his death in June 1935, when the extensive property at 141 Park Street was purchased by local Ford dealer Thomas K. Somers. The Bissonette boardinghouse provided housing for itinerant carpenters and mill workers and stood near the present location of Vachereau and Park Streets. (Goff Nelson Library Collection.)

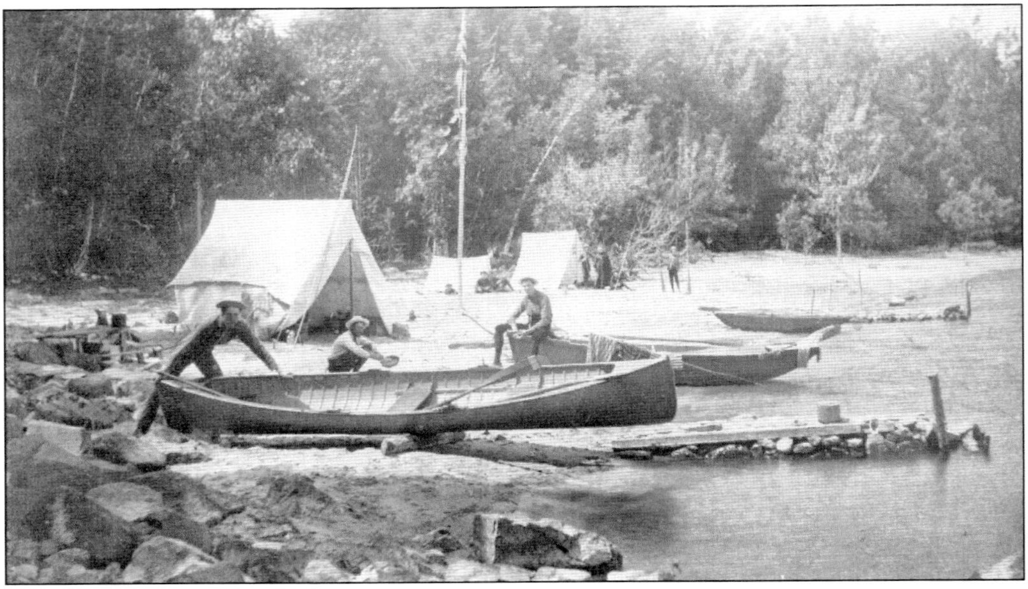

Although sportsmen had always shown interest in the Adirondacks, the publication of William H.H. Murray's *Adventures in the Wilderness; or, Camp-Life in the Adirondacks* in 1869 brought a flood of tourists to the area. Here, the guides who lived off that tourism have set up tents along the shore in preparation for a deer hunt. (Author's collection.)

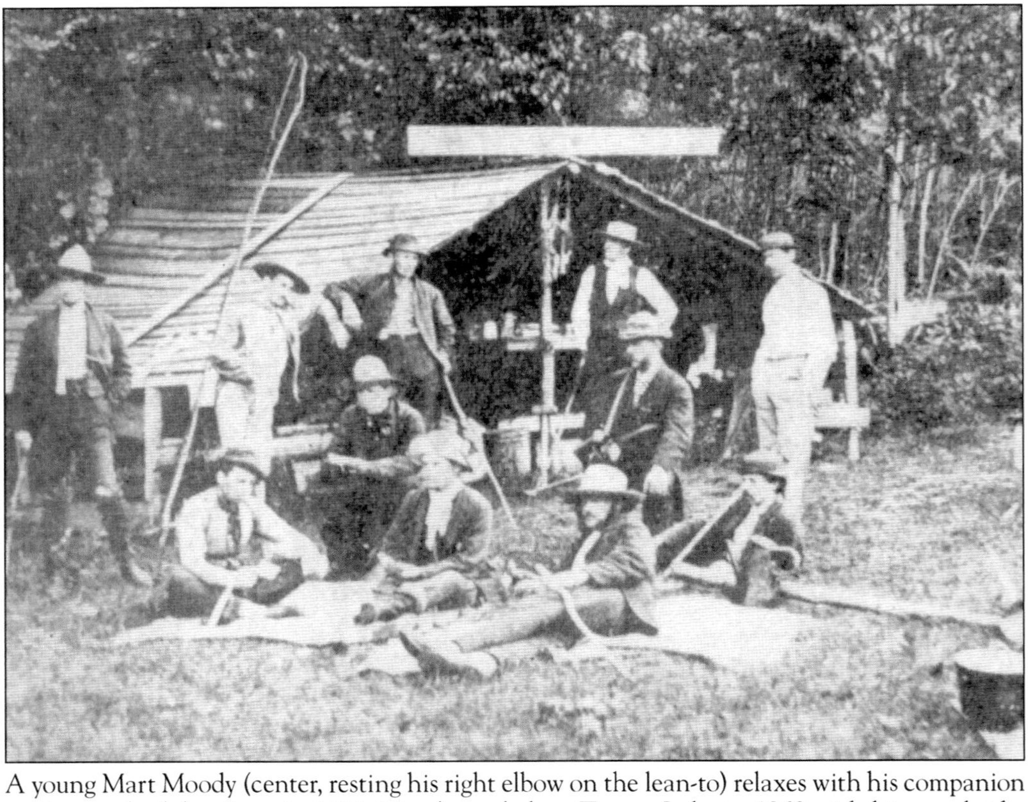

A young Mart Moody (center, resting his right elbow on the lean-to) relaxes with his companion guides on the lake. Born in 1833, Moody settled on Tupper Lake in 1868 with his new bride, Minerva M. Reid, and built the Mount Morris House. (Author's collection.)

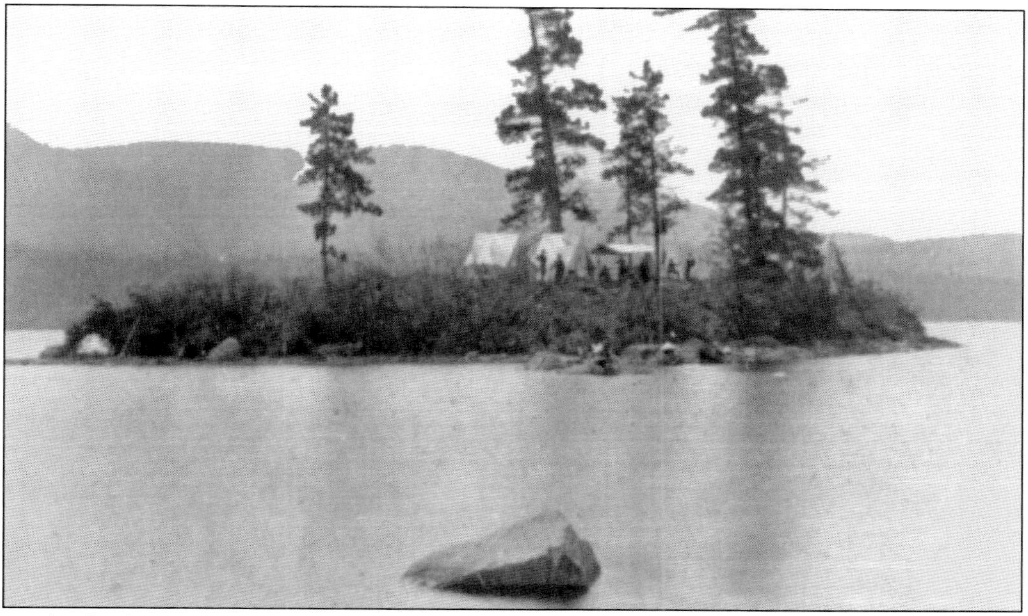

Mink Island was one of Harvey Moody's favorite campgrounds when he guided on Tupper Lake. Harvey was one of the seven sons of Mart Moody's older brother, Jacob, the first permanent settler in Saranac Lake. Another brother of Mart and Jacob, Cortez "Cort" Moody, also an early settler, built a small cabin at the foot of Tupper Lake. (Author's collection.)

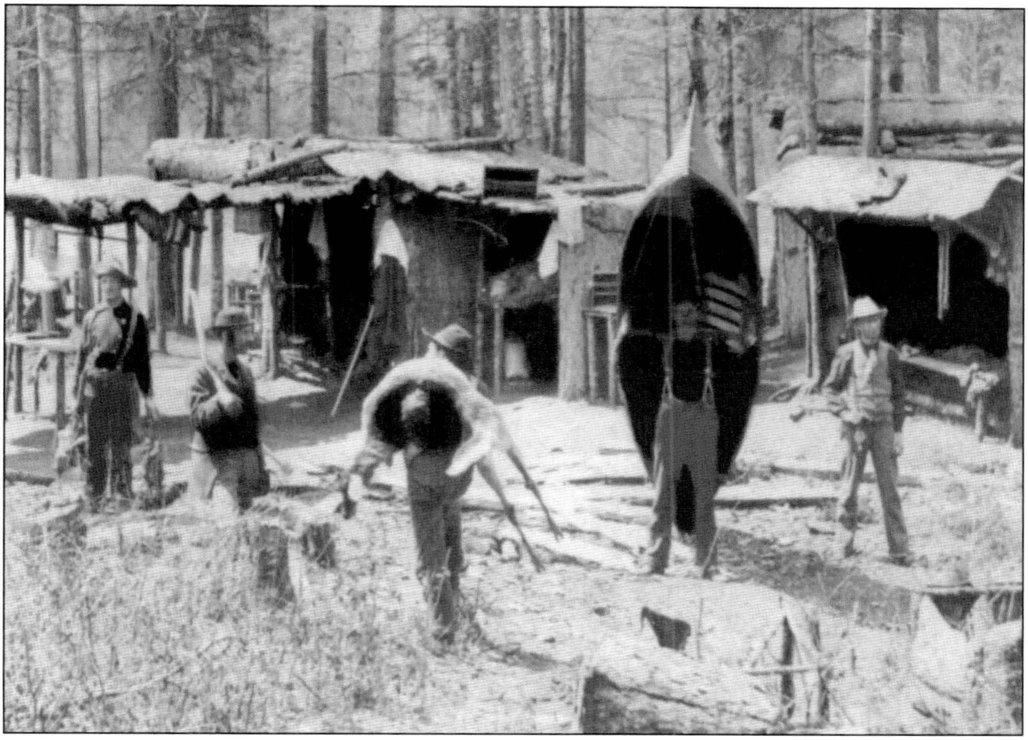

On successful days, the guides' camp would end the evening with a captured deer. On this night, the men would eat venison as they gathered around the campfire recounting the day's exploits. (Author's collection.)

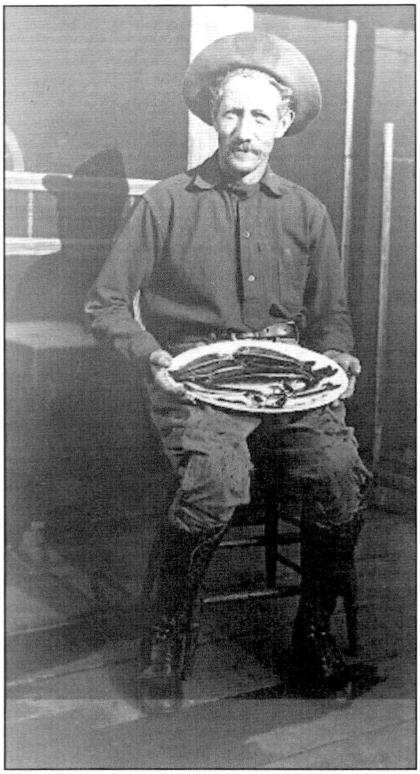

Brook trout and the larger lake trout were a delicacy at the early logging camps and standard fare for the first pioneer families. They are still plentiful in the local waters. (Author's collection.)

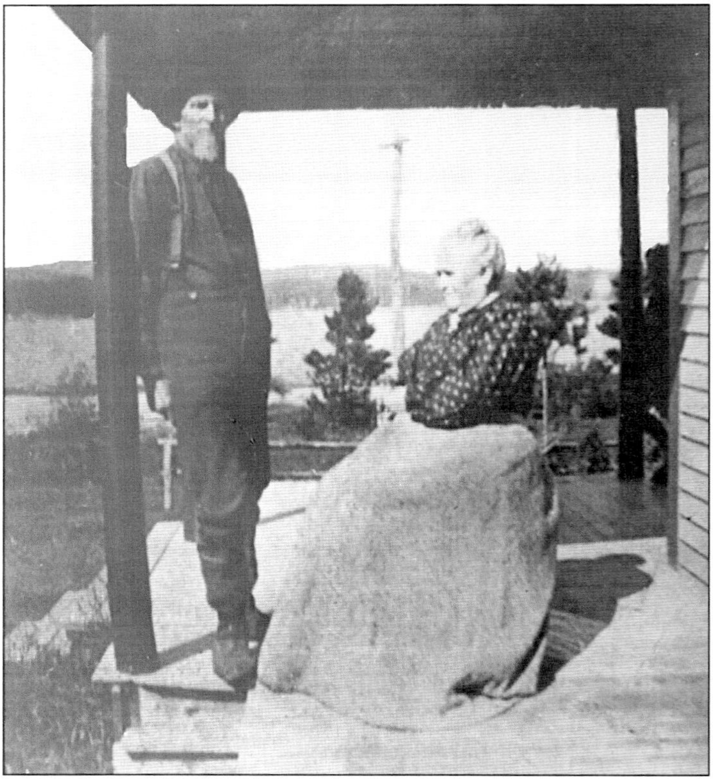

"Uncle Mart" relaxes on his porch overlooking Tupper Lake with his beloved wife, "Aunt Minerva." They married on January 6, 1861, and were affable, well-liked pillars of the wilderness years. "Aunt Minerva" continued to run the Moody Post Office after Mart's death in 1910. (Goff Nelson Library Collection.)

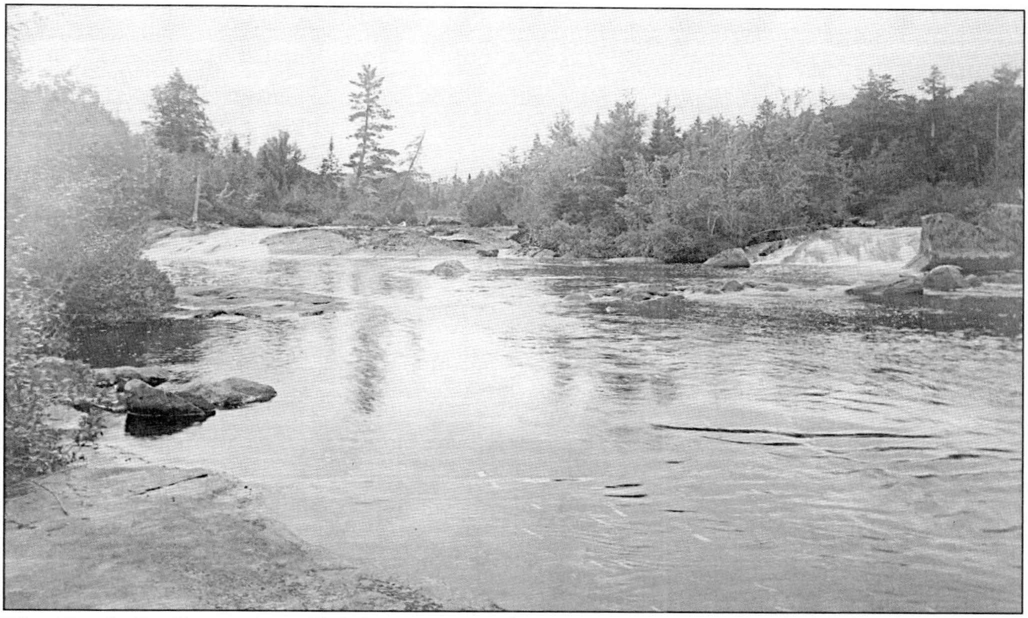

The 18-mile Bog River, also called the Bog River Flow, originates near the sources of the Oswegatchie River in Hamilton County and flows through Lows Lake and Hitchens Pond, cascading into Tupper Lake at Bog River Falls. Seneca Ray Stoddard took this photograph of the river, right before the falls, on his 1888 visit. (Goff Nelson Library Collection.)

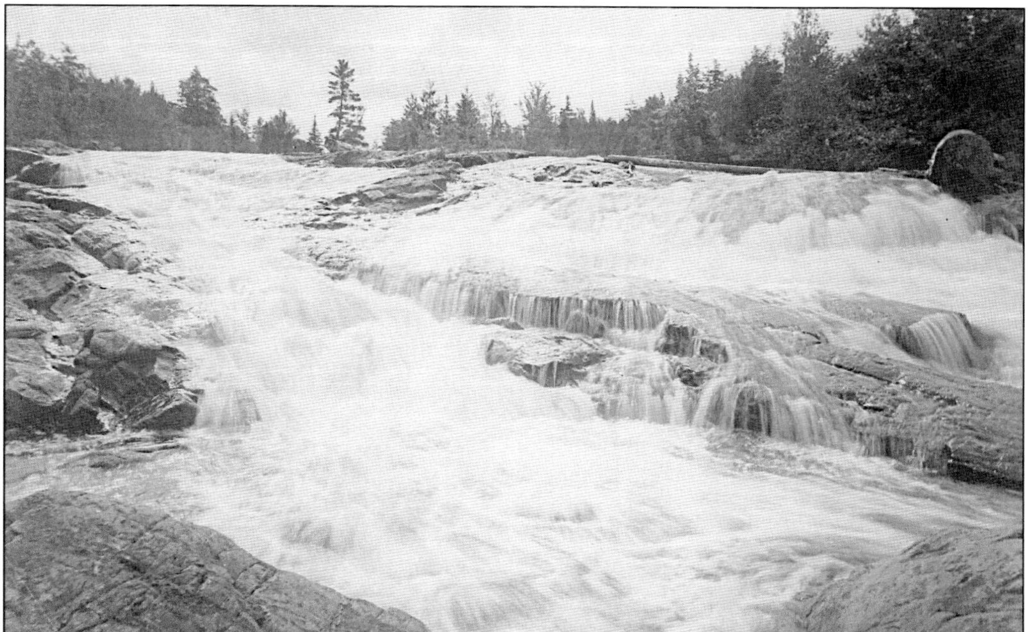

As the river gushes down the exposed bedrock, it creates a thick cloud of white foam where the water meets the air. During summer rains and spring thaw, the aerated water sent food to the base of the lake, making it a fishermen's paradise. The falls are still a popular swimming spot in the summer, and the flat rock makes an excellent waterslide down to the lake. (Goff Nelson Library Collection.)

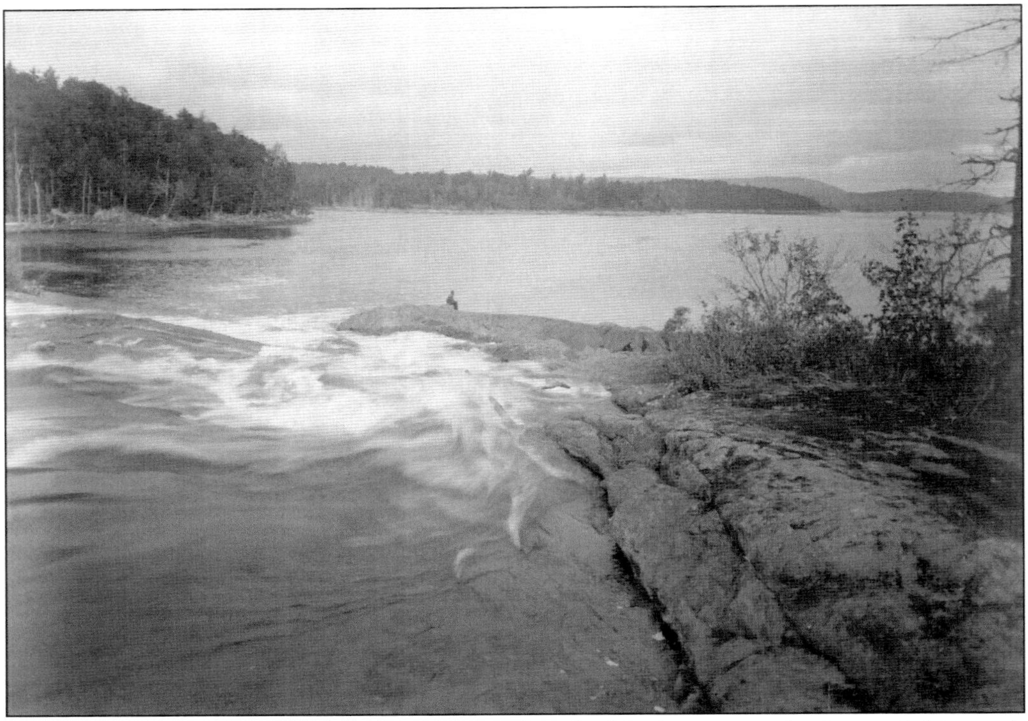
This view from the top of the falls shows Seneca Ray Stoddard sitting on the famous fishing rock that juts out from the shoreline. (Author's collection.)

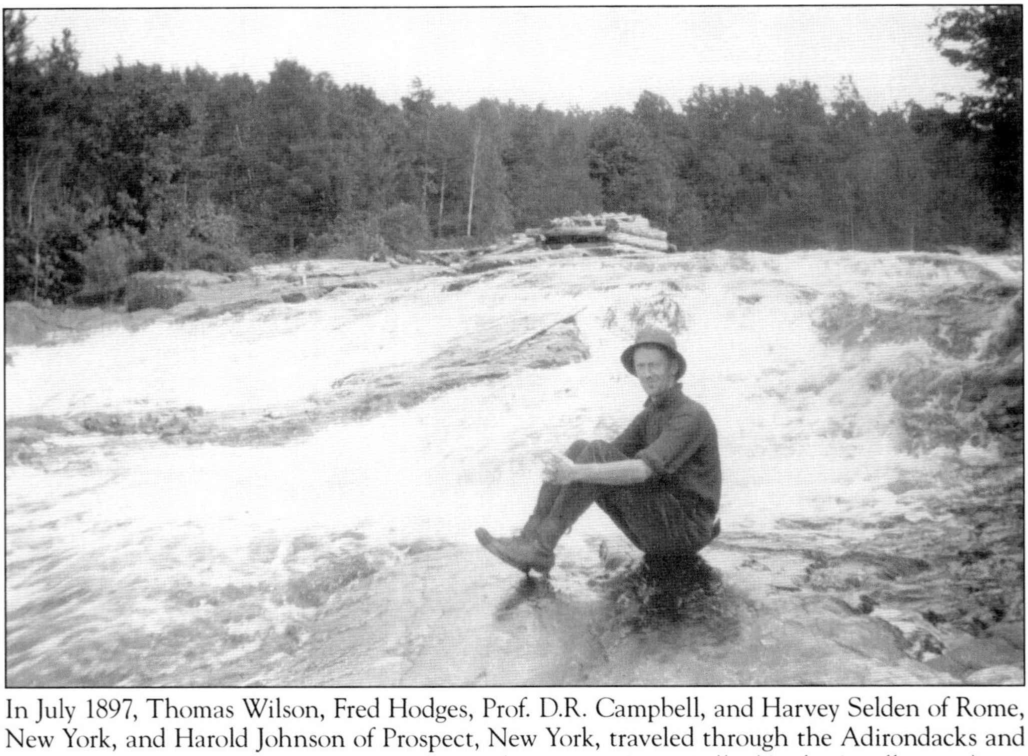
In July 1897, Thomas Wilson, Fred Hodges, Prof. D.R. Campbell, and Harvey Selden of Rome, New York, and Harold Johnson of Prospect, New York, traveled through the Adirondacks and took photographs. Here, Selden poses on a rock near Bog River Falls. (Author's collection.)

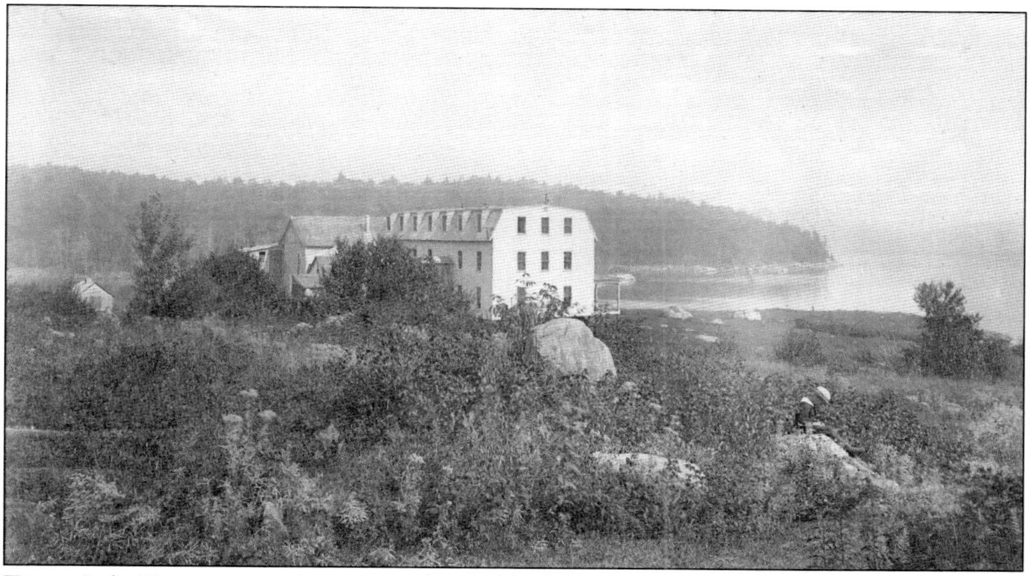

Tupper Lake House was on the western shore of the lake, near the south end. It was about 35 miles by water from Saranac Lake, making it a pleasant day's journey by guide boat. But the opening of John Hurd's Northern Adirondack Railroad made it possible to leave New York City in the evening at 6:25 and reach Tupper Lake House in time for dinner the next night. (Goff Nelson Library Collection.)

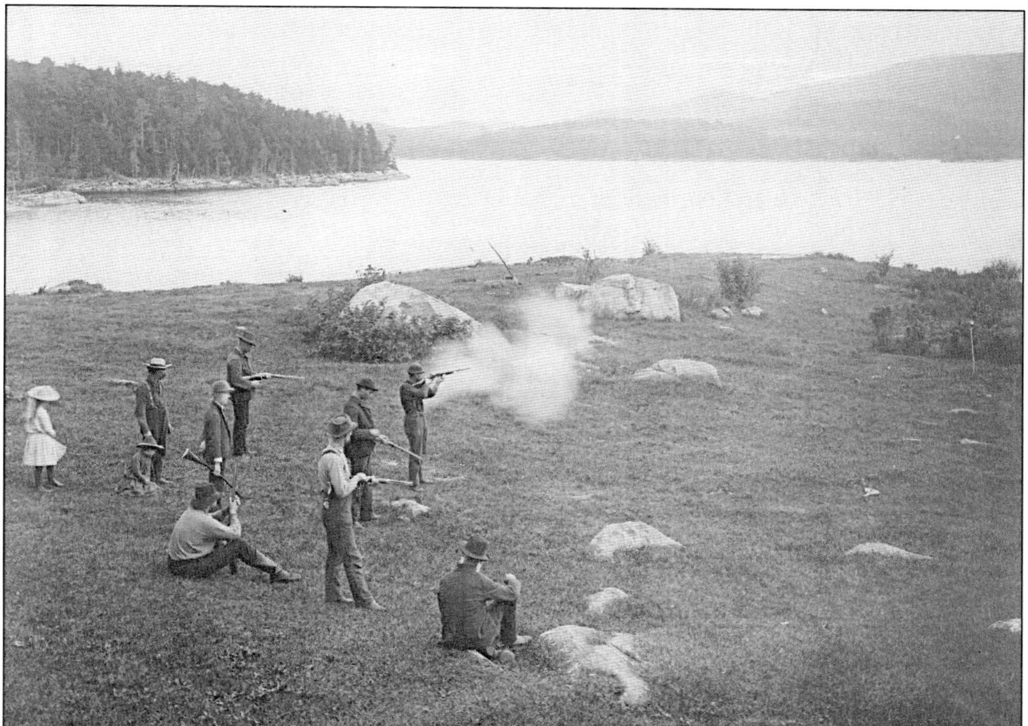

Turkey shoots were common in the early days of the lake when a man's rifle seemed to be just another appendage to his body. This group of sportsmen and guides takes target shots at a can propped on a pole. (Author's collection.)

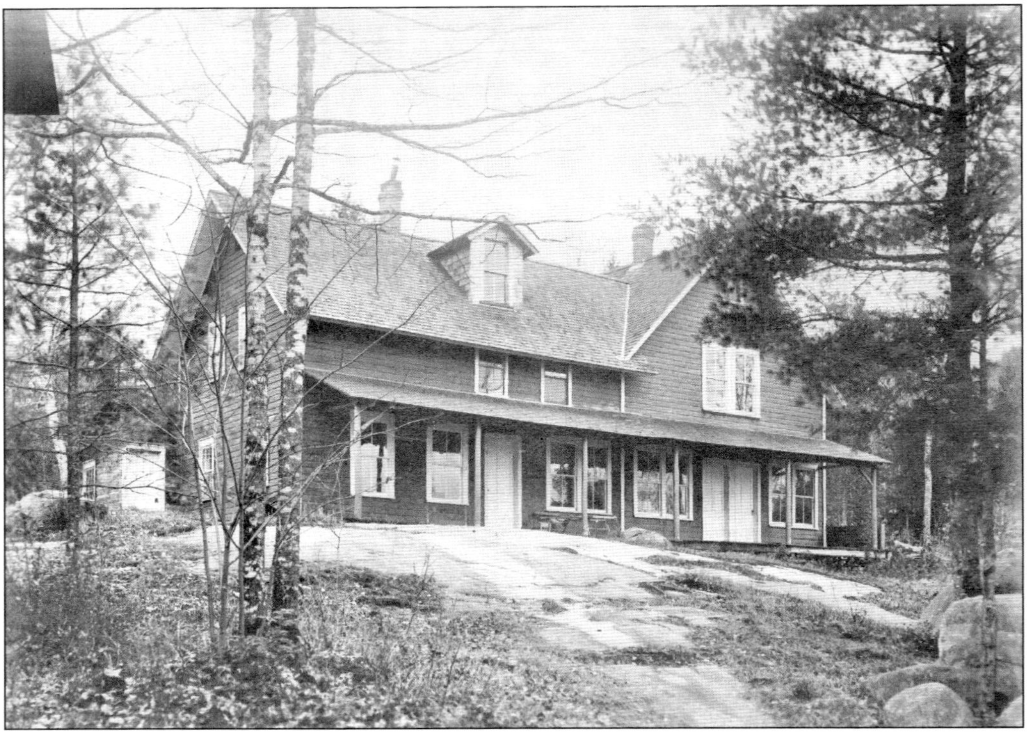

Prior to 1897, Camp Welcome was a small river-driver camp next to Bog River Falls. That year, Charles Lester, along with James and Rachel Cameron, commenced an expansion, adding rooms for summer visitors and hunting parties as well as the log drivers. The hotel stood near the west side of the present bridge over Bog River Falls and was torn down in 1910 by the Cameron family, who moved to Moody and operated Sunset Cottage. (Goff Nelson Library Collection.)

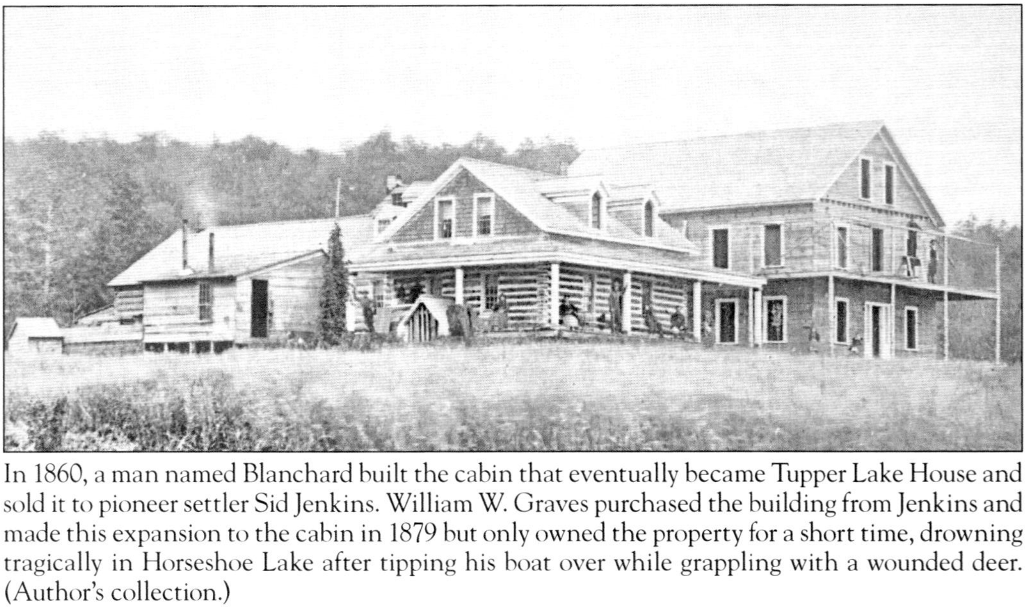

In 1860, a man named Blanchard built the cabin that eventually became Tupper Lake House and sold it to pioneer settler Sid Jenkins. William W. Graves purchased the building from Jenkins and made this expansion to the cabin in 1879 but only owned the property for a short time, drowning tragically in Horseshoe Lake after tipping his boat over while grappling with a wounded deer. (Author's collection.)

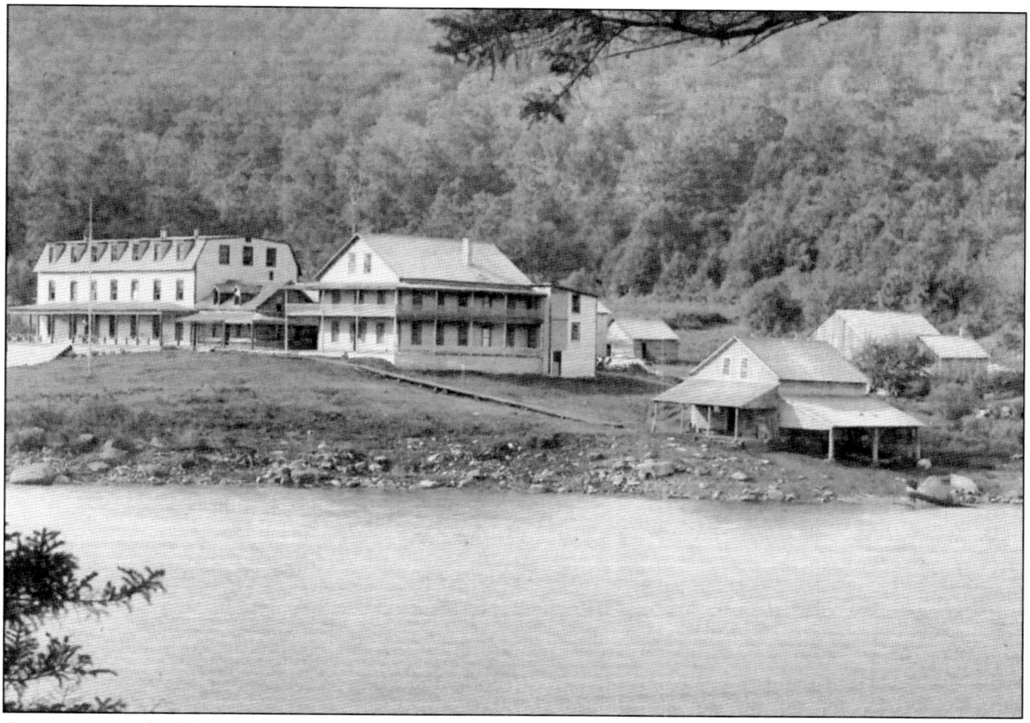

At one time, the Tupper Lake House was operated by Alembert Corey, whose father, Jesse, founded one of the earliest resort inns in the area, Rustic Lodge on Upper Saranac Lake. Tupper Lake House served as a welcome haven for some of the great men of the day, including Pres. Grover Cleveland. (Author's collection.)

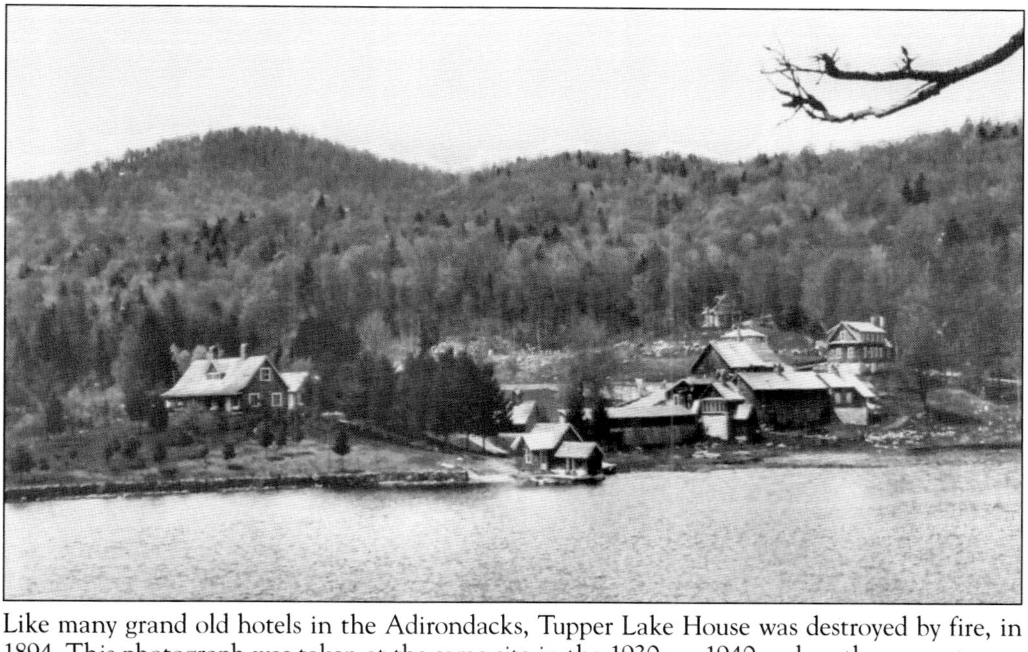

Like many grand old hotels in the Adirondacks, Tupper Lake House was destroyed by fire, in 1894. This photograph was taken at the same site in the 1930s or 1940s, when the property was owned by the American Legion Camp. The hotel is gone, and the water is higher because of the rebuilding of Setting Pole Dam. (Author's collection.)

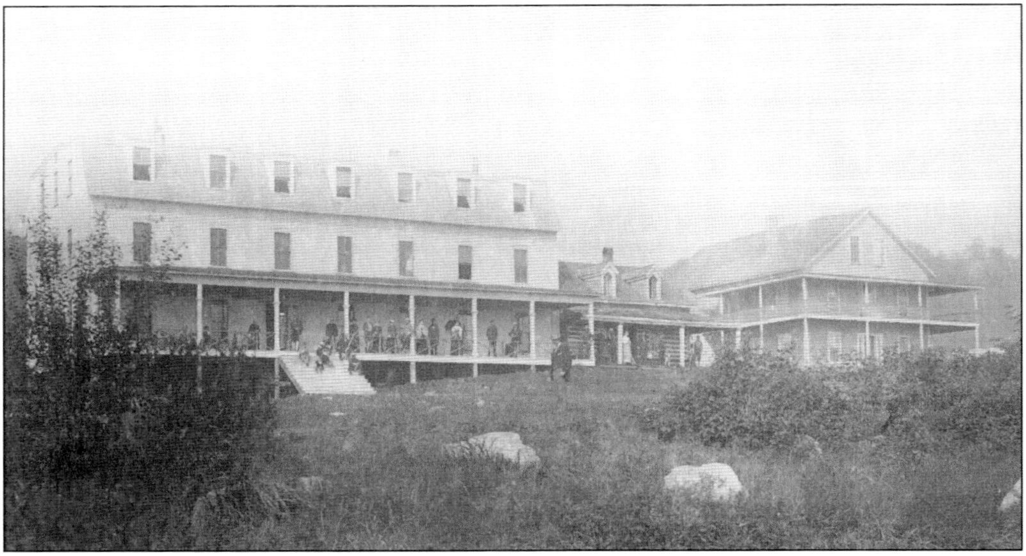

This front view of Tupper Lake House, known at this time as McClure's, shows the progression of the hotel's development, with the original cabin in the center, William Graves's 1879 addition to the right, and the massive addition making it a truly grand hotel to the left. (Goff Nelson Library Collection.)

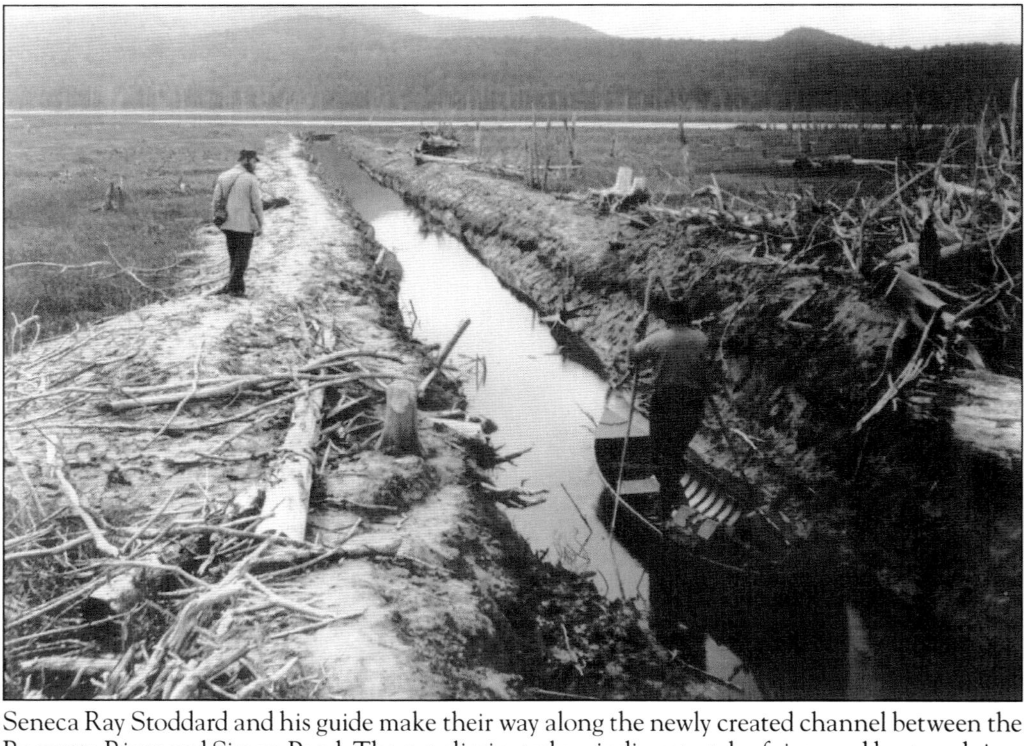

Seneca Ray Stoddard and his guide make their way along the newly created channel between the Raquette River and Simon Pond. The cut eliminated a winding stretch of river and hastened river traffic between Tromblee's Landing and the early Tupper Lake hotels. (Author's collection.)

Two

Early Beginnings

After the Pomeroy Lumber Company harvested the virgin pine and closed down their Tupper Lake operation, its foreman, William McLaughlin, decided to stay on and homestead. He cleared a section of land along the edge of Raquette Pond and enlarged his cow pasture to 40 acres to provide hay for the ever-growing teams of logging horses in the area. The field eventually was to become the site of the Tupper Lake Village; however, it was John Hurd, a visionary railroad man and developer who paved the way.

Hurd began his railroad in Moira with his first road going to St. Regis Falls. After a time, it was extended to Santa Clara, then Brandon, and finally to the shores of the Raquette River and William McLaughlin's cow pasture by 1890. Here, he named his terminus Tupper Lake and built the Big Mill; what was for three decades the largest and most productive lumber mill in New York State. Early historian Fredrick Seaver writes about the fledgling village: "The growth was marvelously rapid, but raw and rough at first. The railroad and lumber interest imported labor and the varieties were many without all being attractive. A single early lot included city toughs, mixed cultures, who were scrapping even before they finished breakfast."

Hurd had met and conquered successive barriers; however, there was one he could not surmount. It was the lack of logs to convert into lumber to carry over his railroad. The Big Mill ran a year.

Hurd tried making wire reels and baskets and similar articles, but the profit and the volume of business was not large enough and the crisis could not be averted. John Hurd went bankrupt. He lived to see prosperity on every side, but the control of his various enterprises passed into other hands and he was unable to share in the prosperity.

For the next nine years, the village grew at exceptional rate. Then, on July 30, 1899, it was almost demolished by fire. The flame originated in the storehouse of King & Page and was carried with almost incredible swiftness to other business buildings on the principal street, the whole being speedily involved in a general conflagration that wiped out 160 buildings. The only redeeming feature, which added in no slight degree to the rebuilding of the village, remained in the fact that Tupper Lake's four large sawmills were not included in the awful calamity. The fire wound up being nothing more than a burp in the village's growth. Within a year, the village was rebuilt and plans were being made to add a chemical factory and a barrel stave mill.

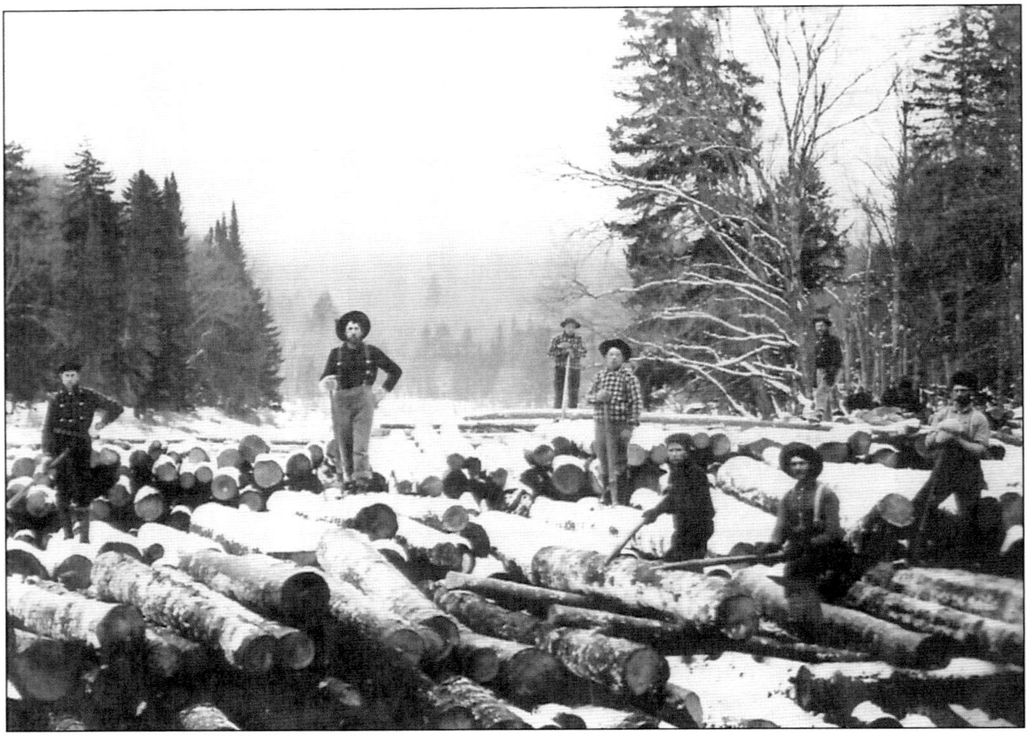

Loggers stand ready with their peaveys as they position logs at the landing along the edge of the Raquette River. After cutting, hauling, and then driving the logs from Townships 26 and 27, they delivered them into Raquette Pond. From the pond, a "union drive" took over and delivered them to the lumber mills down the river at Potsdam, Norwood, and other villages. (Author's collection.)

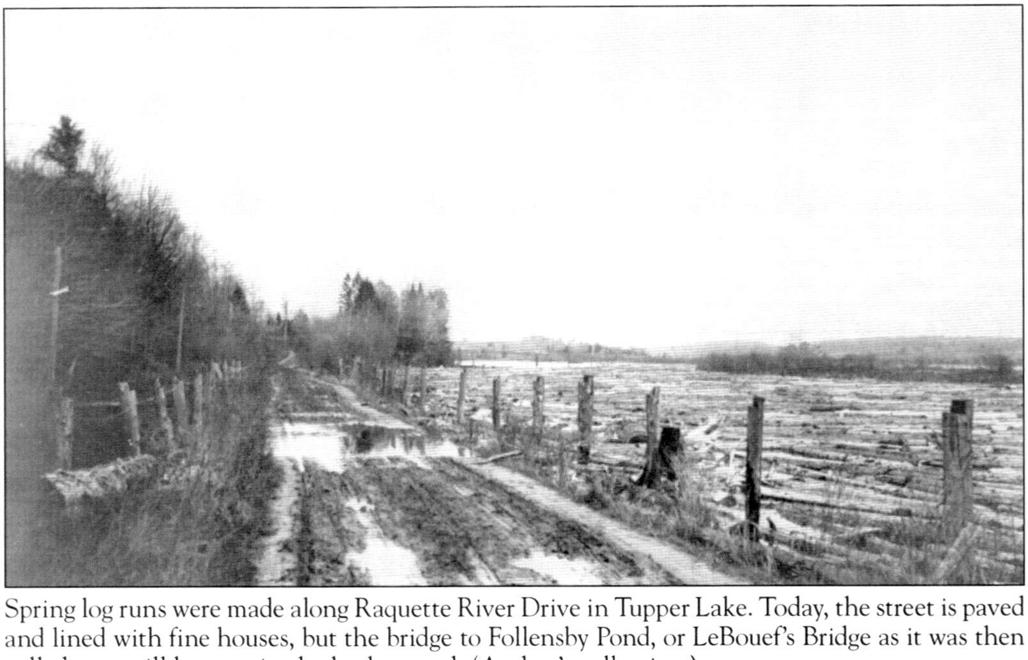

Spring log runs were made along Raquette River Drive in Tupper Lake. Today, the street is paved and lined with fine houses, but the bridge to Follensby Pond, or LeBouef's Bridge as it was then called, can still be seen in the background. (Author's collection.)

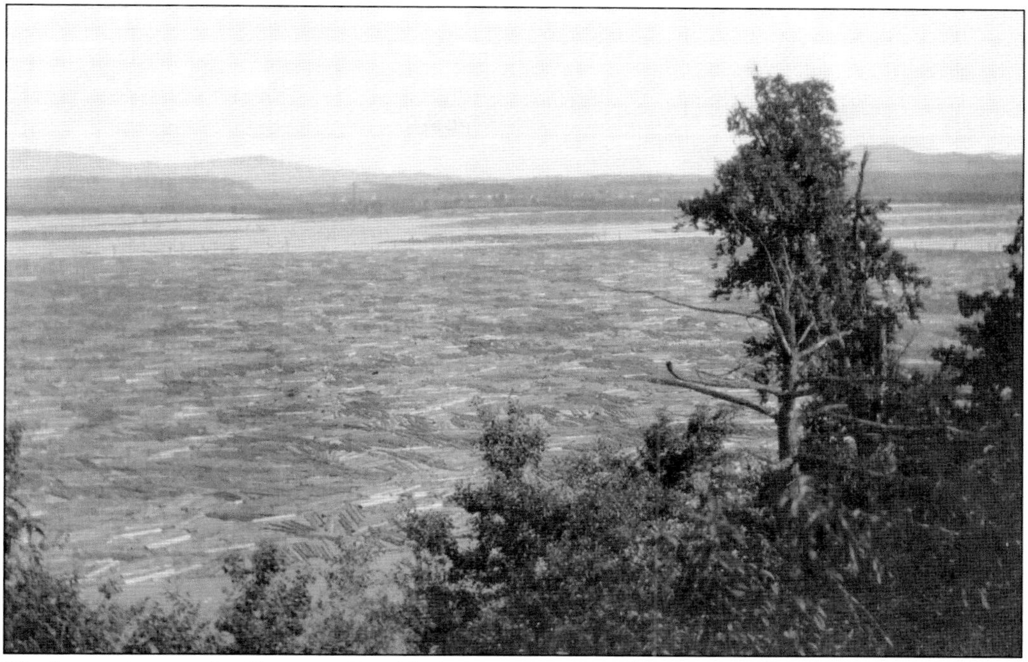

The logs were sorted at Raquette Pond before being sent to the proper mill. Each log was hammer-stamped at the butt by the logging company's mark. Various log crews competed to get their logs driven down the river ahead of the others, creating rivalries, roughness, and ill temper. (Author's collection.)

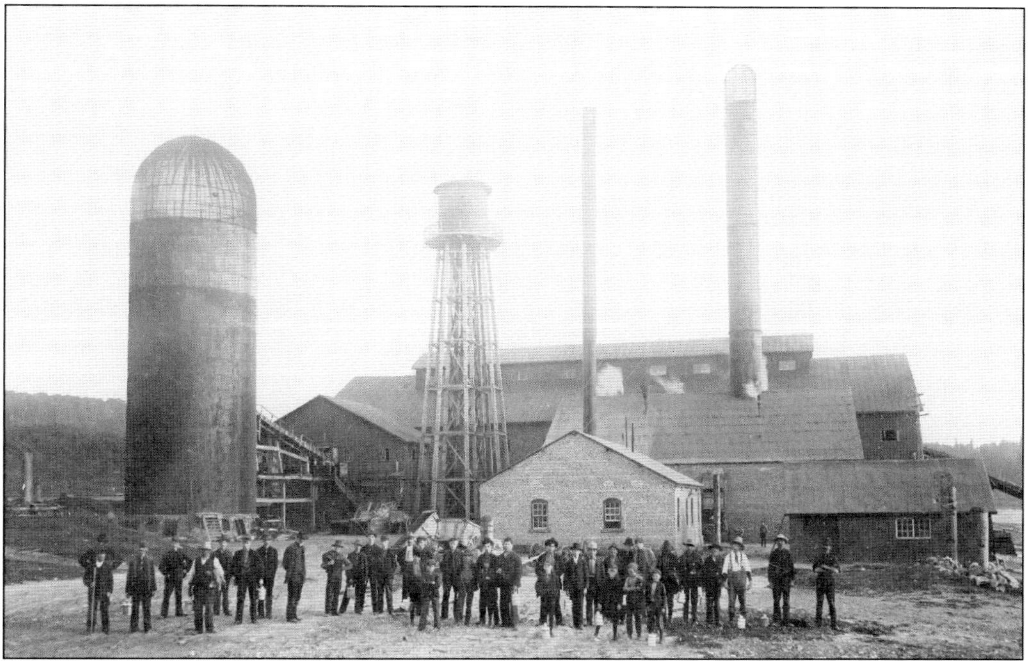

John Hurd's famed Big Mill was erected in 1890 and operated until 1926. As logging flourished for years around the shores of Raquette Pond, this mill and others employed hundreds of Tupper Lake men. It was the economic backbone of Tupper Lake; in fact, most of the early buildings in town were constructed from the lumber sawn from this mill. (Goff Nelson Library Collection.)

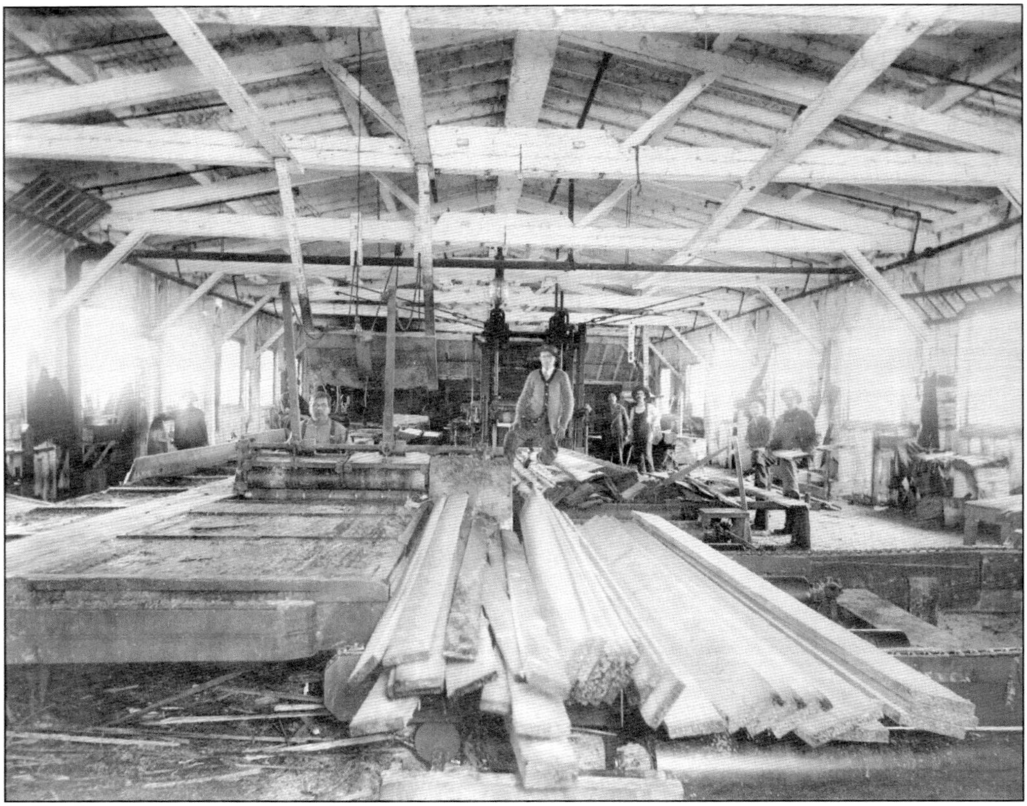

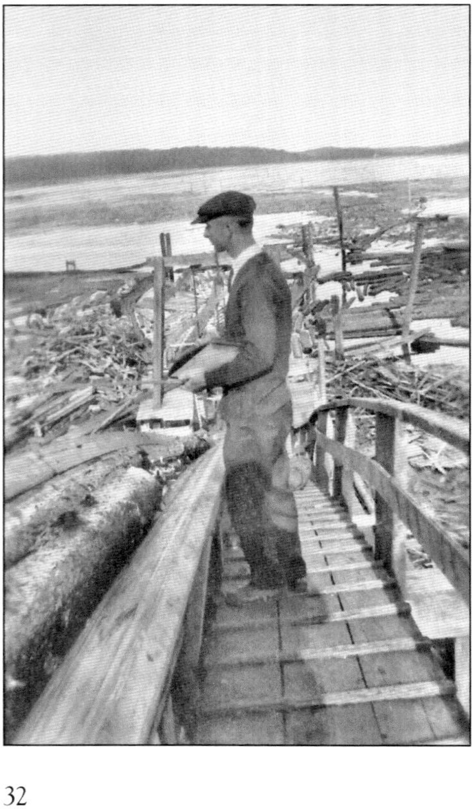

The interior of the Big Mill featured two gangs, two band saws, and two circulars. The annual report of the New York State Forest, Fish, and Game Commission in 1900 shows that the Norwood Manufacturing Company, which operated the Big Mill, had a total cut of nearly 22 million board feet of lumber. (Goff Nelson Library Collection.)

The jack ladder and endless amounts of chain hauled logs from the millpond for sawing. In the early days, pay for labor was $1.65 for a 10-hour day, or $9.90 per week, but millwrights drew $19.80 per week and band-saw fitters took in the large sum of $36 a week. (Courtesy of Bette Sue Martineau.)

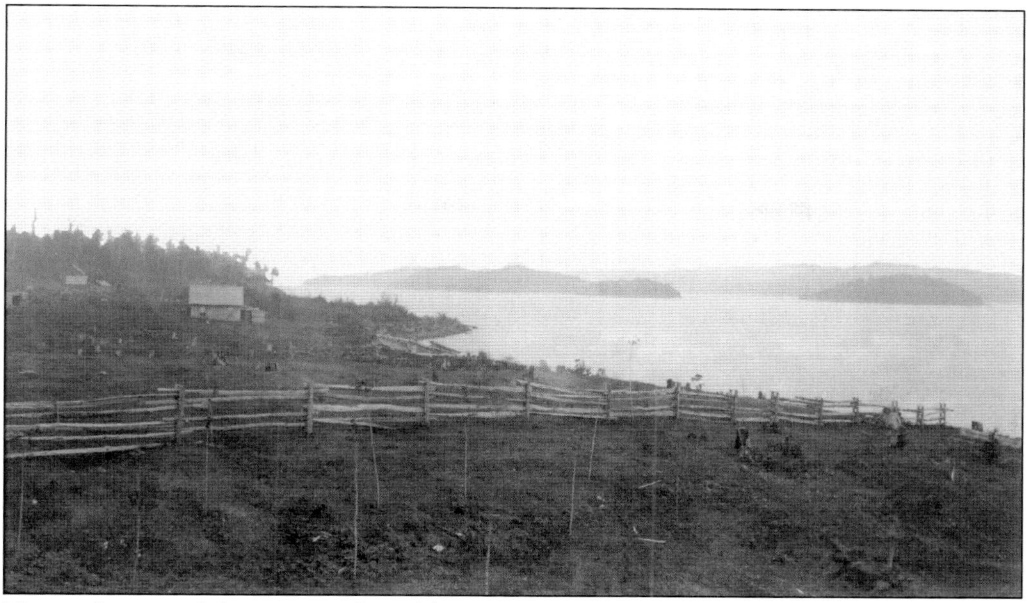

This early view of the pasture cleared by Mart Moody shows Tupper Lake and its islands in the distance. A fencerow runs to the water's edge to protect the newly planted apple trees from being browsed by the cows, which had a small barn among the stumps in the new field. (Author's collection.)

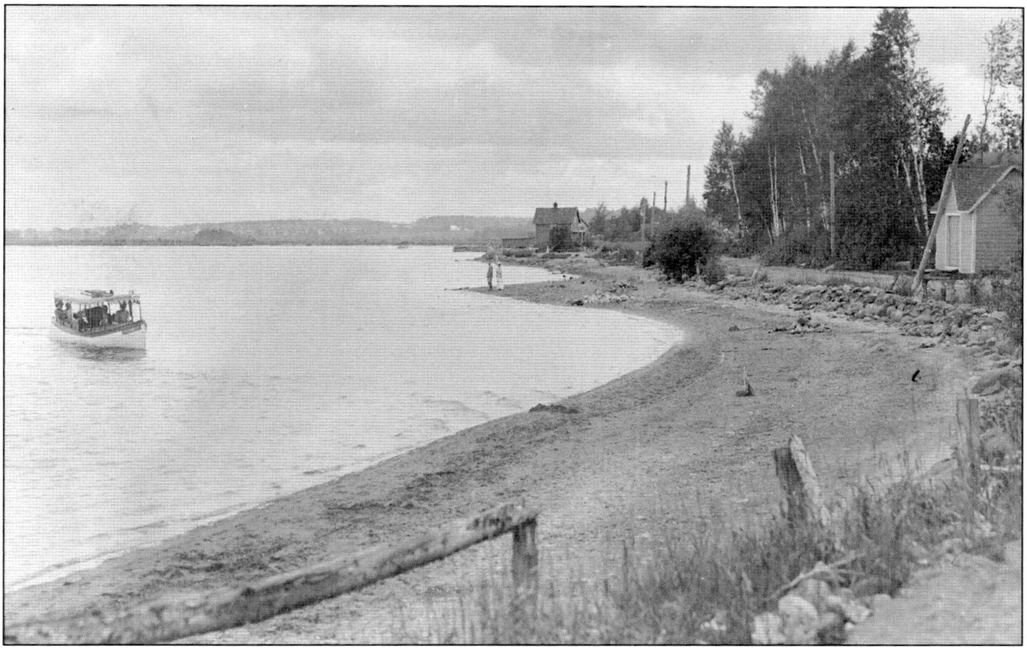

The little steamer *Mermaid* carries its passengers to the shoreline of Moody, which remained isolated for a time because it was still only accessible by water. Eventually, a bridge was built spanning the Raquette River and uniting the two communities. (Author's collection.)

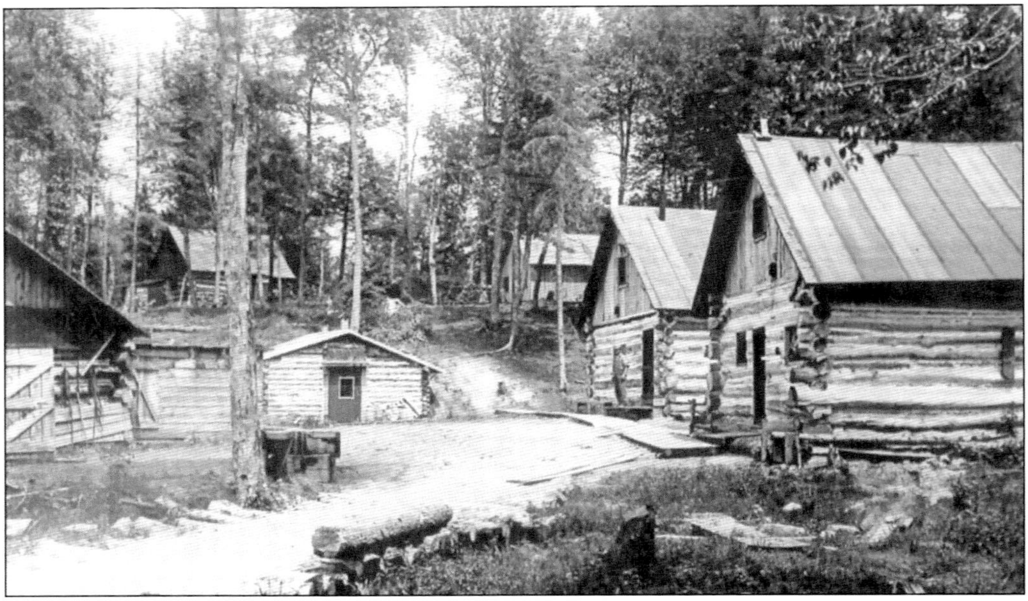

Lumber was king in the early 1900s, and the railroad spurs from Tupper Lake ran like the spokes of a wheel, reaching out to prime timber areas. Log cabins with tar paper roofs sprinkled the community of Conifer. Augustus Lowe's mill at Horseshoe was purchased and moved here by Emporium Forestry Company. (Author's collection.)

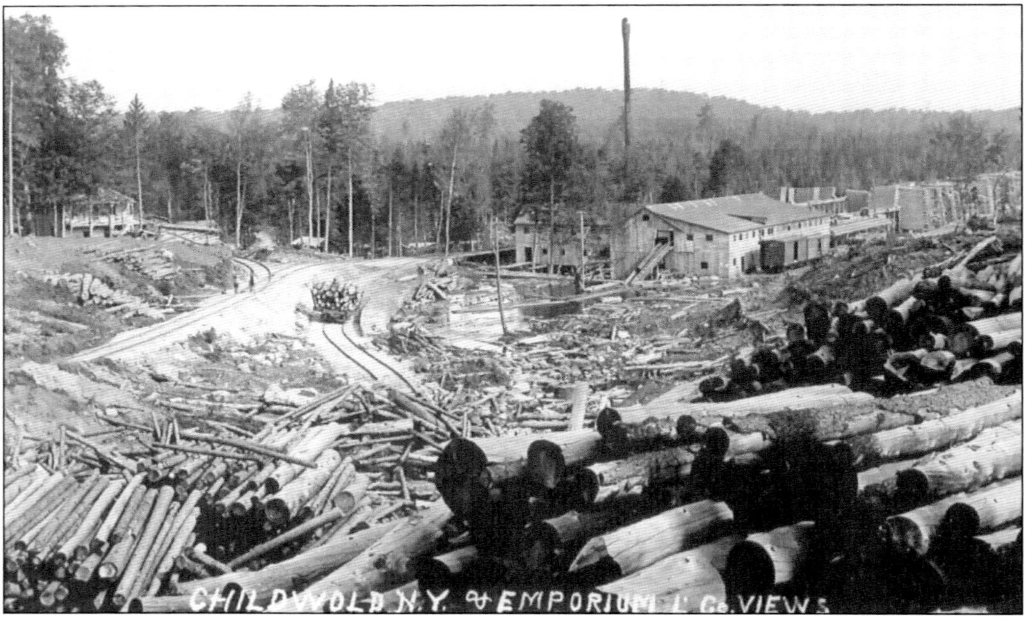

William Sykes and William Caftisch formed the Emporium Forestry Company and opened the Conifer mill in 1911. Soon after, they built the Grasse River Railroad to Cranberry Lake. Many residents moved to lumber camps run by Tupper Lake operators such as John D'Avignon, George Bushey, and Oliver Proulx. (Author's collection.)

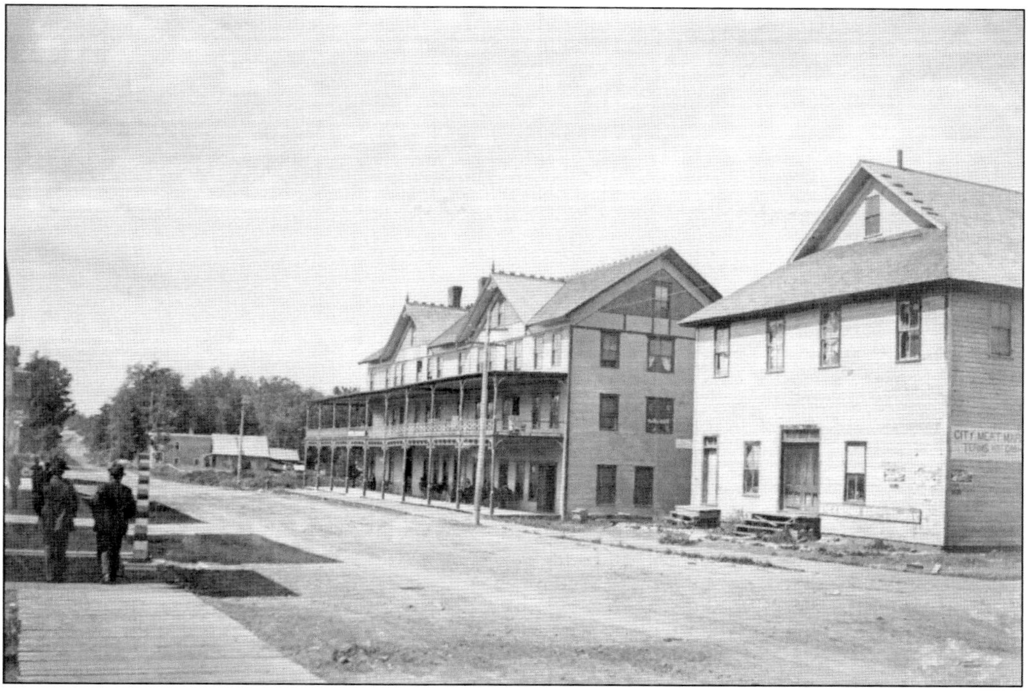

The Hotel Altamont, built in 1890 by John H. and Thomas Weir on Park Street, was the premier landmark of the fledgling village of Tupper Lake for the next 60 years. The adjacent building was a meat market early on and was later known as the old opera house. (Author's collection.)

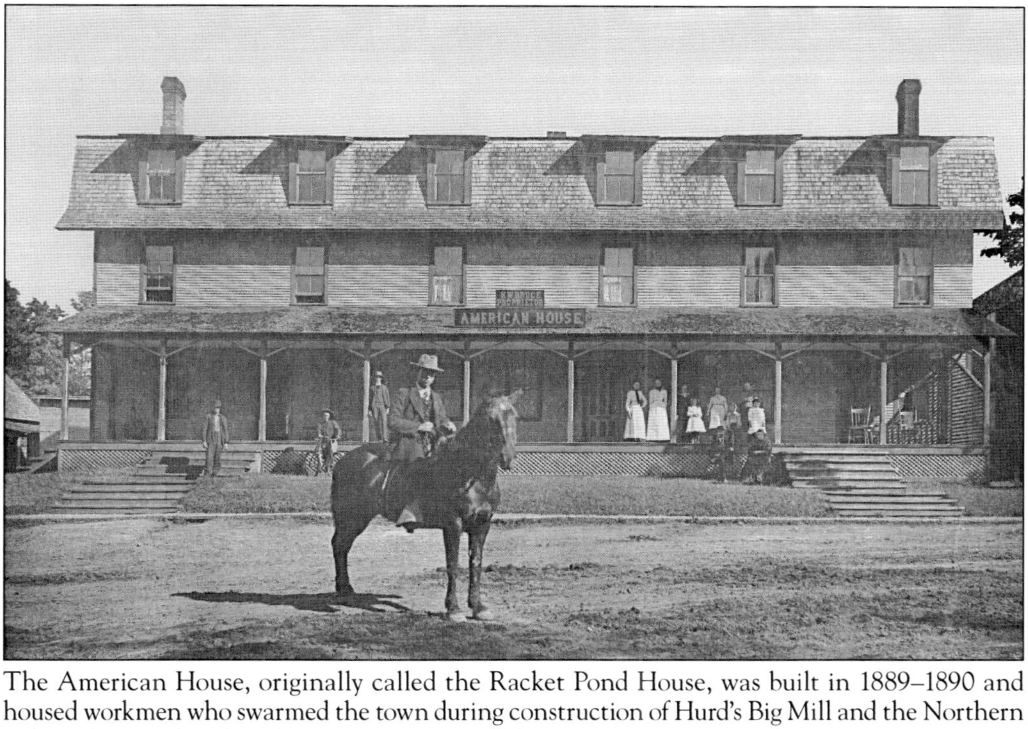

The American House, originally called the Racket Pond House, was built in 1889–1890 and housed workmen who swarmed the town during construction of Hurd's Big Mill and the Northern Adirondack Railroad. It flourished under several owners but entered lean years as the motel era began. (Goff Nelson Library Collection.)

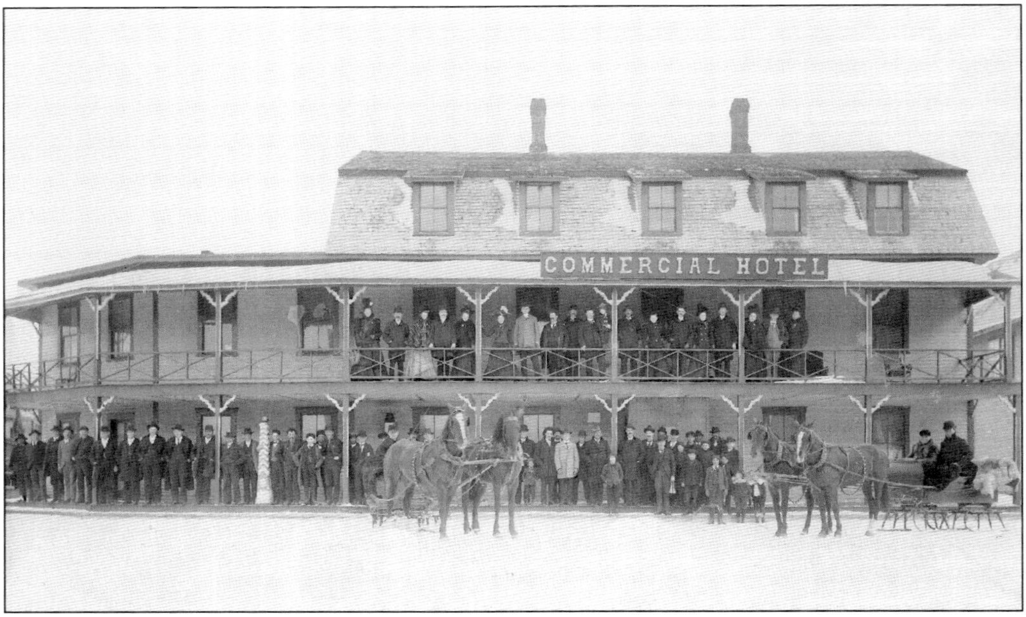

John McConnell, who helped establish the *Tupper Lake Herald* in 1895, had just purchased the Commercial House with his young bride, Katherine, when a dreadful telegram was delivered into their hands. The hotel was beyond any salvage, burnt in the Big Fire of 1899, the August 4 conflagration that took the entire uptown area of the fledgling village. (Goff Nelson Library Collection.)

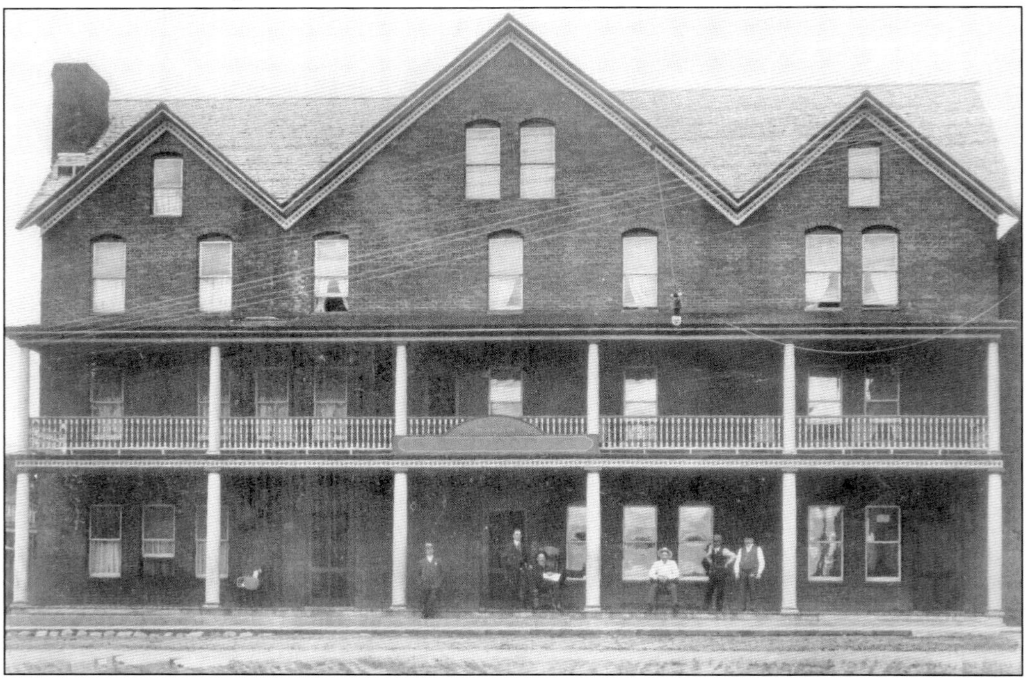

After the Commercial House was lost to fire, Frederick H. LaDuke built the Iroquois Hotel on the same location in 1902. Over the next 20 years, several men ran the hotel, including Thomas Weir, John McConnell, Allen Vosburgh, Ben J. Fountain, William Chambers, and James Shinnock. In the late 1920s, Brahm Bissell purchased it and installed Tupper Lake's first radio station. (Author's collection.)

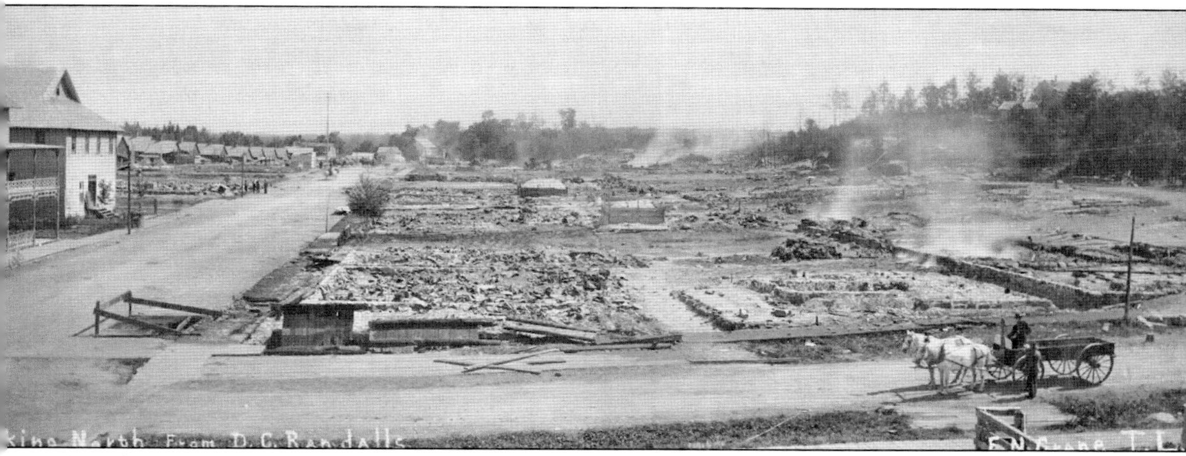

On July 30, 1899, disaster hit this Adirondack boomtown. People read *Franklin County Gazette* with horror: "During the early hours of Sunday morning the most extensive and destructive fire ever known in Franklin County consumed [160] buildings, two-thirds of the prosperous Adirondack Village of Tupper Lake." (Goff Nelson Library Collection.)

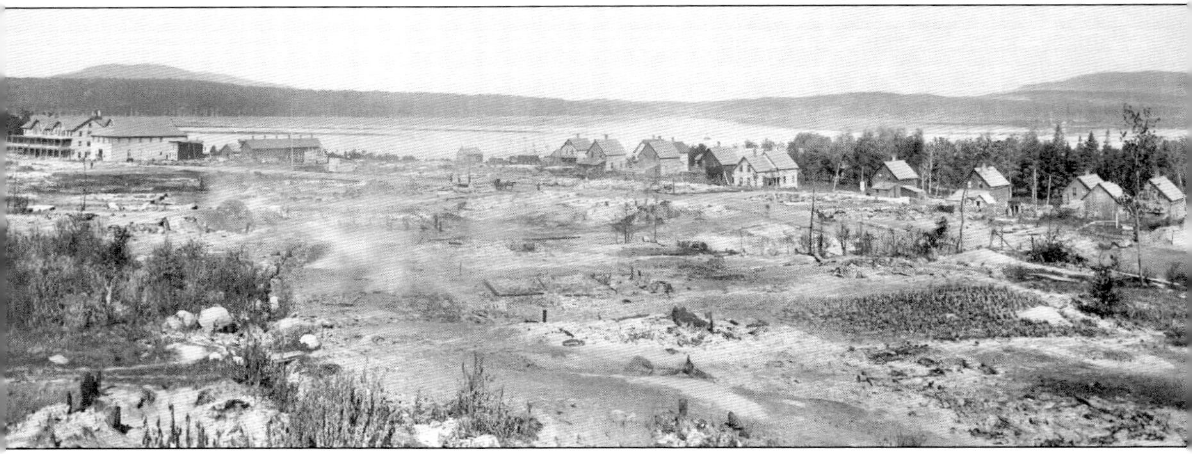

The *Franklin County Gazette* reported that "the flames [were] devouring alike hotels, business blocks, private residences and mills and only stopping when the limits of the village were reached and a mere remnant of the town was left in the midst of blackened rains and general desolation. Although the blow is a crushing one, the citizens of the stricken village are pluckily going about the work of rebuilding and as soon as the losses are adjusted by the insurance companies the construction of a new town will begin." (Goff Nelson Library Collection.)

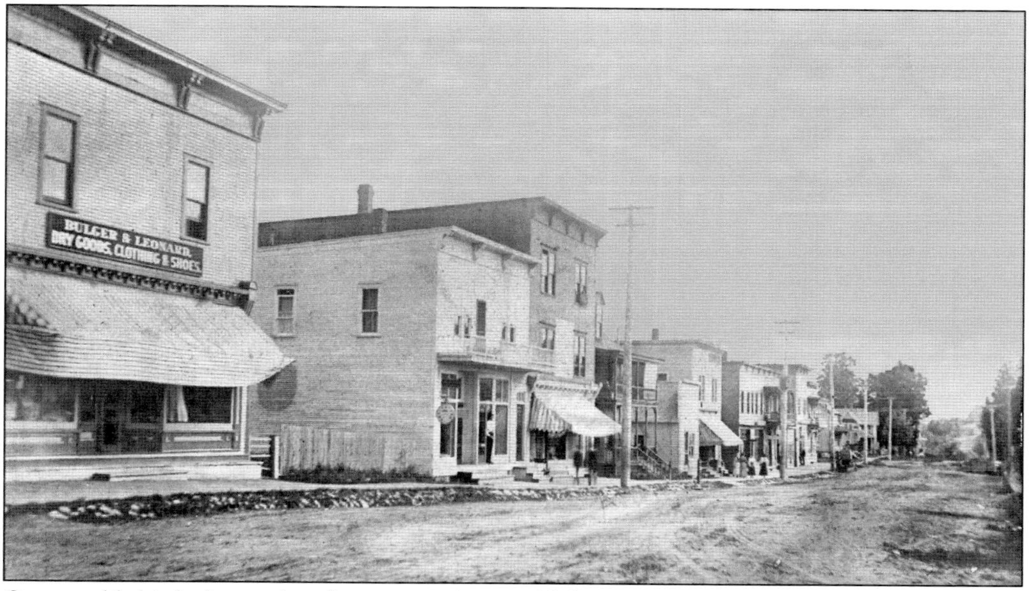

One would think that such a devastating fire would discourage the early pioneers, but the mills escaped the carnage, and thus the jobs were still there. In just a few short years, the village was rebuilt, and this time it was better constructed, with an eye toward fire prevention. This photograph of Park Street, looking west from Cliff Avenue, shows the rebuilt town. (Goff Nelson Library Collection.)

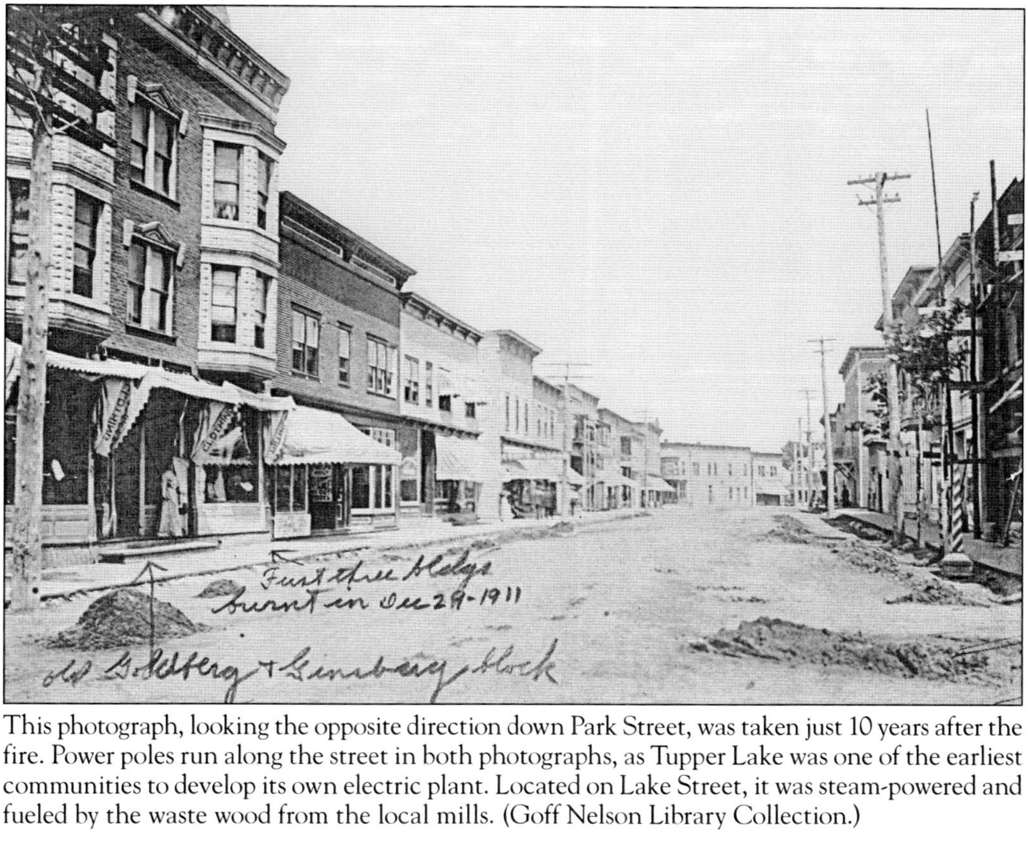

This photograph, looking the opposite direction down Park Street, was taken just 10 years after the fire. Power poles run along the street in both photographs, as Tupper Lake was one of the earliest communities to develop its own electric plant. Located on Lake Street, it was steam-powered and fueled by the waste wood from the local mills. (Goff Nelson Library Collection.)

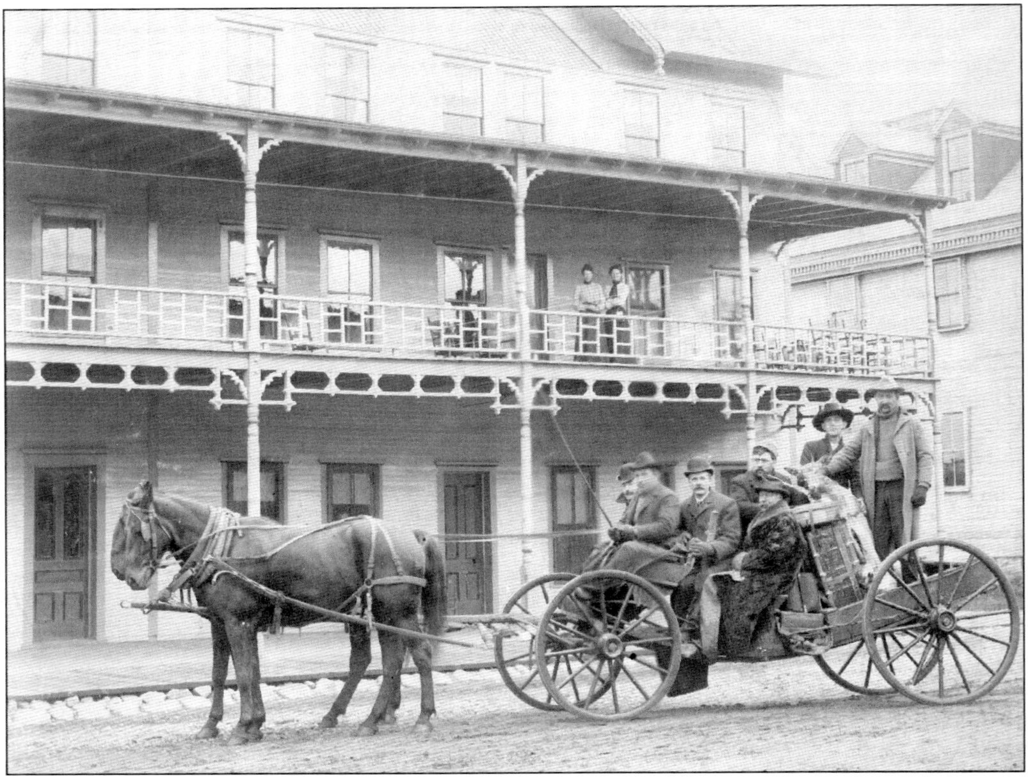

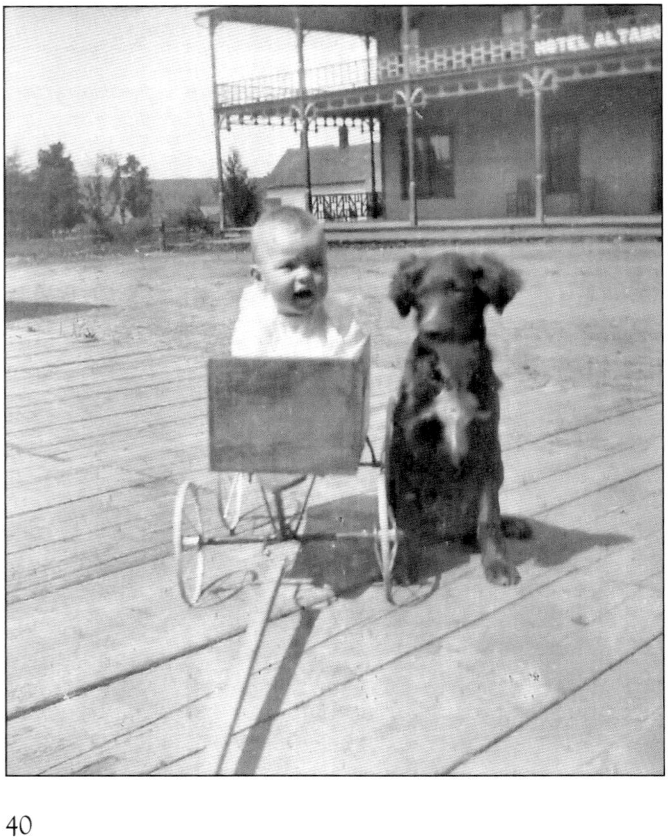

A party of Tupper "sports" poses in front of Hotel Altamont after returning to town with a spike-horn buck. The party included Dan Carter (driving), Bob Mahar (with his hands on the buck), and Charley Lester (seated, in fur coat). The others could not be identified. (Goff Nelson Library Collection.)

Tupper Lake native son John Chaney Goff gets ready for a ride in the baby buggy in front of the Altamont Hotel in 1902. The son of early Tupper settler John B. Goff, he graduated from Tupper Lake High School in the class of 1920. His sister Charity Goff Nelson bequeathed the funds to construct the Goff Nelson Memorial Library. (Courtesy of Bette Sue Martineau.)

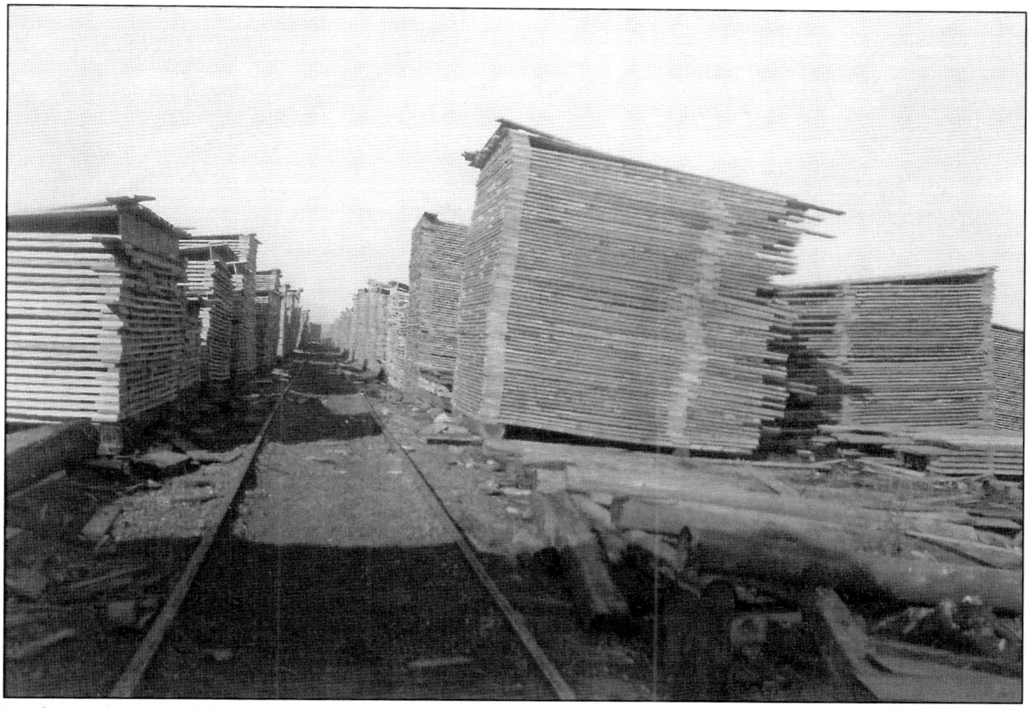

In the early part of the century, lumber was piled by size and species. Rails were laid, and pushcarts were used to move the lumber to the various rows and piles. Each spring, three to four million board feet of pine lumber lay in rows, ready for market, having been sawn throughout the winter. (Goff Nelson Library Collection.)

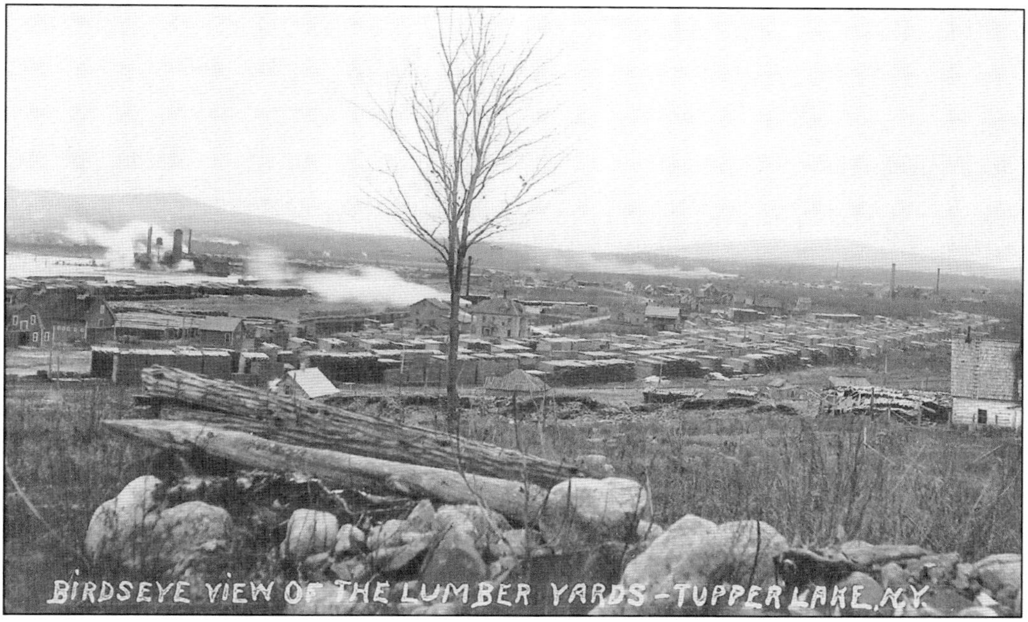

Within 10 years of its birth, Tupper Lake was fast becoming the logging capital of New York State. By 1900, there were 3,045 people living in the pioneer village. As far as the eye could see, there were mills and stacks of lumber ready to be shipped by rail to markets throughout the Empire State and beyond. (Author's collection.)

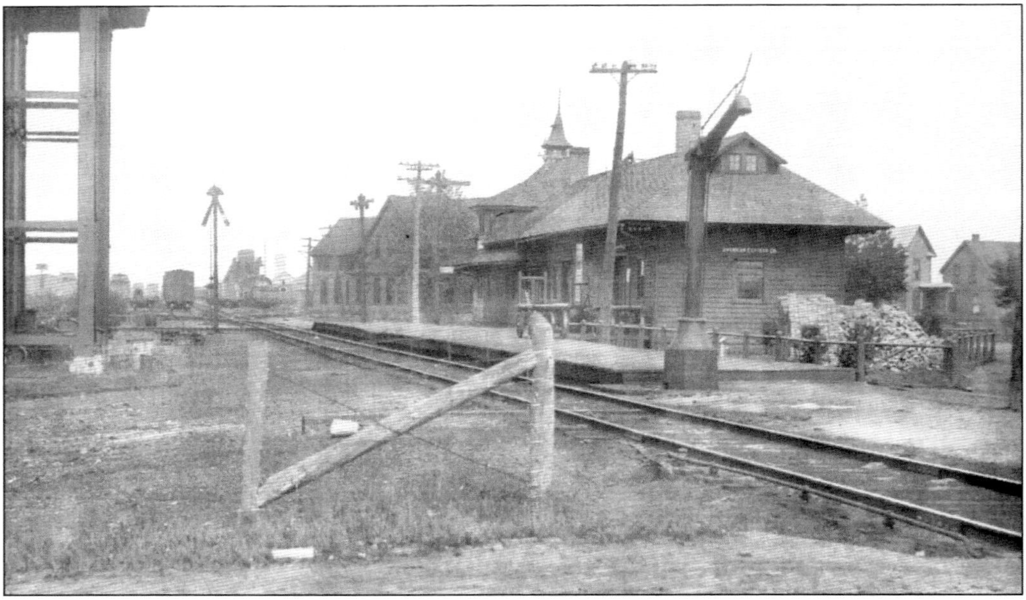

Tupper Lake became a major railroad junction with the arrival of Dr. Seward Webb's Adirondack & St. Lawrence Railroad. On October 12, 1892, a wilderness railroad, a 191-mile route between Montreal and Utica, was completed. A railroad depot was built, and the line was reincorporated as the Mohawk & Malone Railway Company. The following spring, it was leased to the New York Central and a roundhouse, shops, and a sizable railroad yard developed. (Goff Nelson Library Collection.)

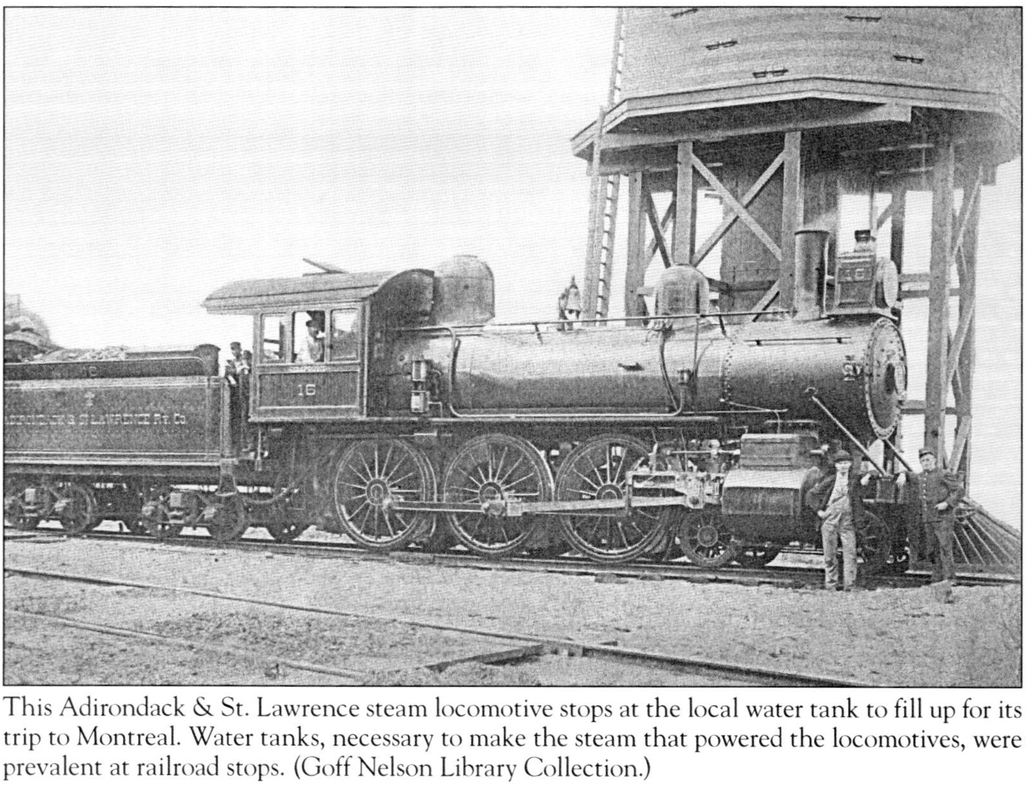

This Adirondack & St. Lawrence steam locomotive stops at the local water tank to fill up for its trip to Montreal. Water tanks, necessary to make the steam that powered the locomotives, were prevalent at railroad stops. (Goff Nelson Library Collection.)

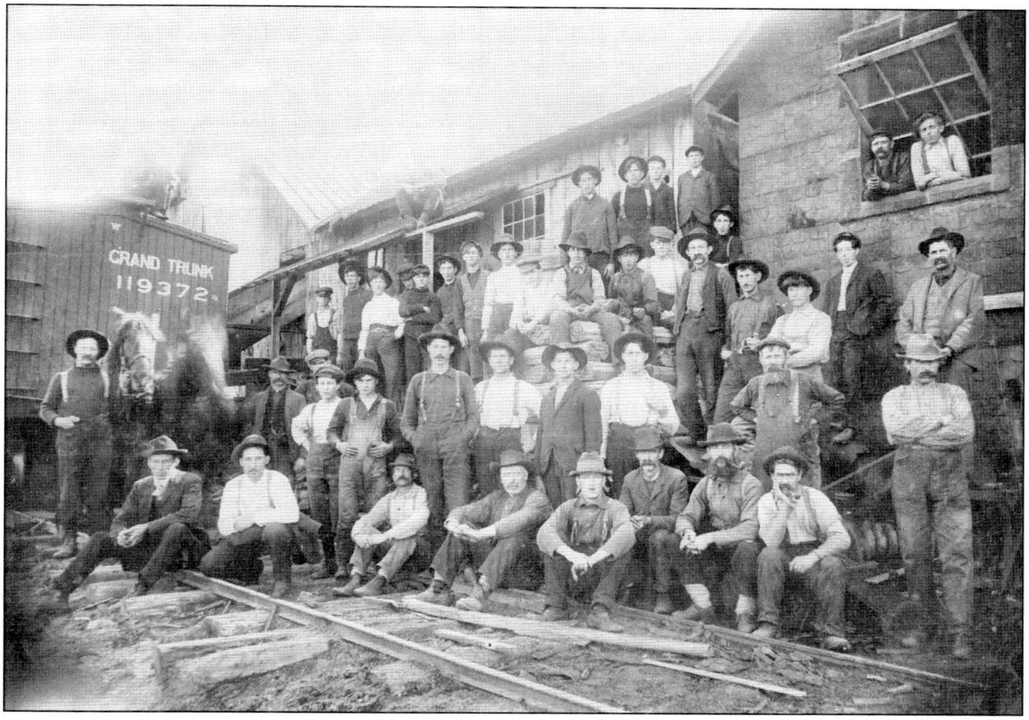

Early Tupper Lake rail workers took a break from the day's labor to pose for this photograph at the New York Central depot. Tupper Lake's sprawling railway yards, driven by the lumber trade, made it a hub for the surrounding Adirondack communities. (Goff Nelson Library Collection.)

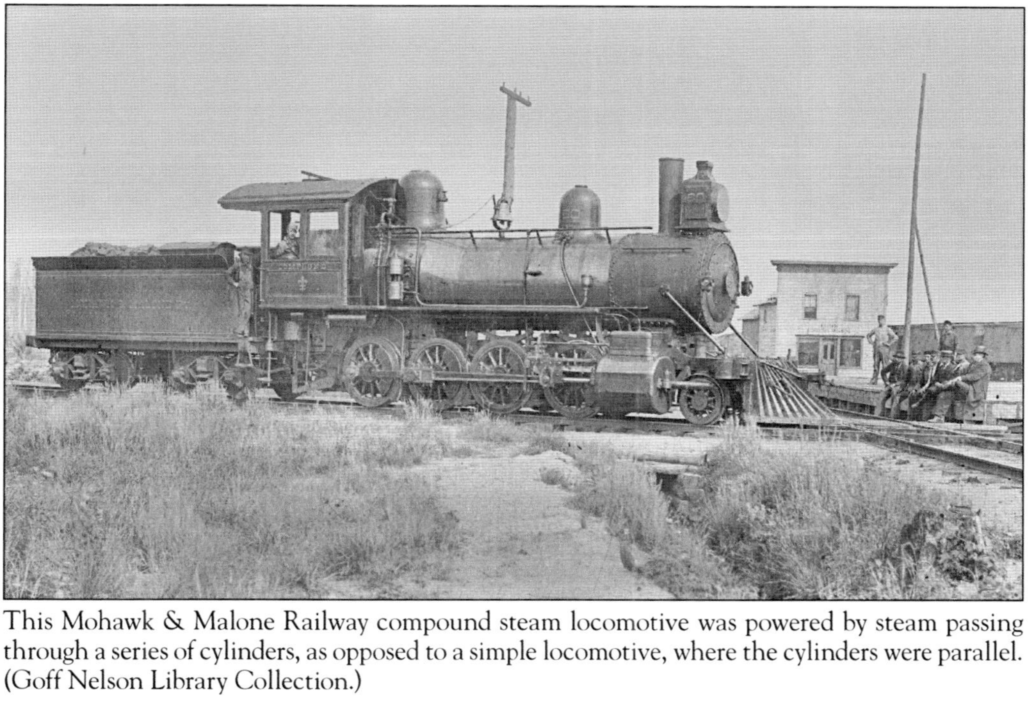

This Mohawk & Malone Railway compound steam locomotive was powered by steam passing through a series of cylinders, as opposed to a simple locomotive, where the cylinders were parallel. (Goff Nelson Library Collection.)

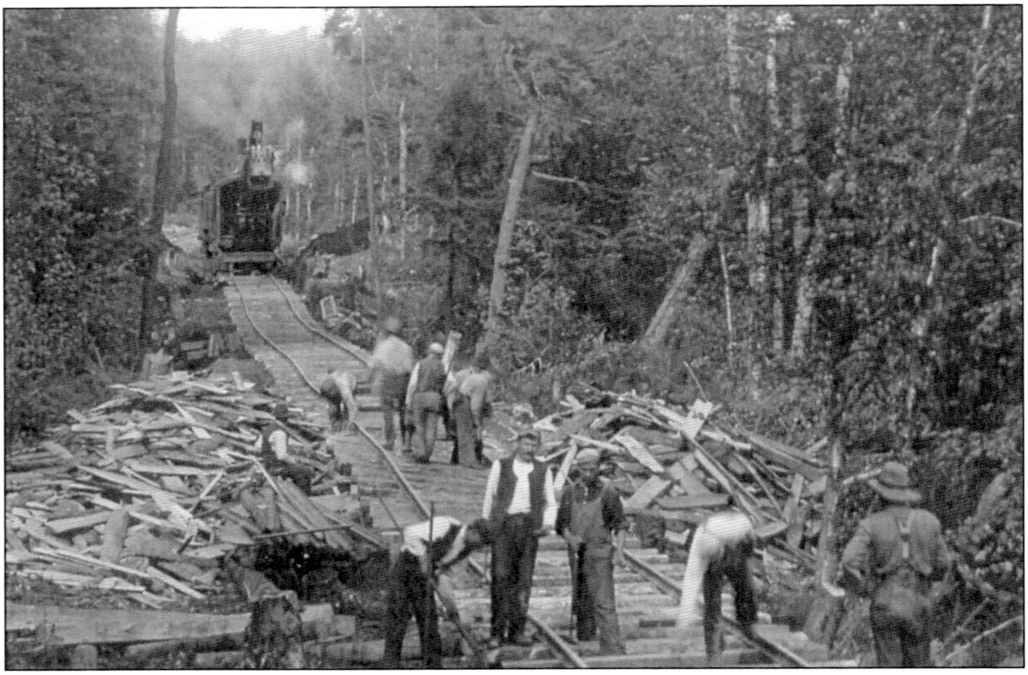

Once the railroad reached Tupper Lake, rail spurs began to web off the main line, reaching out to prime timber areas, formerly too far away or too isolated. These rail workers lay track near Tupper Lake for the Emporium Forestry Company, which built a mill and established the community of Conifer in 1911. (Author's collection.)

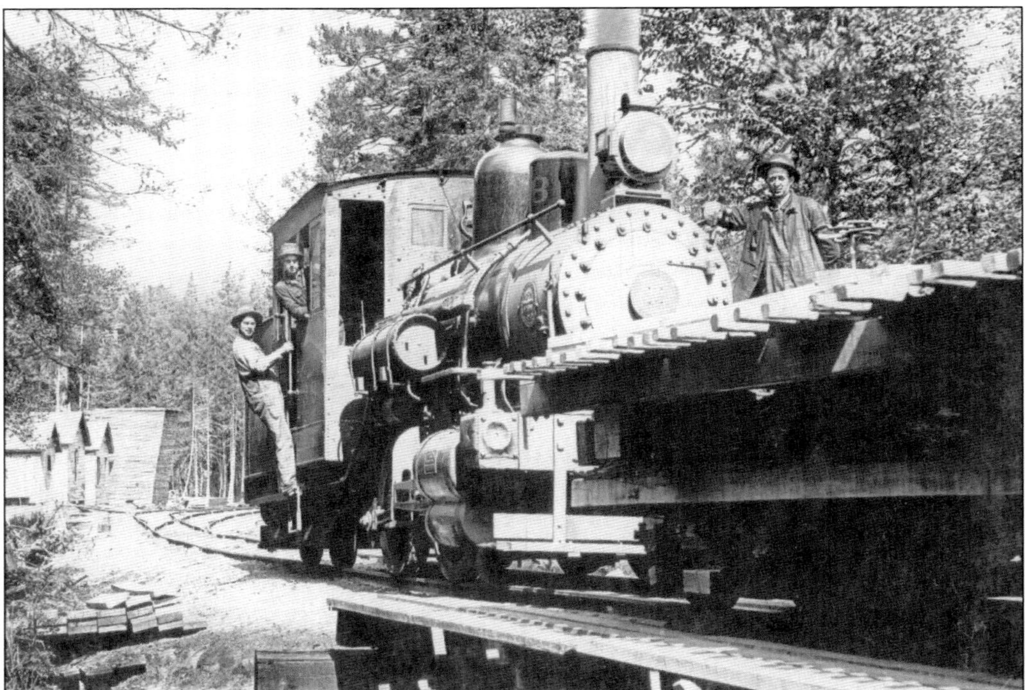

Emporium Forestry's Baldwin Locomotive was a workhorse, often moving lumber and logs from Cranberry Lake to the Childwold Station and the railroad yard at Conifer. (Author's collection.)

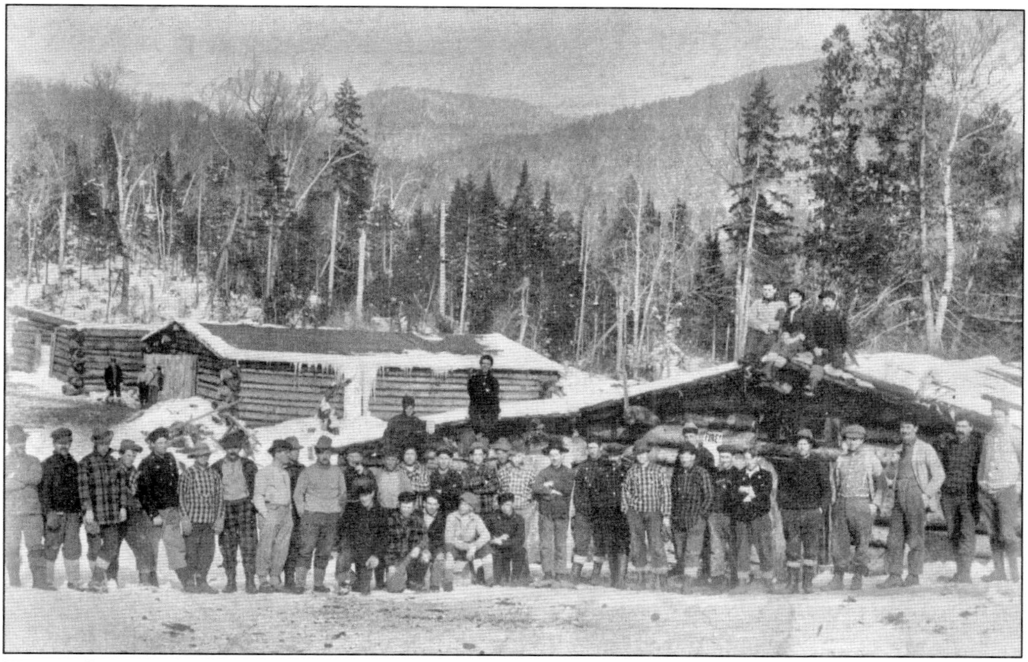

Winter logging camps sprang up throughout the surrounding mountains. This crew established Brickey's Bear Brook Camp, which included a cook shop, blacksmith shop, and living quarters. Bear Brook emptied logs into the Bog River, then over the falls into Big Tupper Lake, where they were pulled by tugboat to the waiting mills. (Photograph by George Dixon; Goff Nelson Library Collection.)

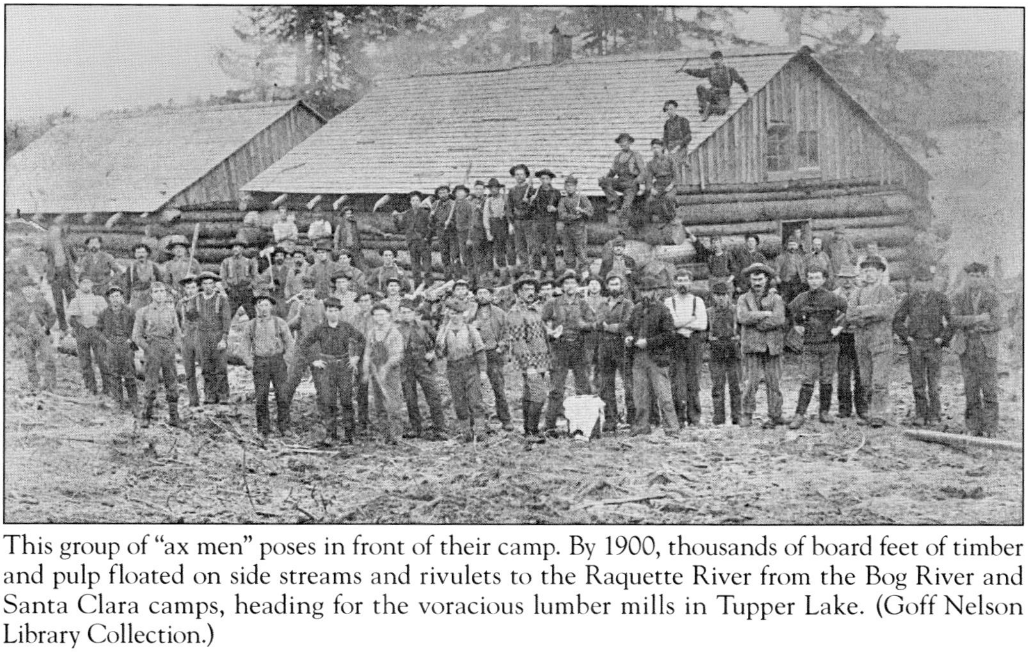

This group of "ax men" poses in front of their camp. By 1900, thousands of board feet of timber and pulp floated on side streams and rivulets to the Raquette River from the Bog River and Santa Clara camps, heading for the voracious lumber mills in Tupper Lake. (Goff Nelson Library Collection.)

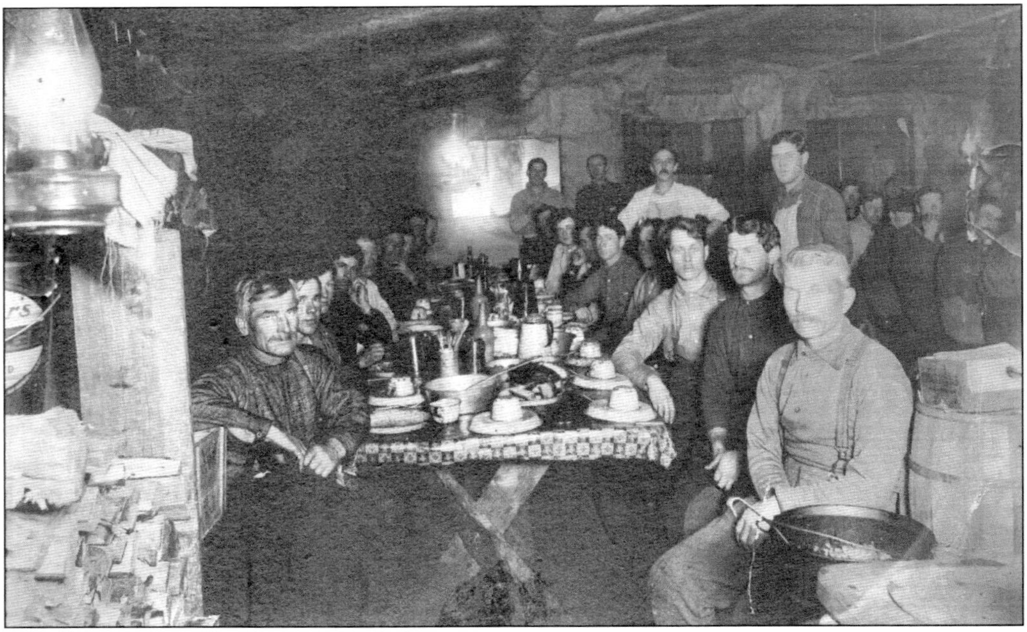

Workers sit down to eat inside a typical lumber camp of the day. Each logging camp employed one or two cooks and helpers to prepare food for as many as 50 to 100 men, who always ate as a group at long tables. The logging companies fed their employees well, knowing thought that healthy, well-fed employees made for good workers who were more likely to be loyal to their employers. (Goff Nelson Library Collection.)

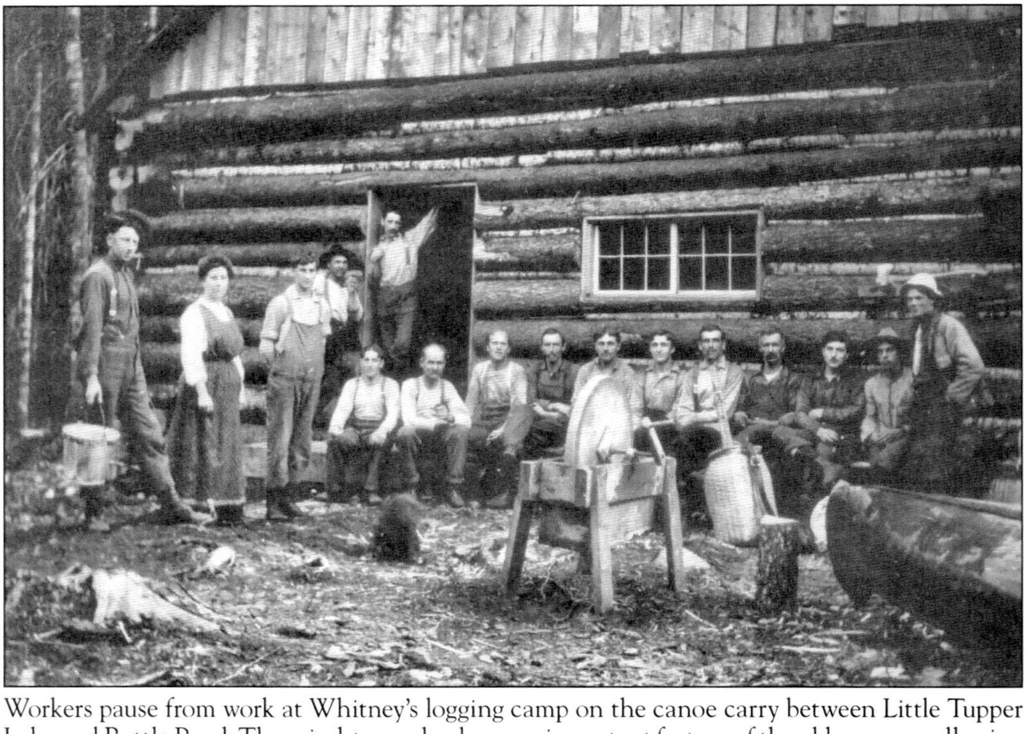

Workers pause from work at Whitney's logging camp on the canoe carry between Little Tupper Lake and Bottle Pond. The grindstone wheel was an important feature of the older camps, allowing loggers to hone their axes and sharpen their peaveys. (Author's collection.)

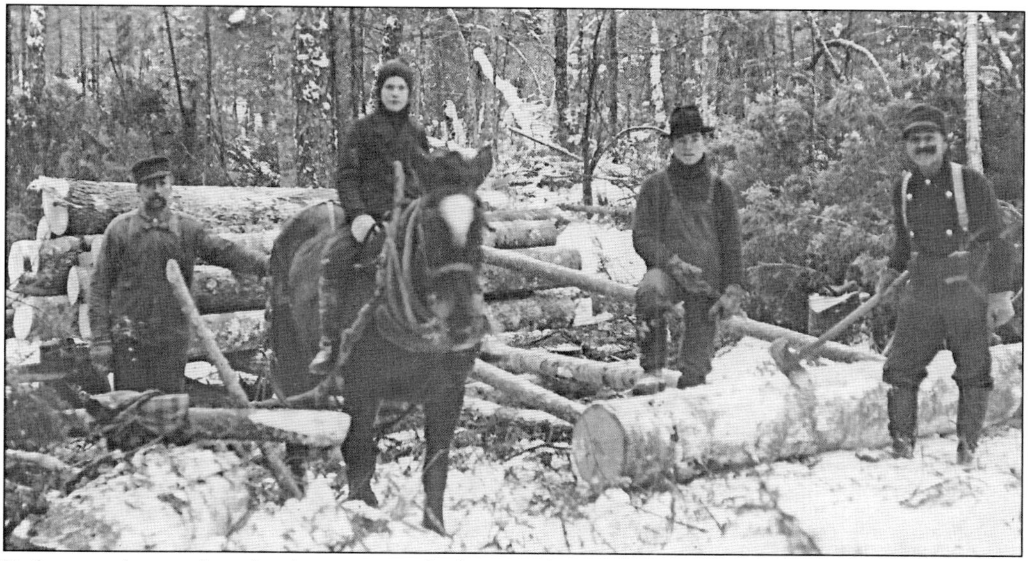

Before mechanized timber harvesting, draft animals were used to assist loggers. Although oxen were sometimes used, the preferred animal was the draft horse. They weighed about 1,600 pounds and had the strength to move cut logs to landings along the rails, streams, and rivers. (Goff Nelson Library Collection.)

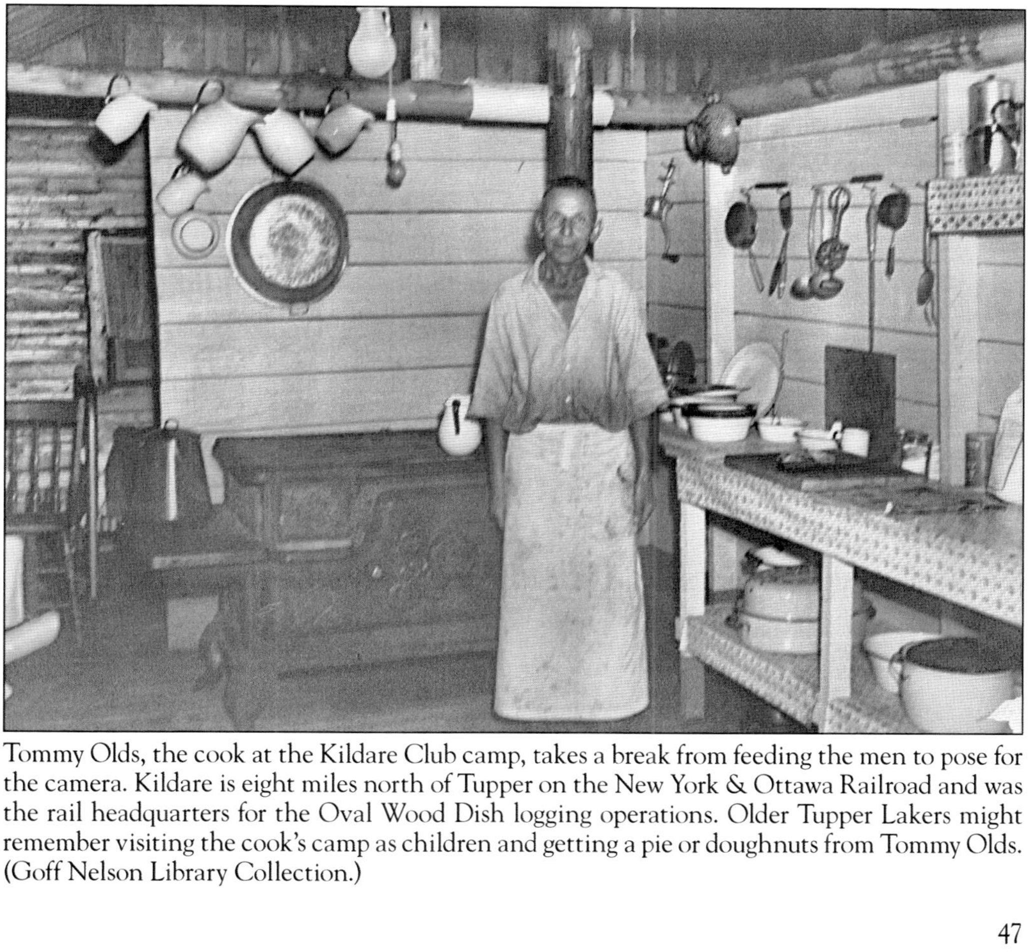

Tommy Olds, the cook at the Kildare Club camp, takes a break from feeding the men to pose for the camera. Kildare is eight miles north of Tupper on the New York & Ottawa Railroad and was the rail headquarters for the Oval Wood Dish logging operations. Older Tupper Lakers might remember visiting the cook's camp as children and getting a pie or doughnuts from Tommy Olds. (Goff Nelson Library Collection.)

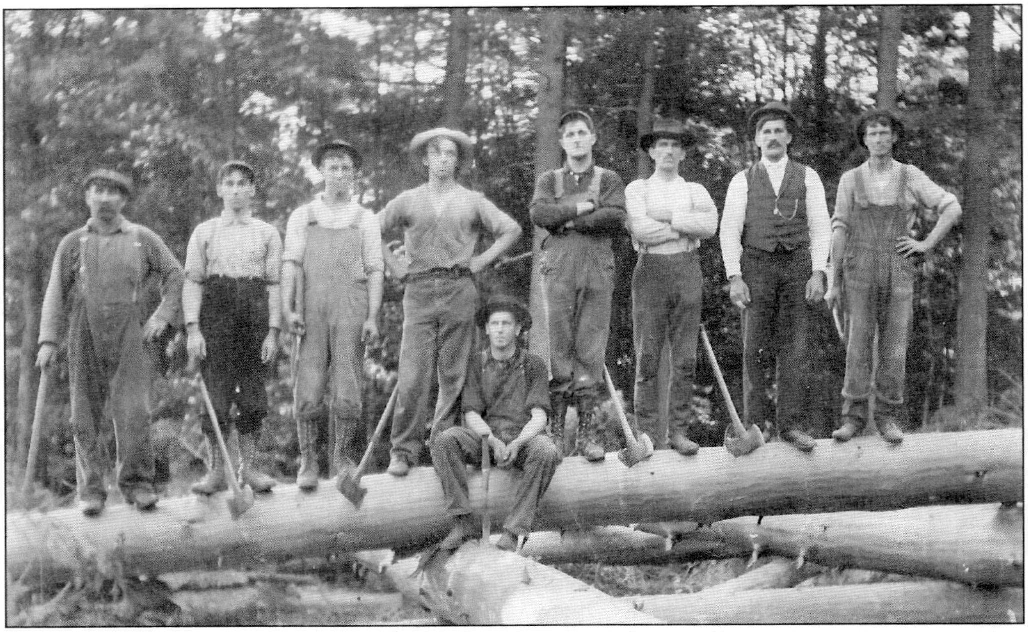

This logging crew poses with their double bit, or two-sided, axes. Primarily used to cut and lop off limbs from the white pine and other softwood logs, double bit axes were very common by the late 1800s. Typically, one blade was sharpened to a finely honed, narrow felling edge, while the second blade was ground slightly blunter and used for knots and rough cuts. (Goff Nelson Library Collection.)

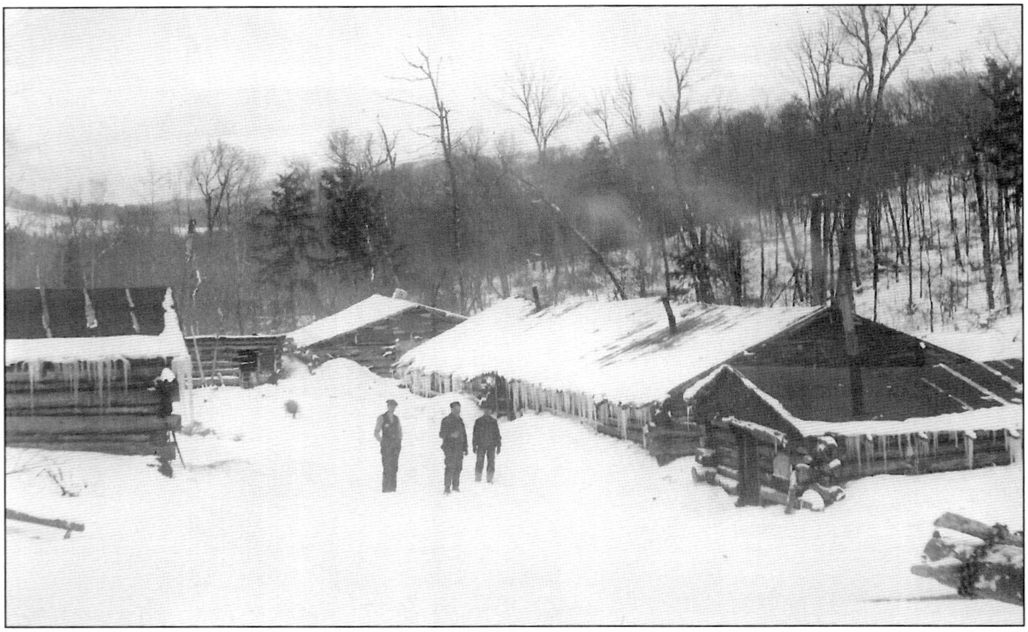

Shown here in 1912, the Peter LeBoeuf camp, on Boulder Brook in the Bog River watershed, was a typical lumber camp with a bunkhouse, cook shanty, and other buildings necessary for the work of the men, horses, and oxen. For the most part, logging was a winter activity and tended to be temporary. Pictured are, from left to right, Frank Eldred, Jack Timmons, and either Fred or Pete LeBoeuf. (Photograph by McCormick Studio; Goff Nelson Library Collection.)

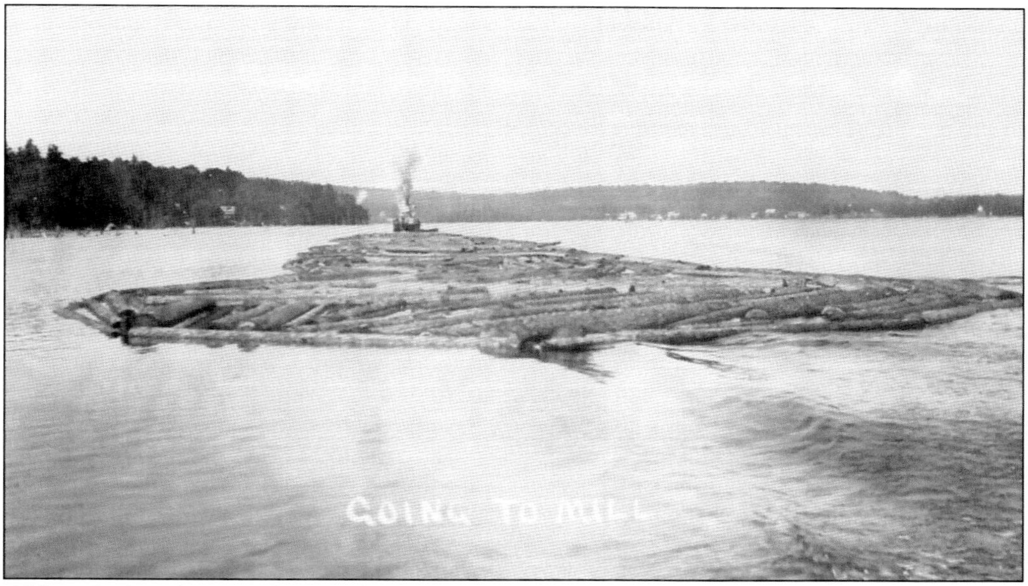

Although this photograph was taken on nearby Cranberry Lake, the sight of a tugboat hauling a log boom to the local mill was a common scene on Tupper Lake in the early 1900s. Over the years, many major lumber firms harvested timber through Tupper Lake, stamping the end of each log with a marking hammer to distinguish their cut. (Author's collection.)

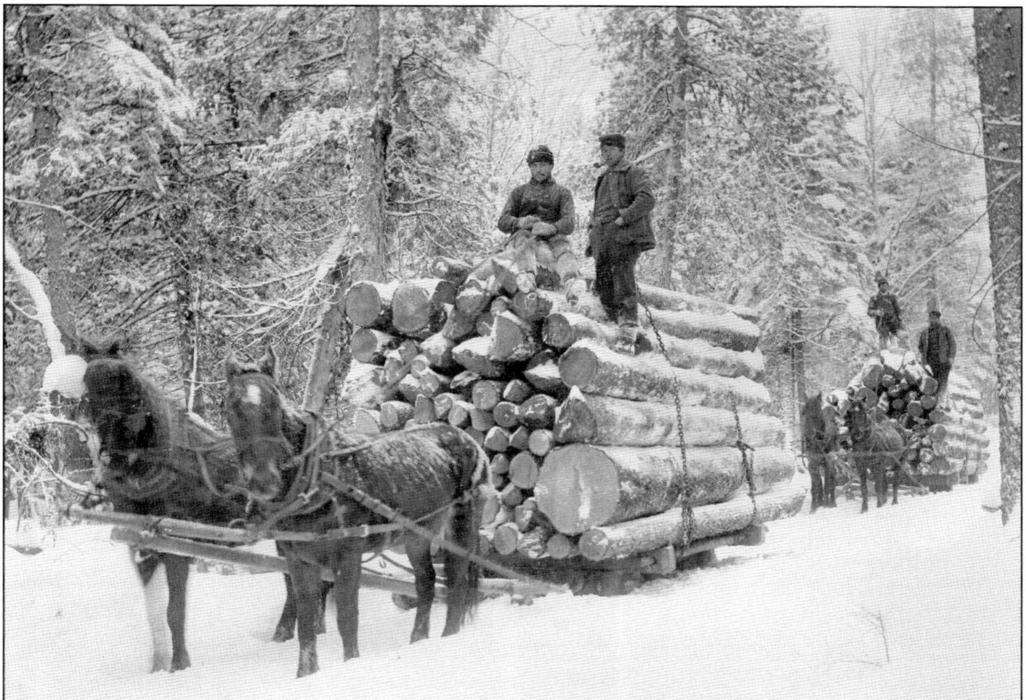

In winter, logs were transported to riverbanks or rails by log sleds. When the ice melted, they were floated down the river to sawmills. Camps usually had 2 foremen, about 70 men, 20 teams of horses, and 7 yoke of oxen. (Goff Nelson Library Collection.)

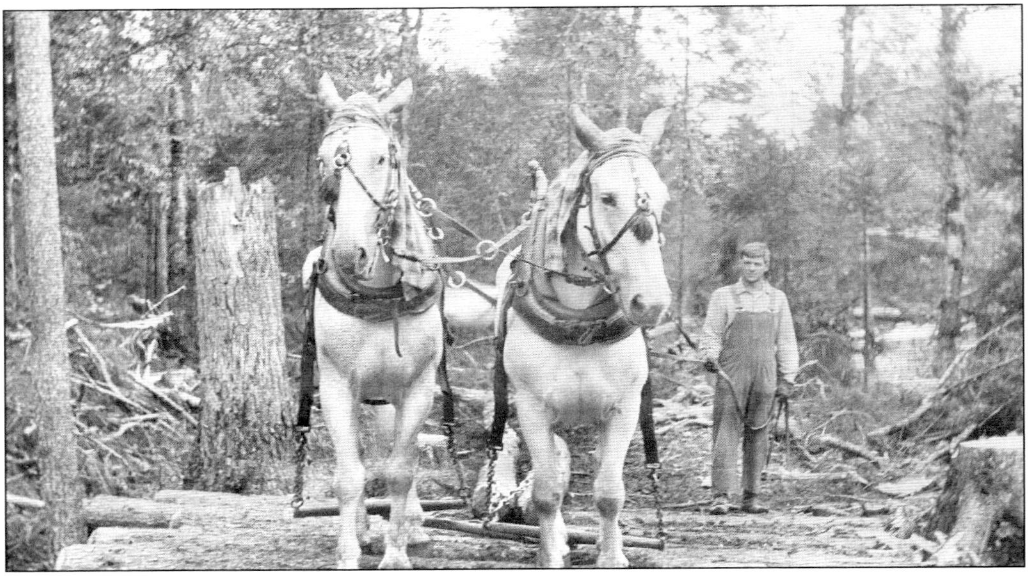

Before the arrival of tractors, teams of horses would "skid" the logs out of the woods to the landings, where a lumberjack would "buck up" the fallen trees to log lengths. To be a successful skidder man, the bond between a teamster and his team of horses was critical. (Goff Nelson Library Collection.)

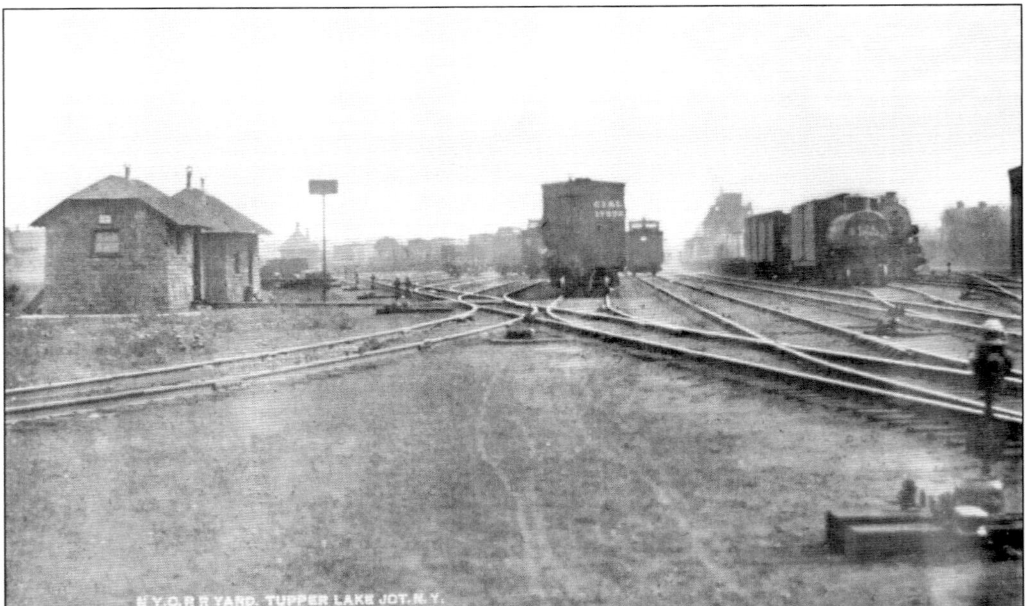

As the junction point for Hurd's and Webb's railroad, downtown Tupper Lake became the Adirondacks' leading rail center, with a sprawling freight shed and offices, extensive yard facilities, water towers, a coal chute, and a roundhouse where 40 men were kept busy maintaining the locomotives operating over the Utica–Montreal and Tupper–Ottawa lines. (Goff Nelson Library Collection.)

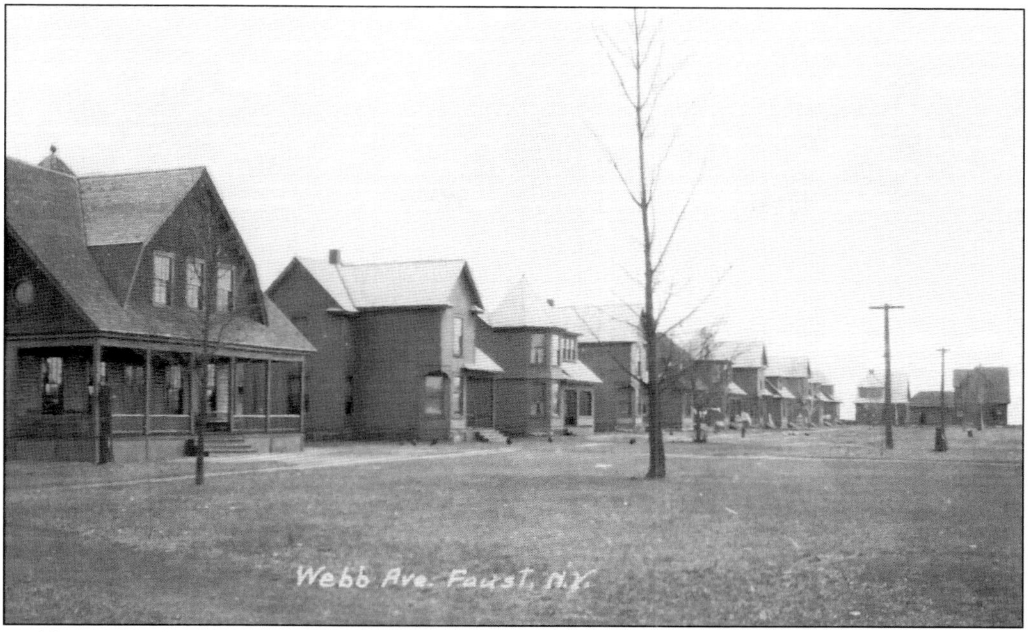

Webb Row was built specifically to house the workers who worked on the railroad and their families. Dr. William Seward Webb's Mohawk & Malone Railway crossed the northern Adirondacks at Tupper Lake Junction. (Author's collection.)

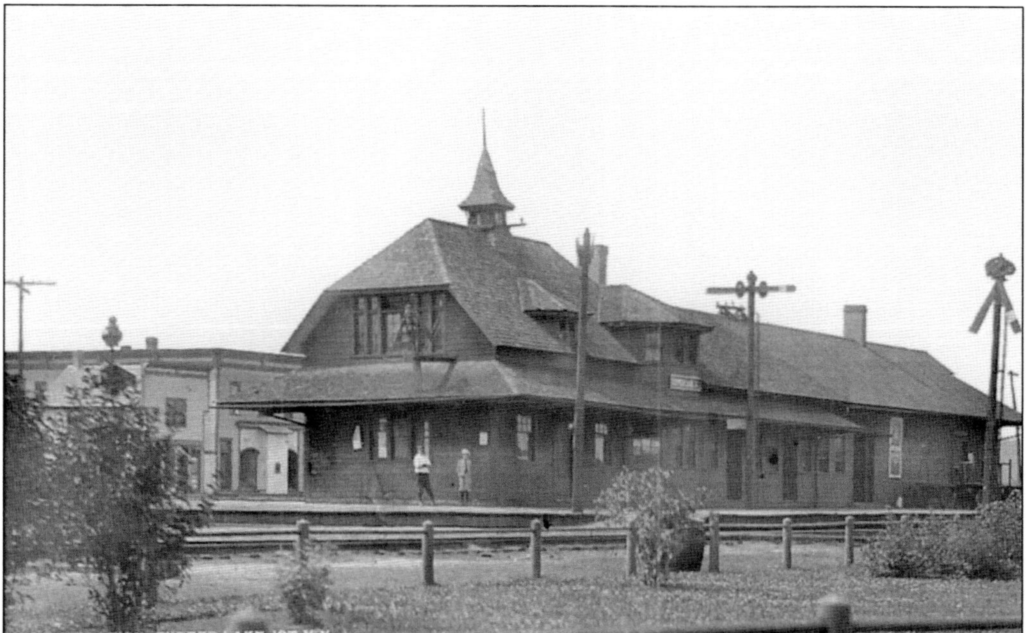

The railroad station at Tupper Lake Junction opened in 1892, reaching from Malone Junction to Childwold Station with a branch from Lake Clear Junction to Saranac Lake. In a 1906 foreclosure sale, the station passed into the hands of the New York Central Railroad, which added freight and passenger service into their operation in 1914. (Author's collection.)

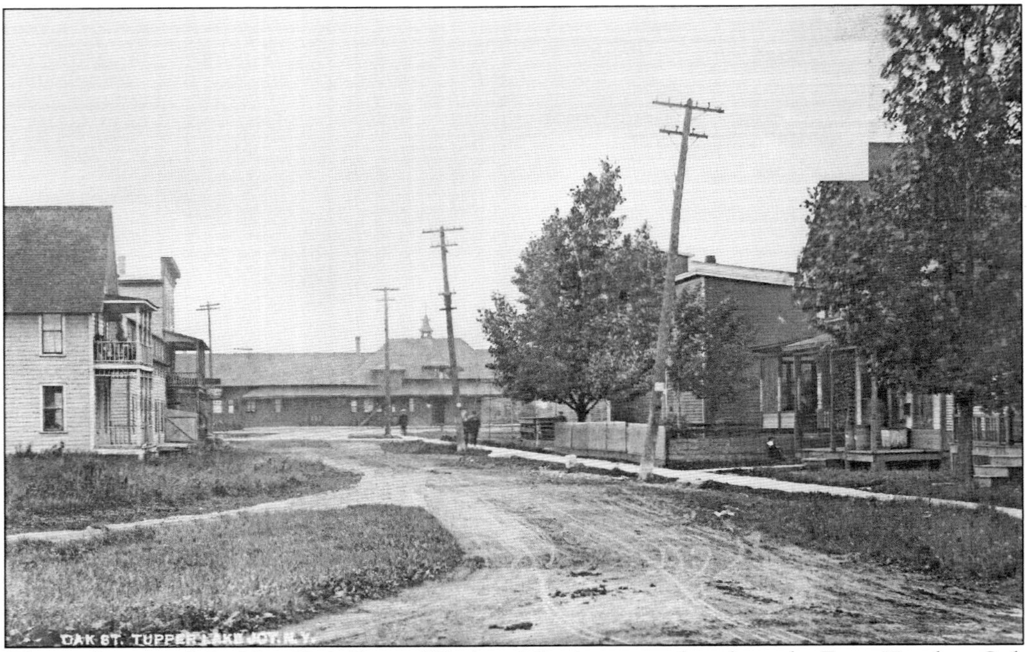

This early view of the New York Central Railroad Station was taken from the Faust Hotel on Oak Street. Paved roads and automobiles would not arrive for several years. (Author's collection.)

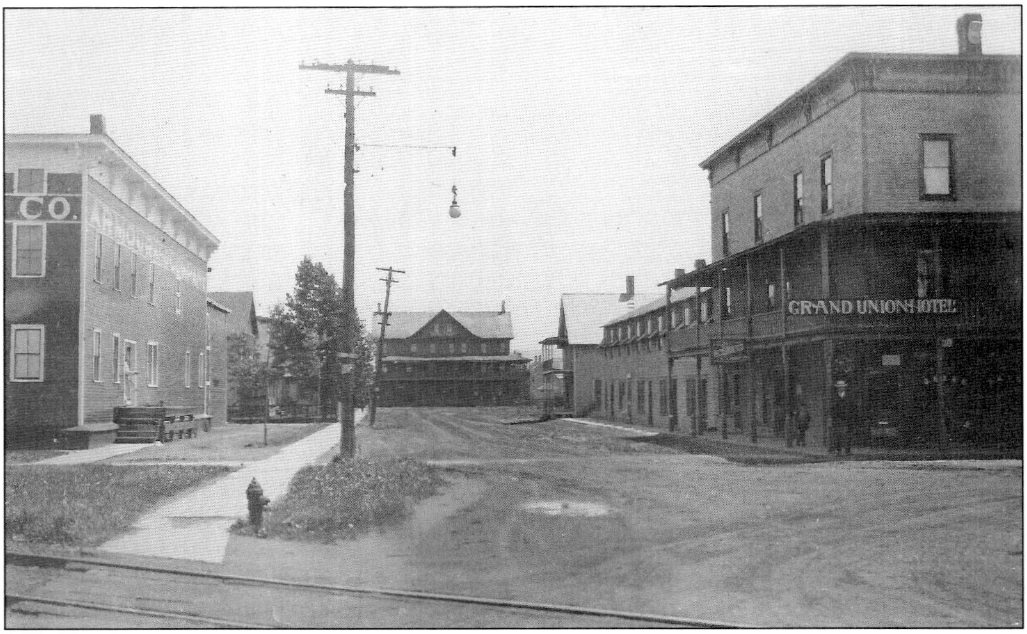

This photograph was taken of the Faust Hotel from the train station. For 60 years, the Faust was a familiar landmark in downtown Tupper Lake. Frank Dowd built it in 1895 and later became the Faust postman. To the left is another longtime fixture, the Armour meatpacking building, and to the right is the Grand Union Hotel, the only of these buildings still standing. (Author's collection.)

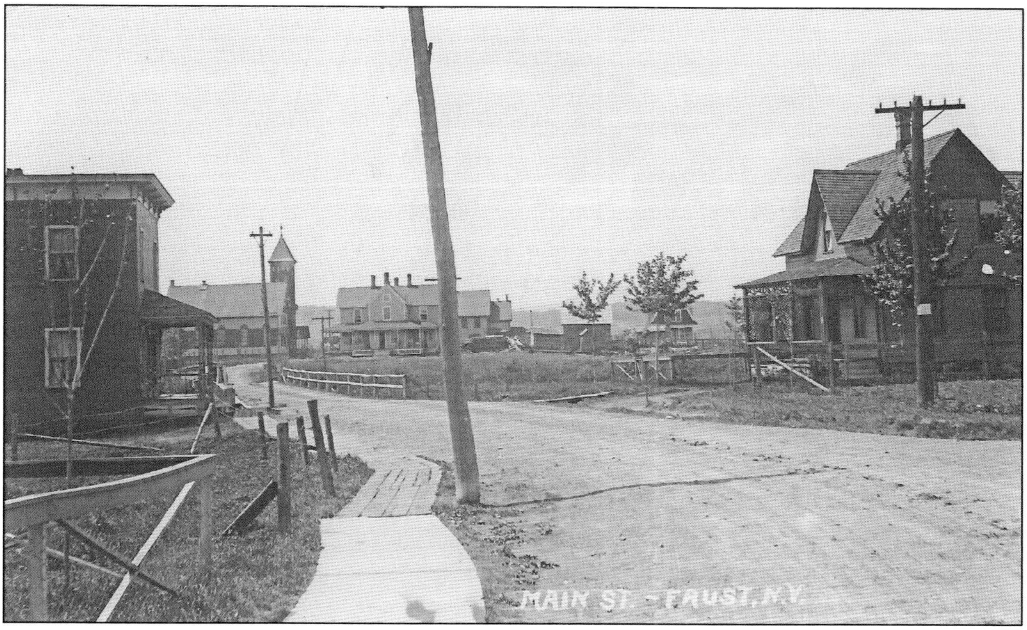

Looking northwest from the railroad tracks is the original Holy Name Church. Built in 1904, it was destroyed by fire in 1922. (Author's collection.)

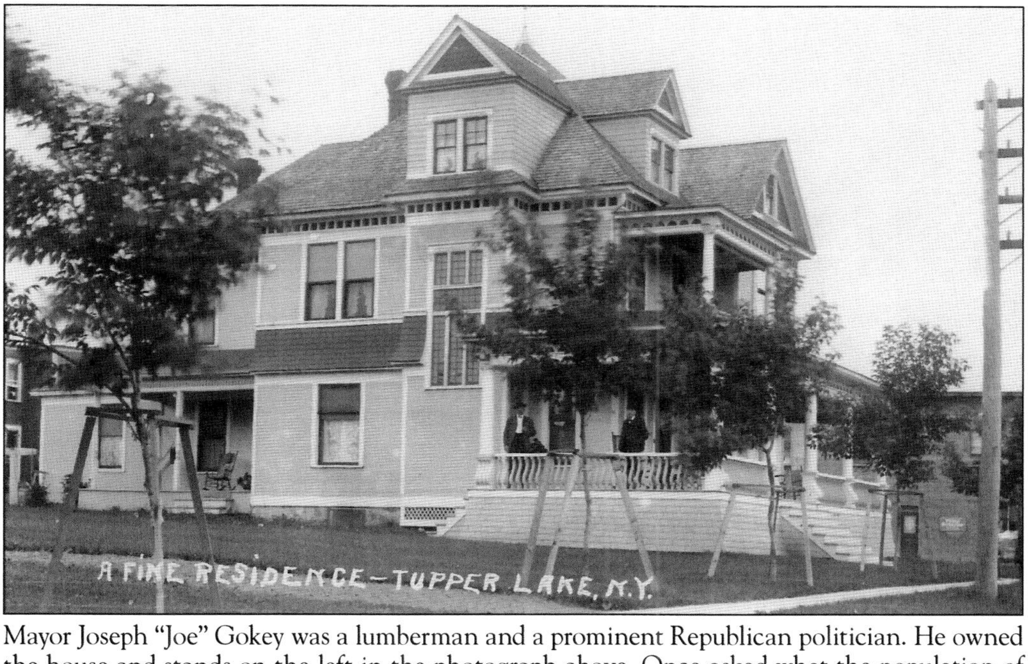

Mayor Joseph "Joe" Gokey was a lumberman and a prominent Republican politician. He owned the house and stands on the left in the photograph above. Once asked what the population of Tupper Lake was, he replied, "Mostly Spruce and Hemlock."

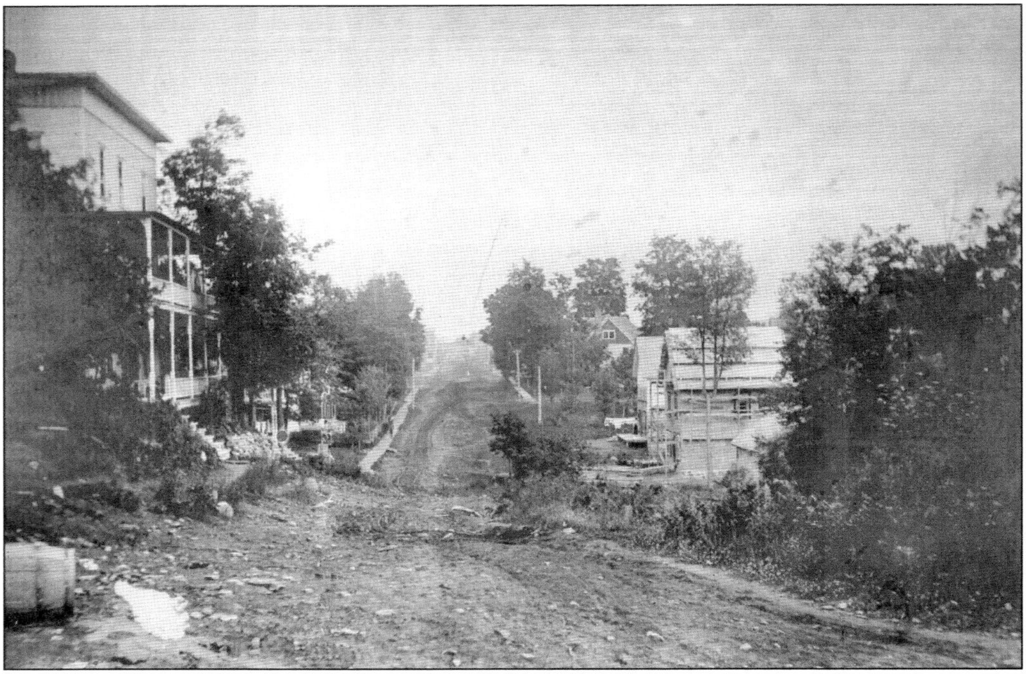

The Globe Hotel, on the left side of the dirt road, was built in 1890 and was later owned by Barney Seigel of Seigel Hardware, who changed the name to Alta Cliff. Grace Brown once stayed at this hotel with the father of her unborn child, apparently thinking that the trip would end in marriage. However, Chester Gillette was planning murder, not marriage, and it was the last day the attractive young woman would spend on this earth. That murder would become Upstate New York's most famous murder case. (Goff Nelson Library Collection.)

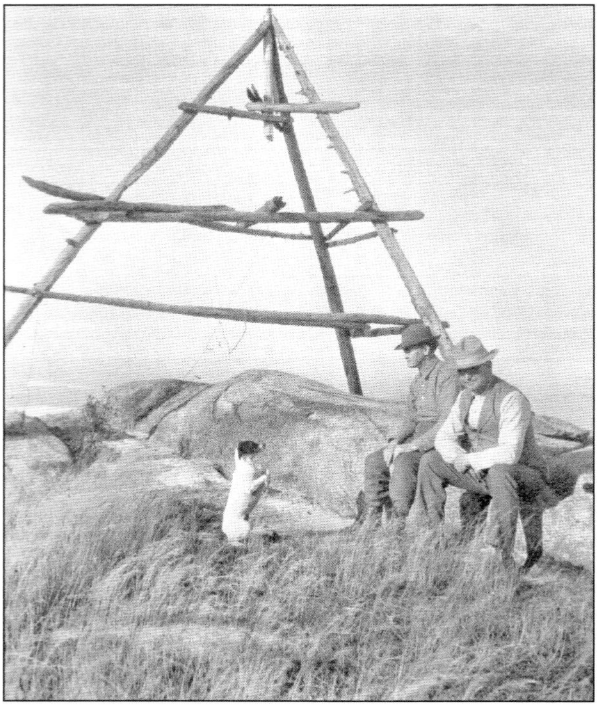

Two men and their dog sit atop Mount Morris next to the remains of a survey tripod. Later, the town built a ski center on the side slopes, marketing it as Big Tupper. (Goff Nelson Library Collection.)

Three

The Town Matures

After the turn of the 20th century, new technology changed Tupper Lake forever. Horses and sleds were replaced with automobiles and motorized tractors. The small subsistence farms that grew hay to feed the logging horses began to enlarge and diversify to serve the ever-growing community. The dairy industry grew from subsistence farms, which began sell milk, cheese, and food crops. Laborers came to town to work the woods and mills. Hotels and boardinghouses were built and itinerant merchants began to settle in the community. With the railroad firmly established, the logging industry expanded and new mills were established to produce a diversified list of products, from furniture parts to wooden spoons and bowls. The buildings lost in the great fire were rebuilt to be more substantial, and many had firewalls.

The heated millpond, or "hot pond," was invented around 1890. This innovation made it possible to run sawmills year-round, creating permanent jobs.

Early loggers cut trees only in winter because it was easy to move logs on sleds across the snow to nearby frozen waterways. The logs would sit on the frozen lakes and rivers until spring, when the water would carry the logs downriver to the sawmill. The logs were then sorted and delivered to the local mill. Hot ponds located right next to mill buildings made logging easier. Exhaust steam from the mill, or hot water from another source, was pumped into a standing body of water to keep it partially thawed all winter. Cut logs were piled into the heated water, where they thawed and softened. A shed or roof was often built over the hot pond, so that even the sections of log floating above water would be warmed and full logs could be sawn.

Mountain lumbering also accelerated during this time. The Santa Clara Lumber Company ran log jobs to the top of Mount Seward, one of the highest mountains in New York. The logs were drawn six miles down the mountain to Calkin's Brook, from there passing into Cold River and eventually reaching the Raquette River and the mill at Tupper Lake, miles from where the trees had grown.

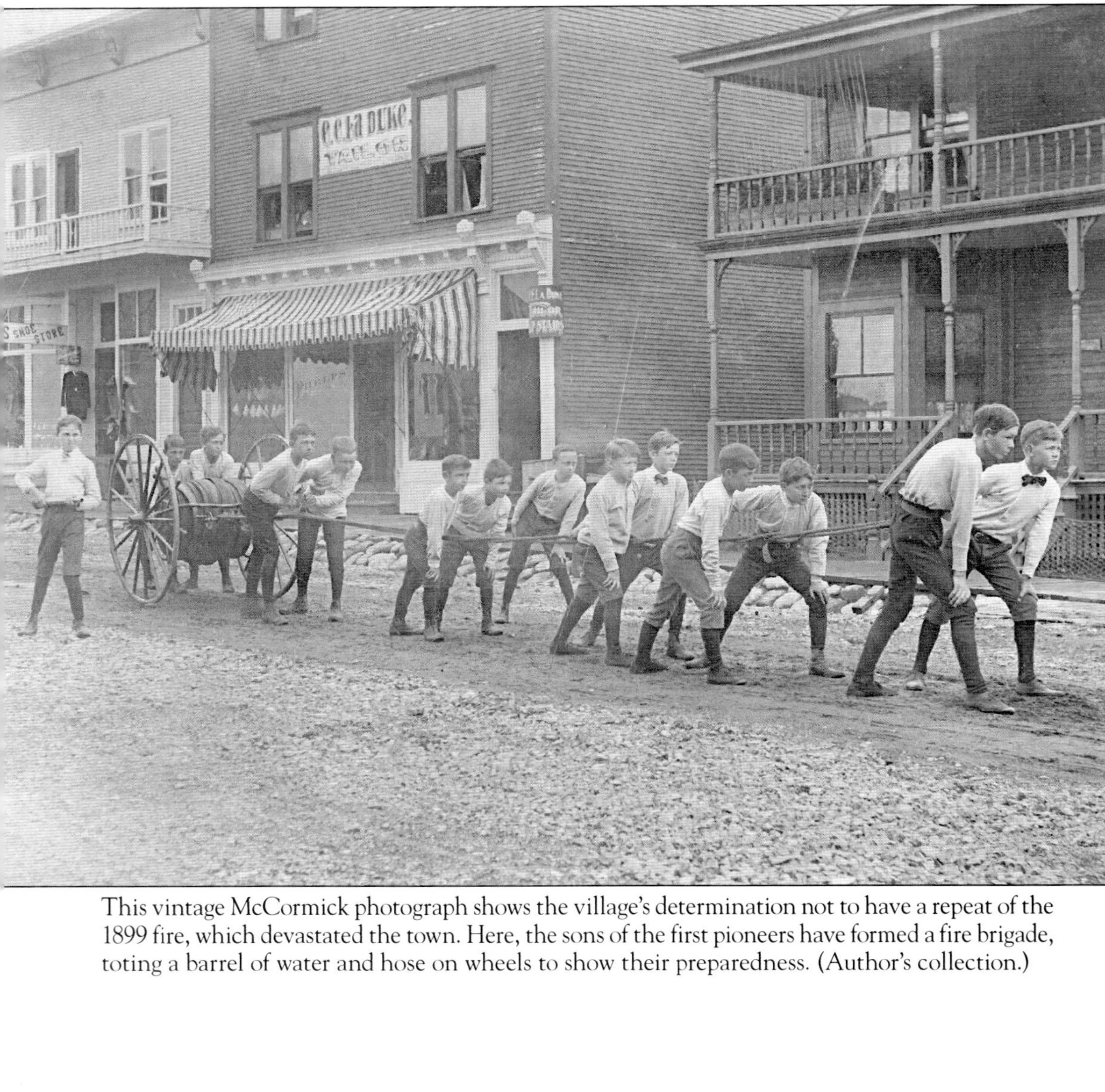

This vintage McCormick photograph shows the village's determination not to have a repeat of the 1899 fire, which devastated the town. Here, the sons of the first pioneers have formed a fire brigade, toting a barrel of water and hose on wheels to show their preparedness. (Author's collection.)

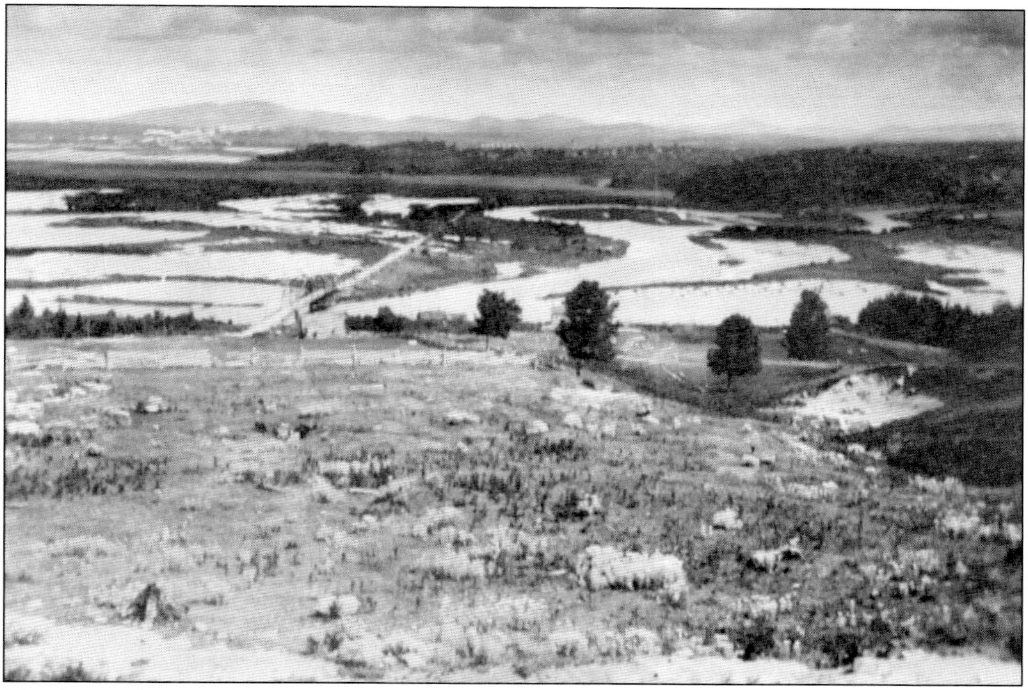

Moody Marsh, named in memory of the Moody family of river guides, is part of one of the largest contiguous wetlands in the Adirondacks. Until 1894, when the steel bridge was constructed, Moody residents crossed on a log bridge. The route followed along the lake's east shore to the crossing, where the carriage road was often under water to the height to the buggy's plank seats. (Goff Nelson Library Collection.)

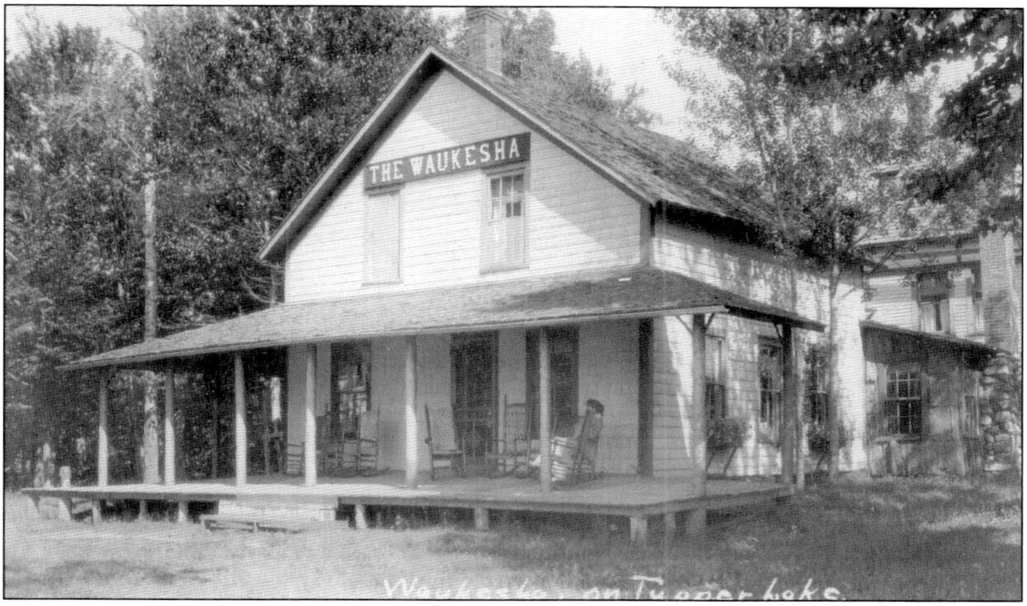

After "Uncle Mart" Moody sold his first hotel, he built another a half-mile down the road. He called it Redside Camp after the brook that emptied into nearby Tupper Lake. In 1893, he sold again to Mr. and Mrs. Jabez Alexander, who enlarged the camp, changed the name to the Waukesha, and ran it successfully for the next 56 years. (Author's collection.)

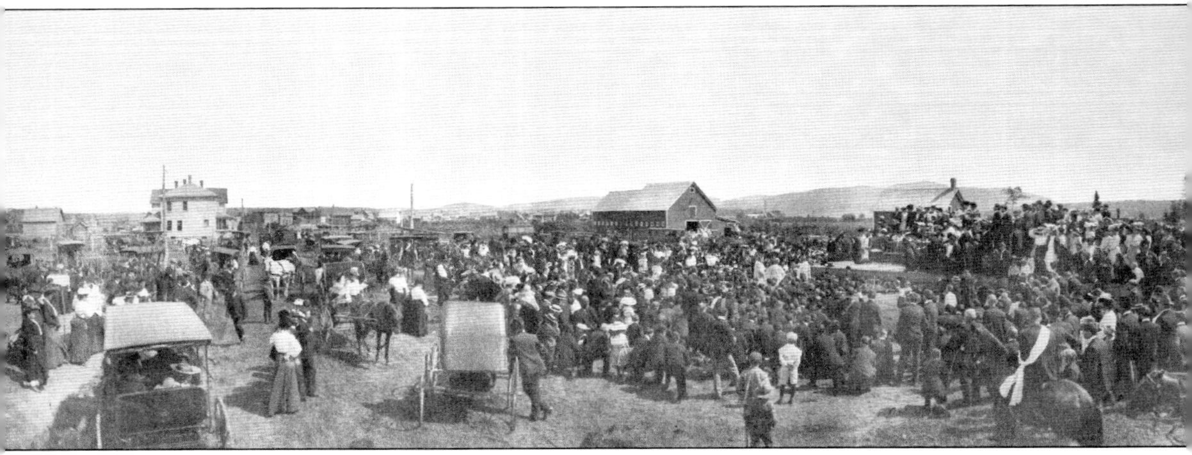

The Holy Name Church was incorporated on January 20, 1904, after Father Constantineau, reverend of the St. Alphonsus Church, ceded the Faust area for a new parish. Rev. Alexander Klauder drew the plans for the original church. All of Faust celebrated the laying of the cornerstone, and the church was completed in 1910 at a cost of $30,000. Unfortunately, the church succumbed to fire in 1922. Despite substantial financial costs, the congregation came together and erected a new church by 1924. A handsome brick church, it still stands today on the corner of Underwood and Main Streets. (Goff Nelson Library Collection.)

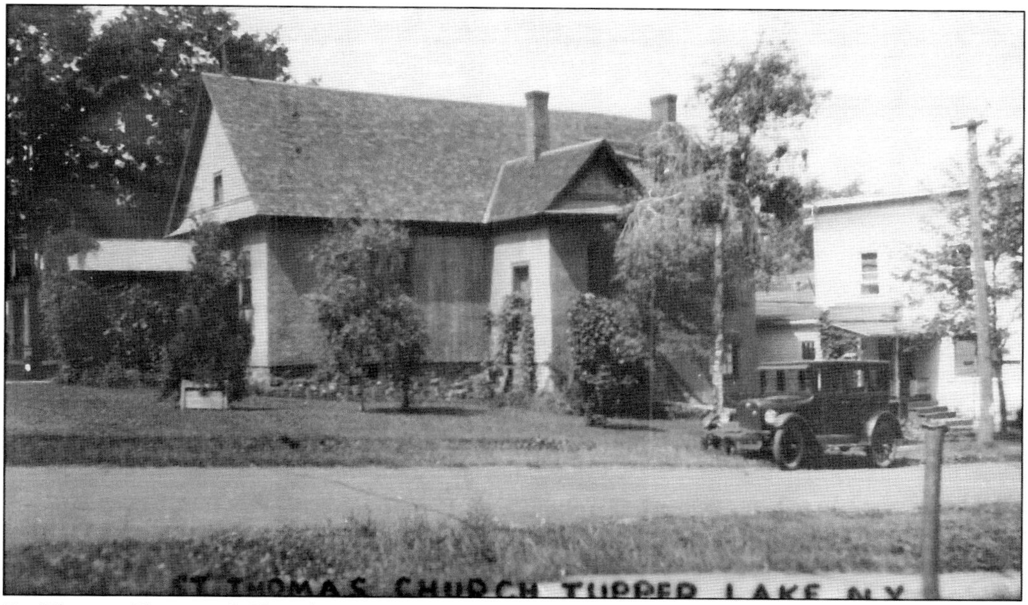

St. Thomas Episcopal Church was erected in 1899 by J.H. Wert for $500. It was a plain building and looked more like a residence than a church. Before it was constructed, pioneer John Hurd ran a Sunday morning "Gospel Mission Train" for early settlers. (Author's collection.)

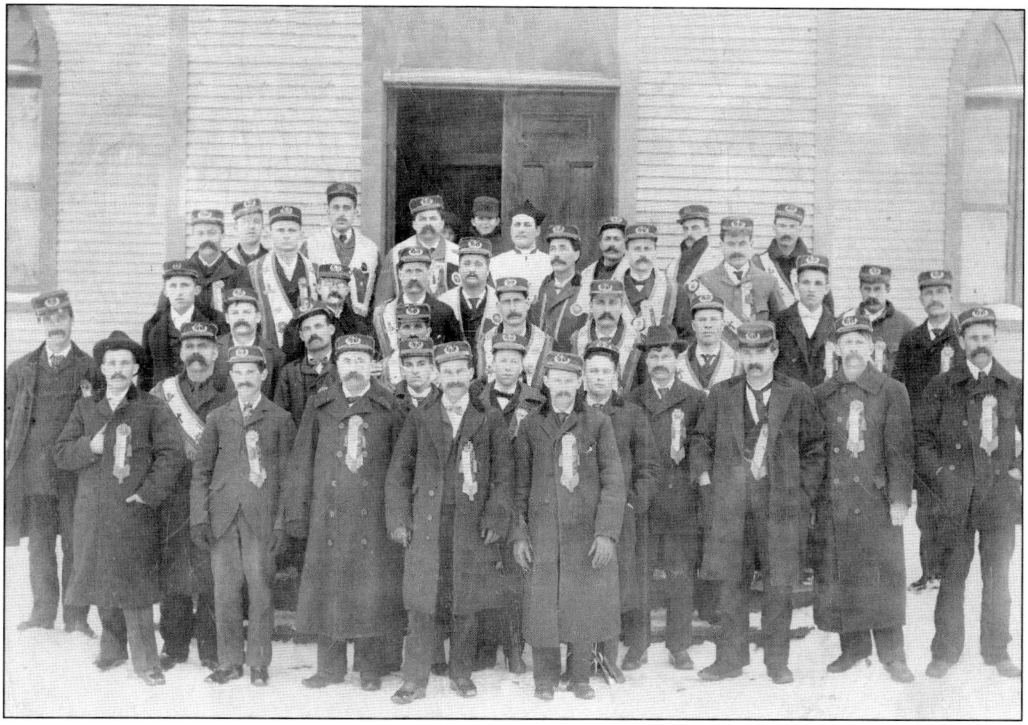

The logging industry attracted a large contingent of French Canadians who eventually made their homes on Tupper Lake. The Saint-Jean-Baptiste Society, created by journalist Ludger Duvernay in Lower Canada, evolved out of the belief that if one helps oneself, heaven will help that person. The society declared June 24 to be St. John the Baptist Day, the national day of the Quebecers. (Goff Nelson Library Collection.)

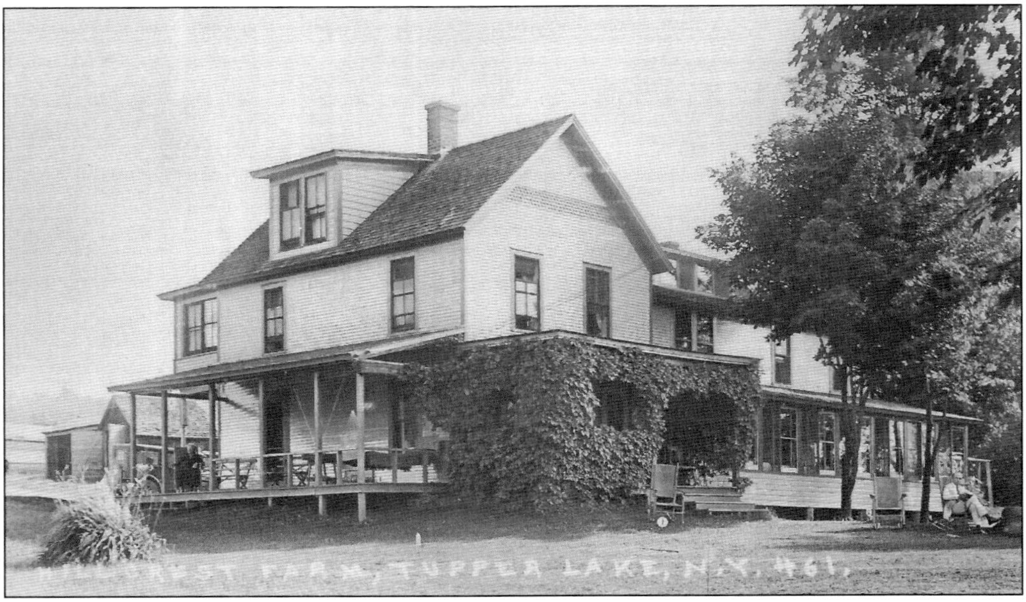

In 1907, Charles and Alice Hathaway established Hillcrest Farm in Moody, running it as a boardinghouse. Charles died in 1931, but Alice continued to run Hillcrest until her retirement in 1968. The farm was famous for their "Choke Dogs," a name given by Hillcrest patrons for the stack of buckwheat pancakes they served with maple syrup from the farm's sugar bush. (Author's collection.)

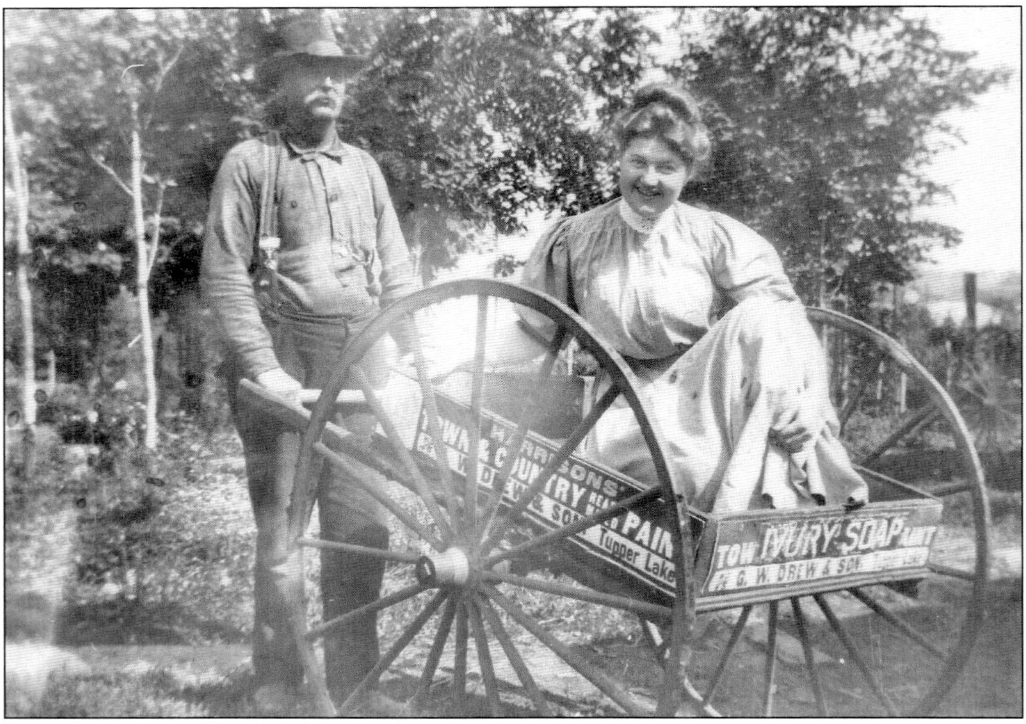

The handcart this couple plays in features an advertisement for G.W. Drew & Son. Ernest A. Drew and his wife first came to Tupper Lake just after the big fire in 1899 and ran this furniture and undertaking business until 1920. (Author's collection.)

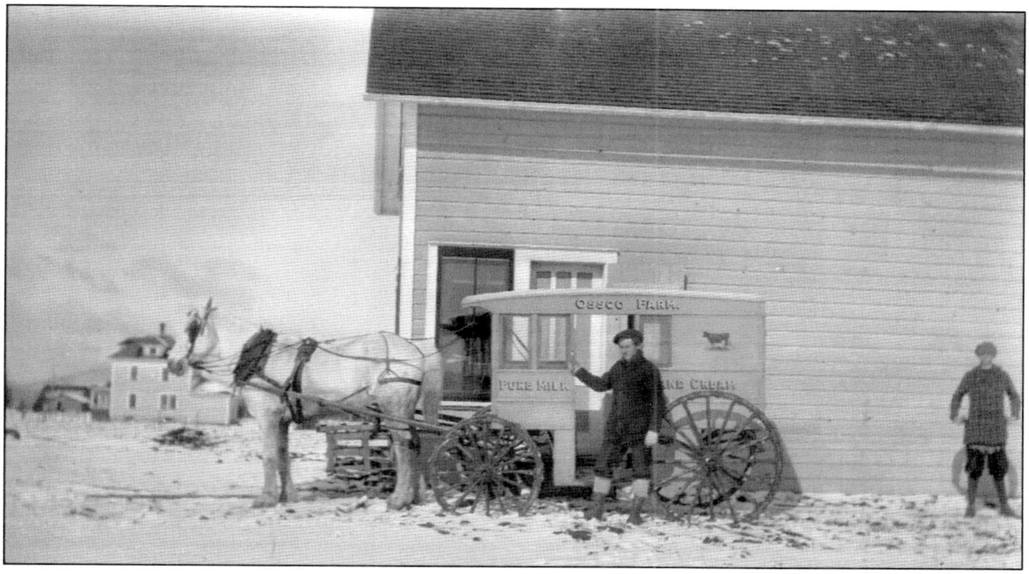

The Ossco Farm milk wagon delivered to Tupper Lake in the early 1900s. Albert and Lavina Hosley, who ran Ossco Farm, named for an Iroquois word meaning "beautiful view," sold the farm to the residents of Tupper Lake, who donated it to the Veterans Administration for the establishment of Sunmount Veterans Hospital. (Author's collection.)

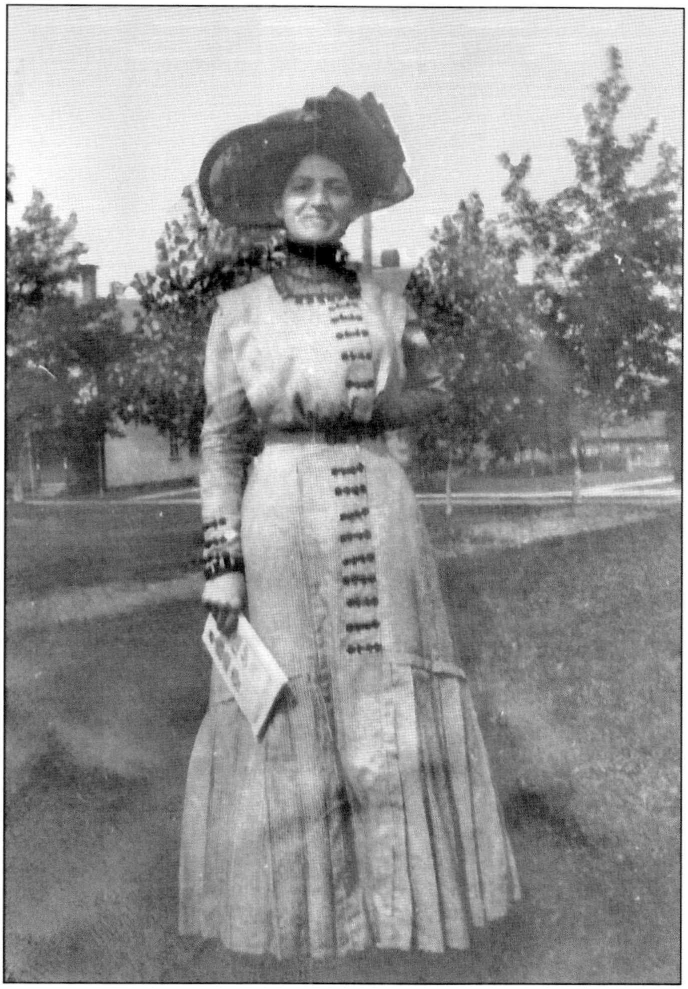

Mary (Vincent) Baker was one of Tupper Lake's first businesswomen, purchasing a dry goods store in the Foote Block and opening a ladies' finishing store. She was also a milliner and made many stylish hats for the ladies of Tupper Lake. (Joy Vincent-Moody.)

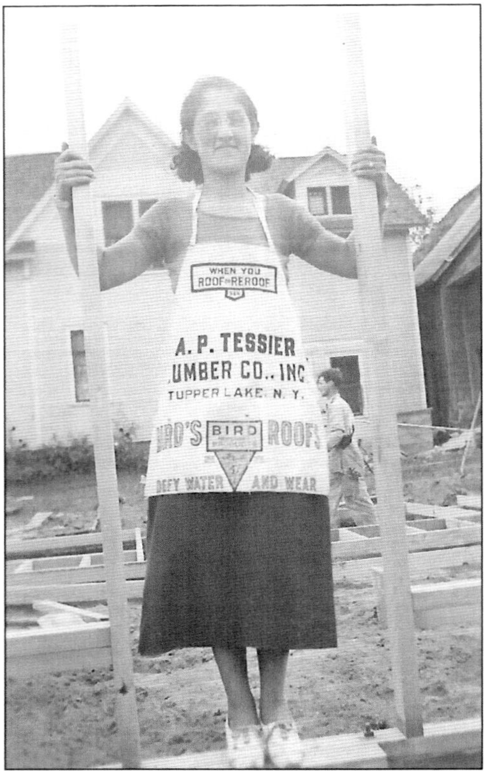

Mildred (Payrot) Vincent was born in March 1913 in Loon Lake. She lived in Tupper Lake and worked for many local businesses, including the A.P. Tessier Lumber Company and Mrs. Charles Murray's Boardinghouse. (Joy Vincent-Moody.)

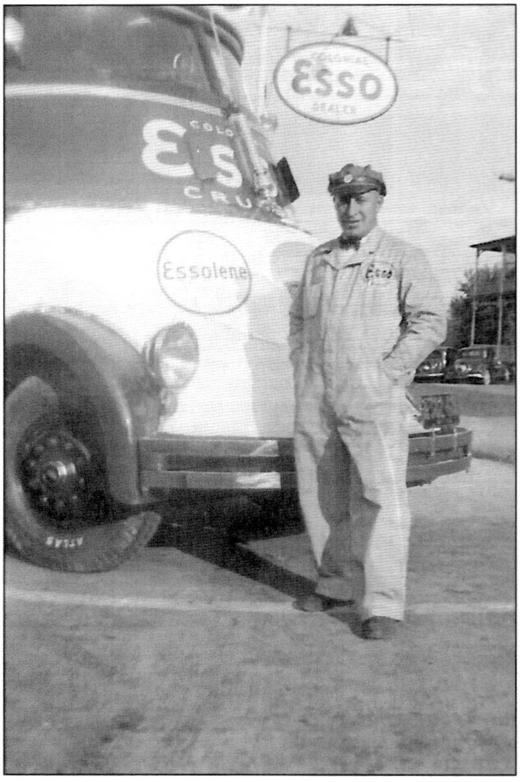

George Telesford Vincent stands alongside the "Esso Cruiser," a unique bus-like motor vehicle. The cruiser had a crew of seven men and was equipped with an electric galley and sleeping quarters. It also had a fireproof projection booth and screen to show talking pictures and broadcast radio. It visited communities throughout New York to promote motor safety. (Joy Vincent-Moody.)

A man of many hats, George Vincent drove for the Adirondack Motor Bus Company and later opened up the Esso Service Center in Faust. He also ran one of the early taxi services and stepped in to run the Colonial Hotel and Grill at 47 Main Street when Dan Datolla was called to active military service. (Joy Vincent-Moody.)

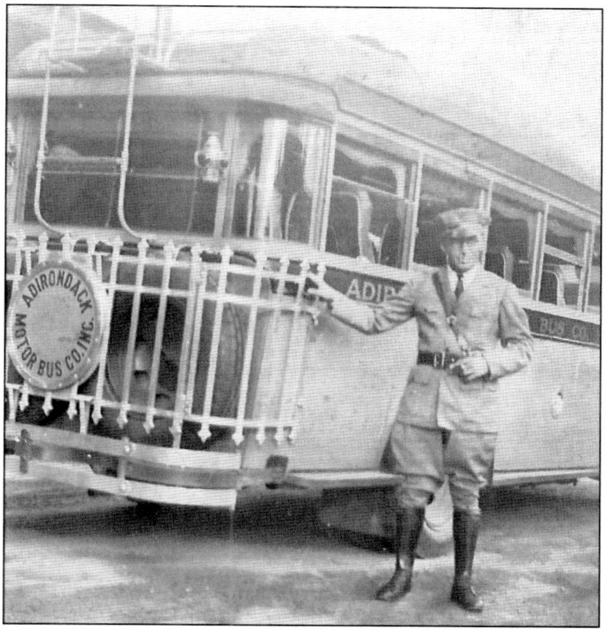

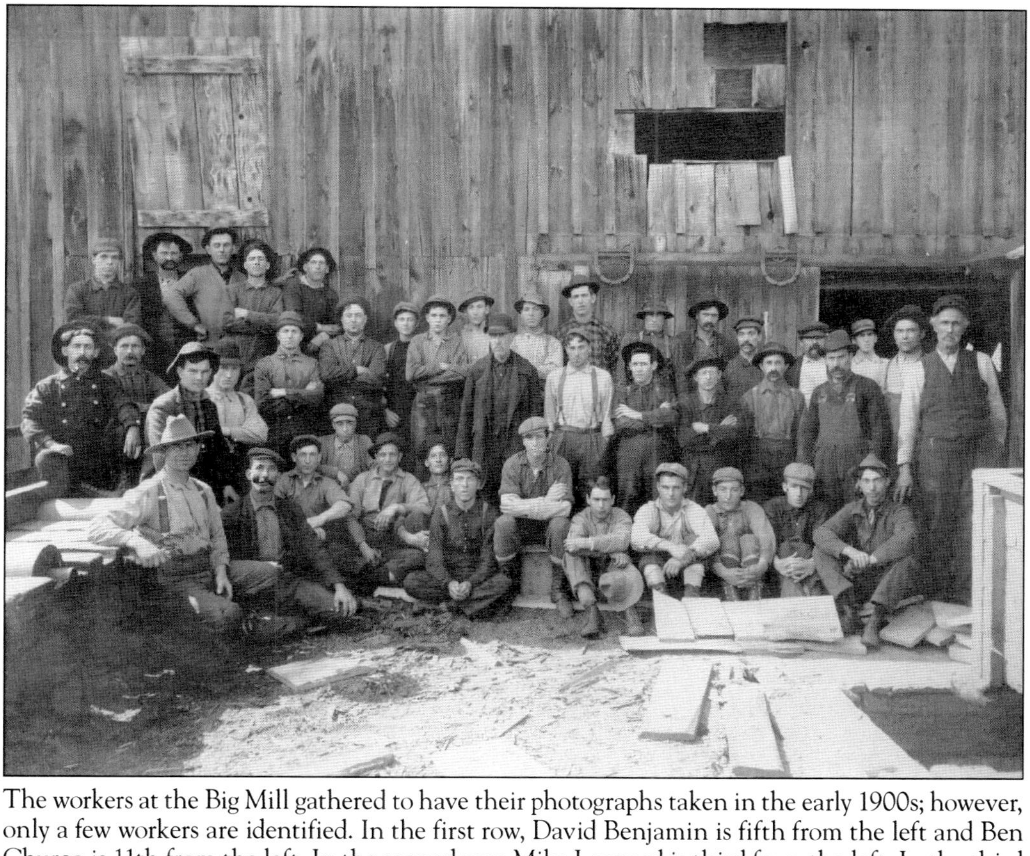

The workers at the Big Mill gathered to have their photographs taken in the early 1900s; however, only a few workers are identified. In the first row, David Benjamin is fifth from the left and Ben Churco is 11th from the left. In the second row, Mike Leonard is third from the left. In the third row, fourth from the left is William Staves and fifth from the left is Ernest Martin. (Goff Nelson Library Collection.)

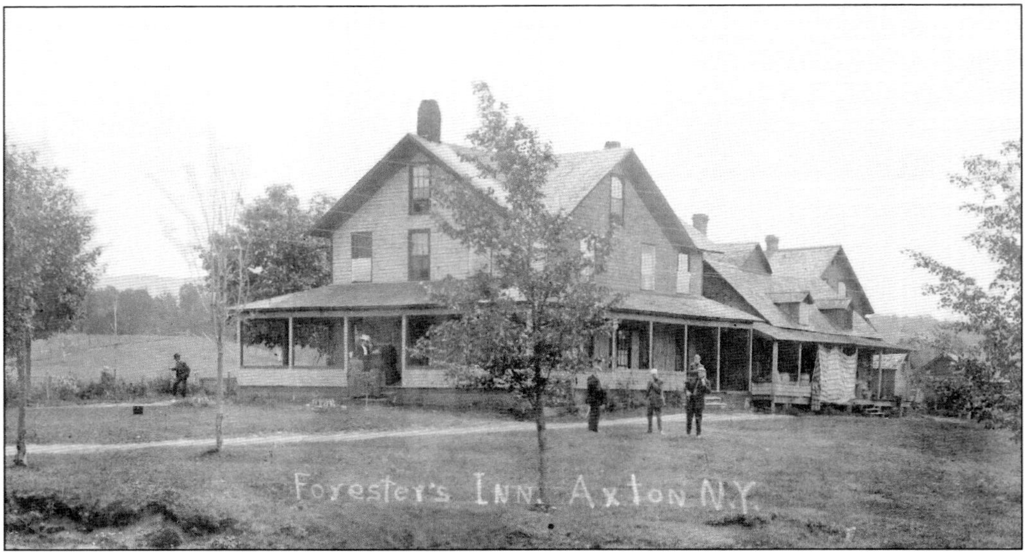

Forester's Inn was the headquarters for several professors, their families, and a number of students from Cornell College of Forestry in Ithaca. Axton—shortened from Ax Town—began as a logging camp for the Santa Clara Lumber Company. But the community grew and was used to house the many teams of horses for log jobs in the Raquette River watershed. Towering pines cover every trace of Axton today. (Author's collection.)

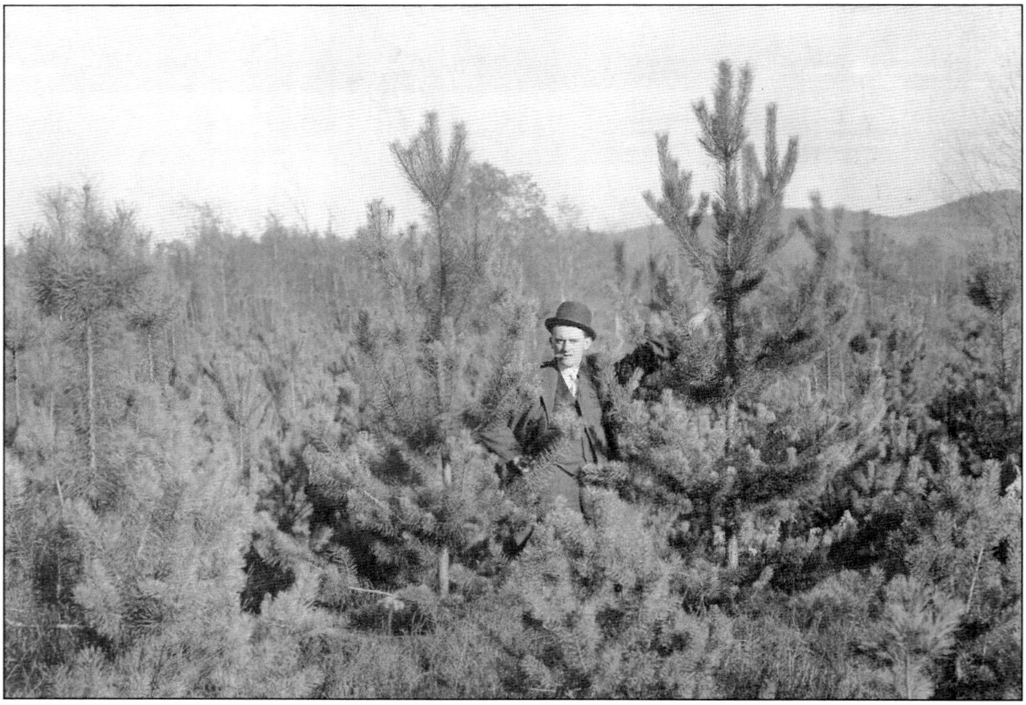

While the man in this photograph is unidentified, it was taken by early Tupper Lake photographer Frank McCormick, who had a studio. The trees look to be young Scotch pine and were probably planted by the Civilian Conservation Corps (CCC) during the Depression at Cross-Clearing, approximately six miles from Tupper Lake at the end of the Brooklyn Cooperage railroad line. (Author's collection.)

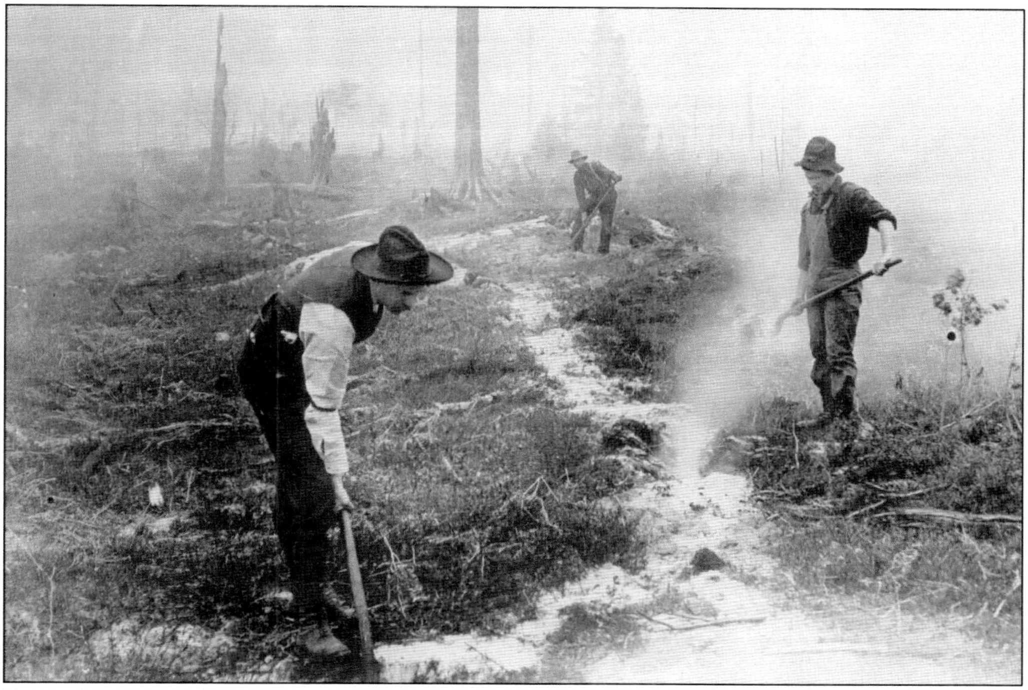

Forest fires ravaged the Tupper Lake area around 1900. Many were started by sparks from coal-fired locomotives, poor logging practices, or careless campers. Many men fought fires to protect the town, including George Sisson, who incorporated a steam fire engine from Utica to protect the Tupper Lake mills from a raging conflagration just one week after the big fire decimated the town in 1899. (Author's collection.)

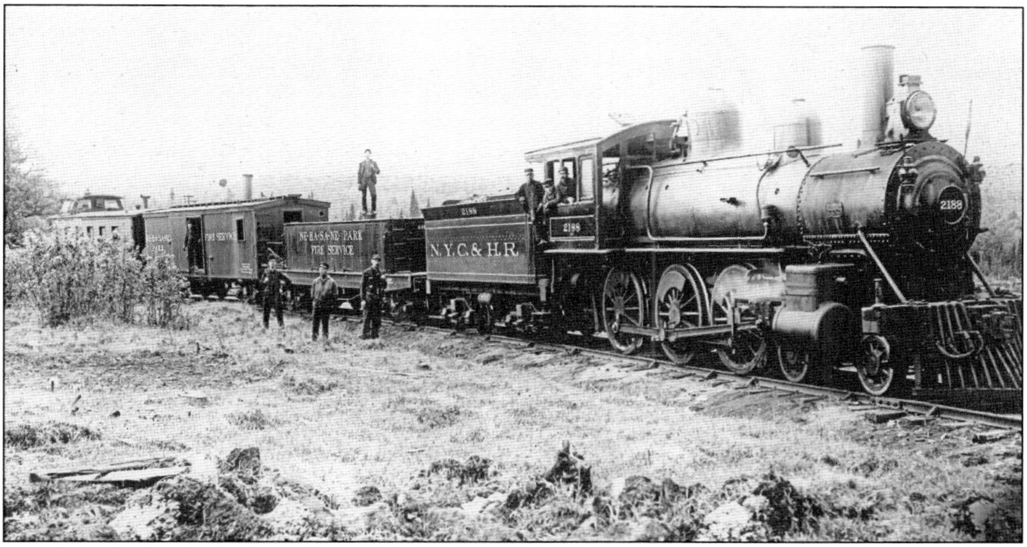

Dr. William Seward Webb acquired control of the Herkimer, Newport & Poland Railroad in 1890 and completed the first and only railroad through the heart of the Adirondacks. The junction with John Hurd's Northern Adirondack Railroad sparked the village of Tupper Lake into being. Webb also established Nehasane Park, a 115,000-acre game preserve, and pioneered forest conservation work. He established this fire train in an effort to fight the raging forest fires of the day. (Author's collection.)

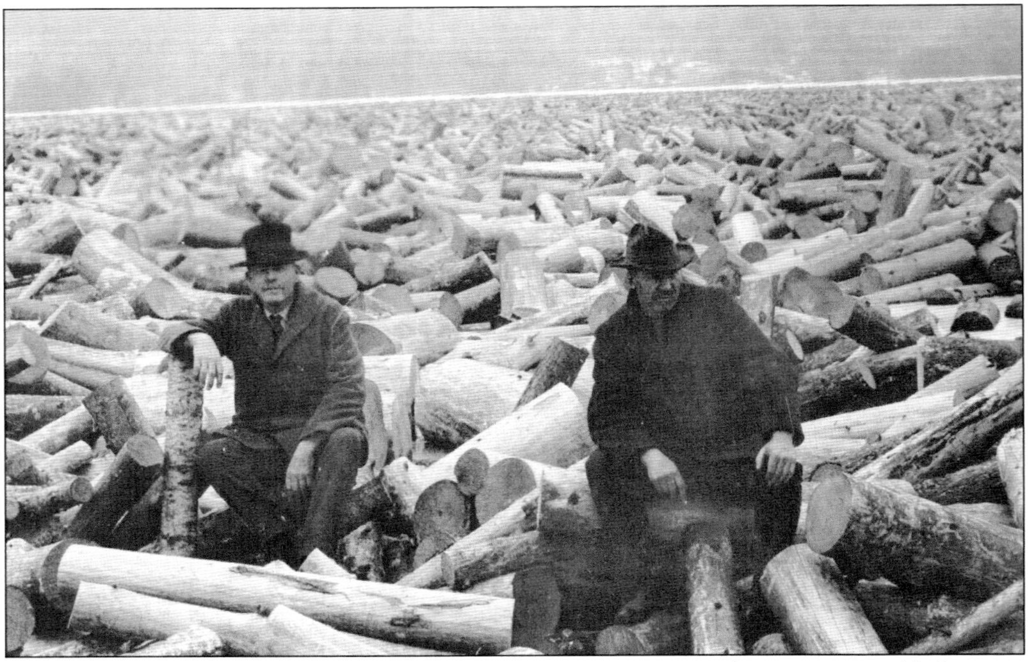

Two employees sit atop pulpwood on Rock Island Bay in Tupper Lake. It was most likely on its way to the plant built in Underwood by the Champlain Realty Company, a subsidiary of the International Paper Company, for delivery to the paper company's Piercefield mill. (Goff Nelson Library Collection.)

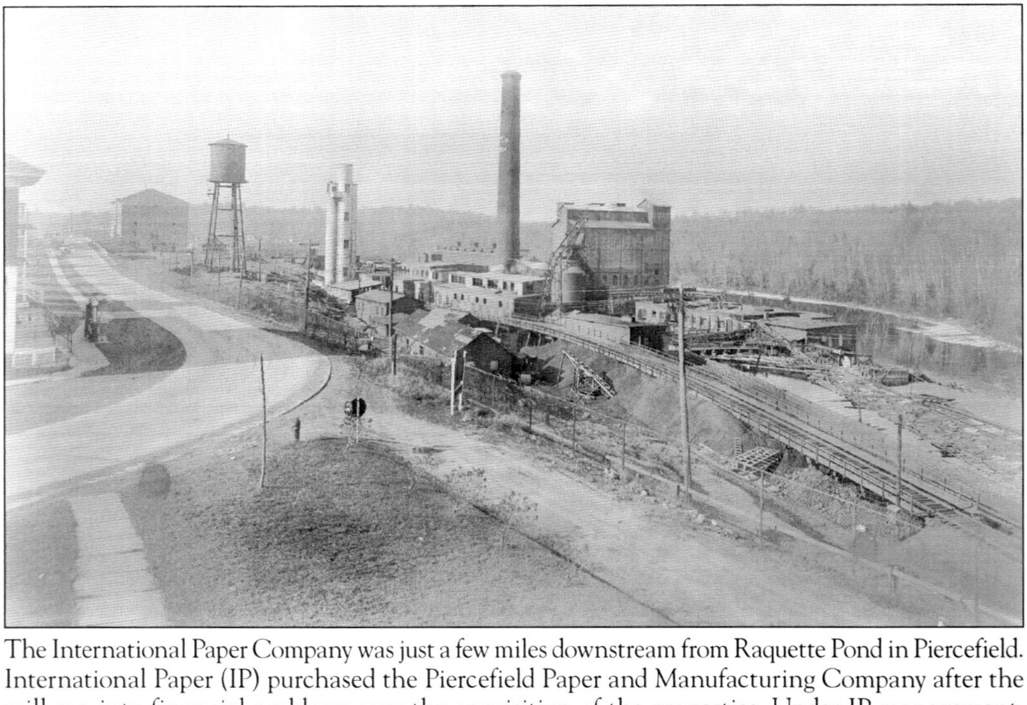

The International Paper Company was just a few miles downstream from Raquette Pond in Piercefield. International Paper (IP) purchased the Piercefield Paper and Manufacturing Company after the mill ran into financial problems over the acquisition of the properties. Under IP management, the mill flourished, producing a record pulp consumption of 24,400 cords in 1900. (Goff Nelson Library Collection.)

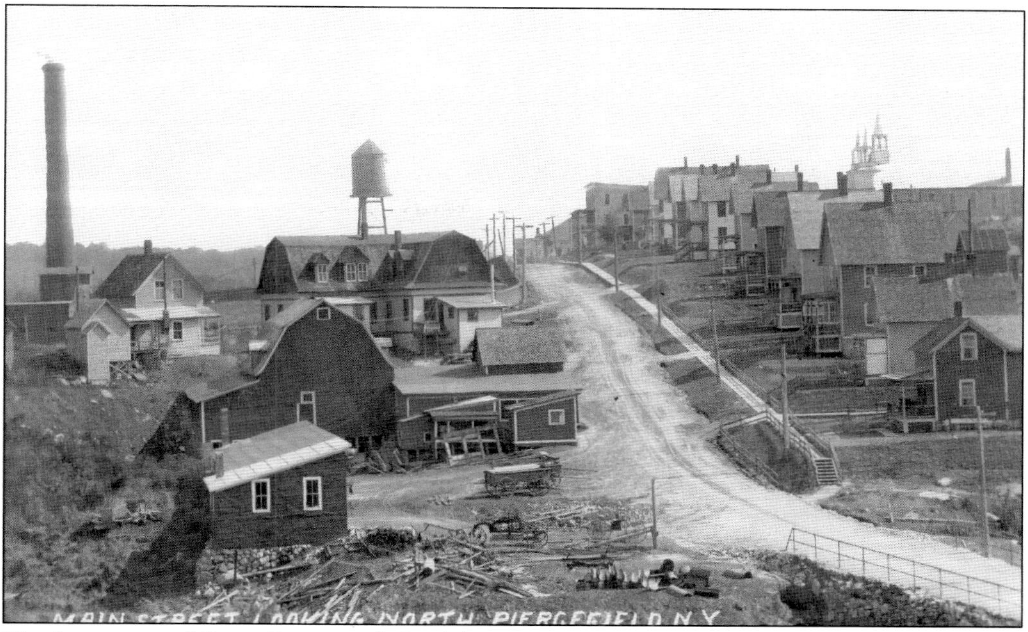

The International Paper Company helped the town prosper. At its peak, the community boasted a population of about 1,000, with two churches, a modern school, and the International Hotel. A large community house was built to include a movie theater, a dance hall, bowling alleys, a basketball court, and a restaurant. (Goff Nelson Library Collection.)

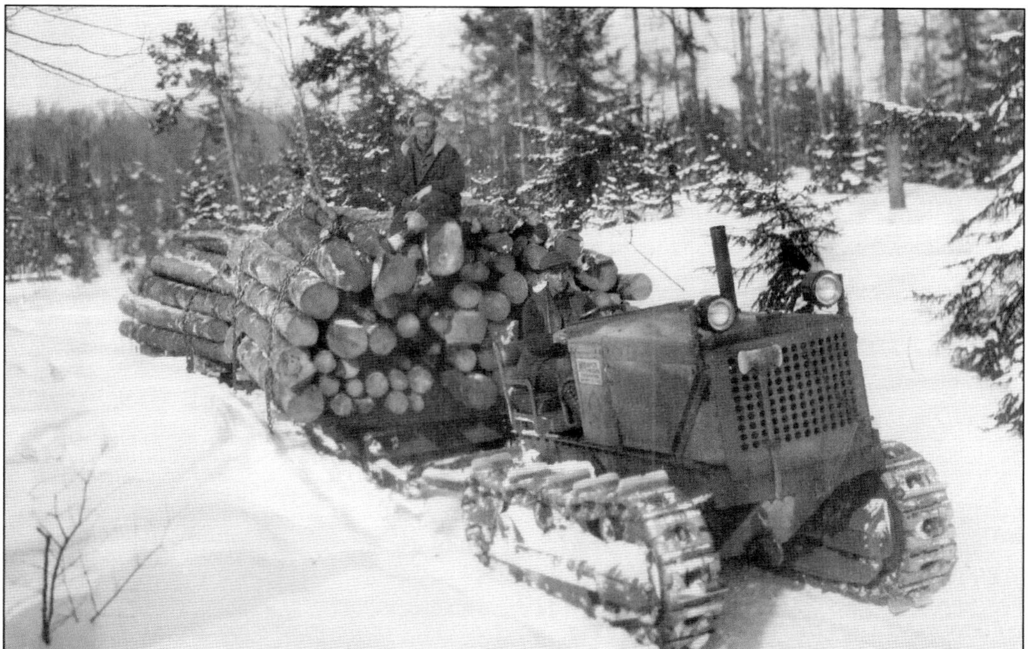

With the invention of the combustion engine, the job once done with teams of horses was replaced by the tractor, which took over the transporting of logs to the landing. (Goff Nelson Library Collection.)

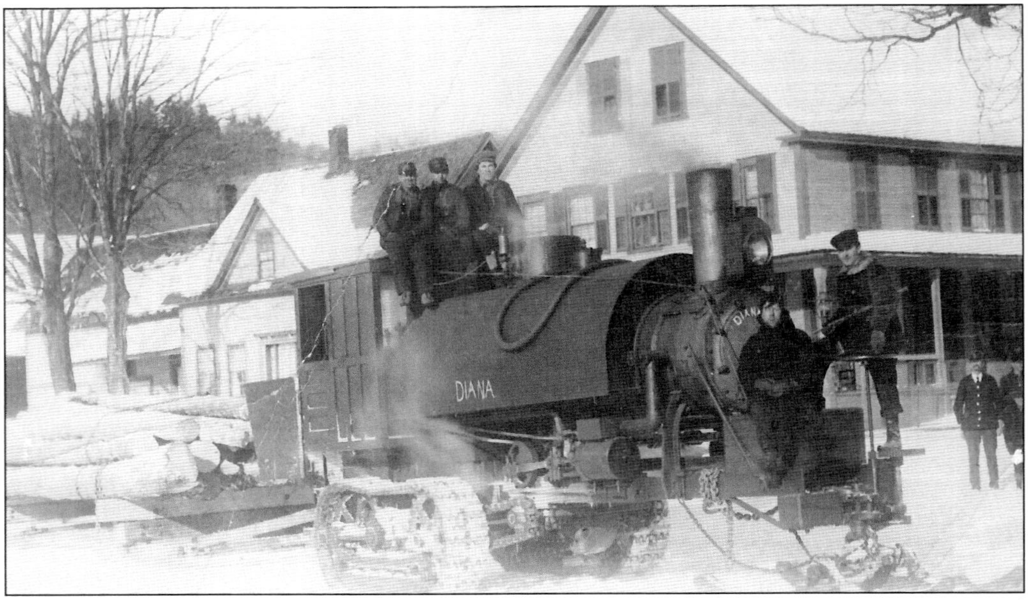

The Lombard Steam Log Hauler, patented on May 29, 1901, was the first successful commercial application of a continuous track for vehicle propulsion and led to the development of the Linn Tractor, which was widely used in Tupper Lake. A log hauler could tow a string of sleds filled with logs over snow and ice. (Author's collection.)

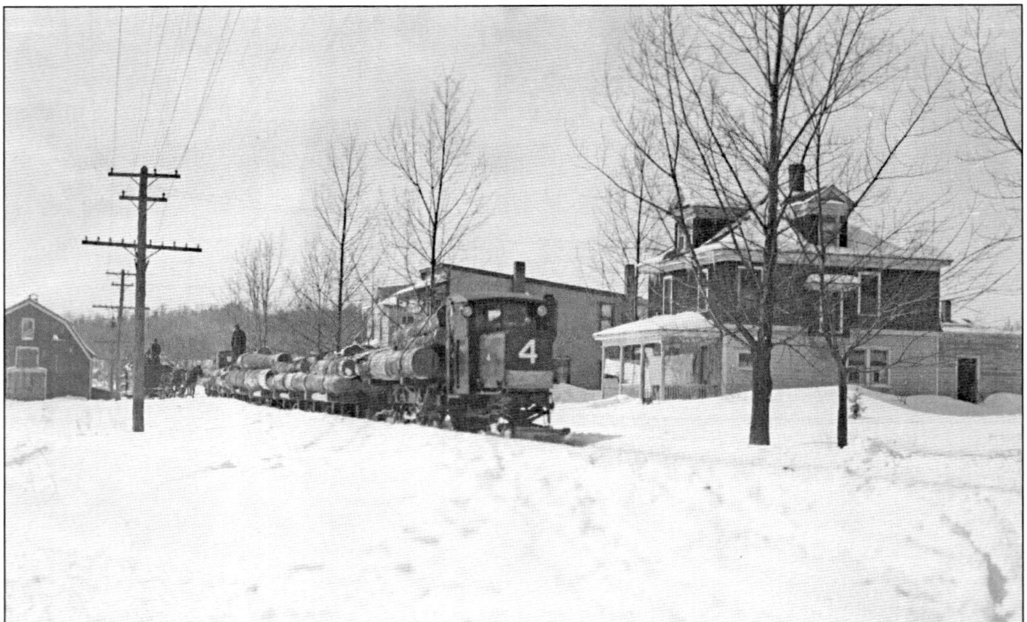

With such large payload ability, the Linn did not require trailers or wagons to move a load, and no dead weight—or ballast—was needed for traction. They hauled freight beyond the ends of the rail lines, as they are in this photograph, and could carry loads of logs directly to the Tupper Lake mills. Later, they added large V-shaped plows and were enlisted to remove snow on rural roads and side streets. (Goff Nelson Library Collection.)

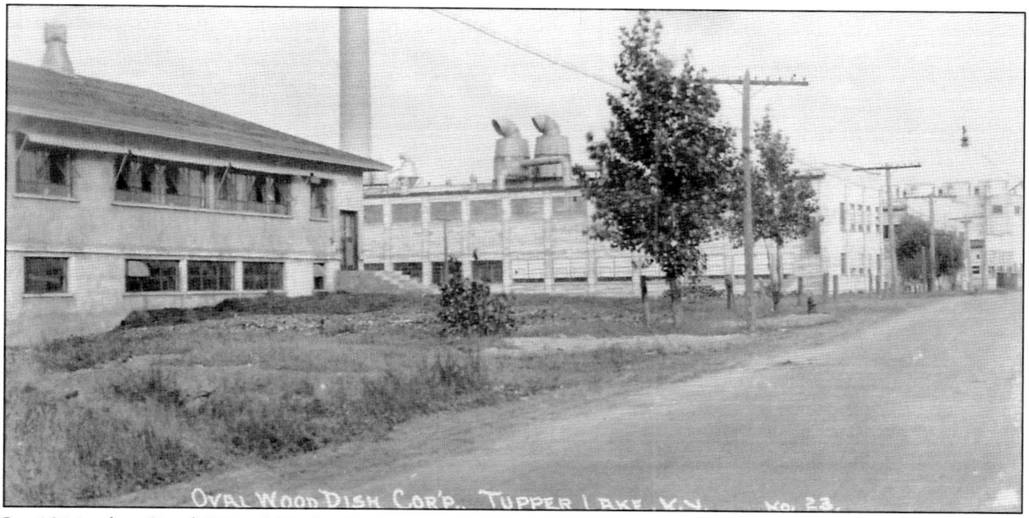

In 1914, the Oval Wood Dish Corporation purchased the company's first timberlands in the Adirondacks from the Santa Clara Lumber Company. They acquired the majority of Follensby Tract together with a portion of the Mount Morris Tract and lands in Township 22. For the next 50 years, they were one of the premier employers of the community, until they were sold to the Adirondack Plywood Corporation in 1964. (Goff Nelson Library Collection.)

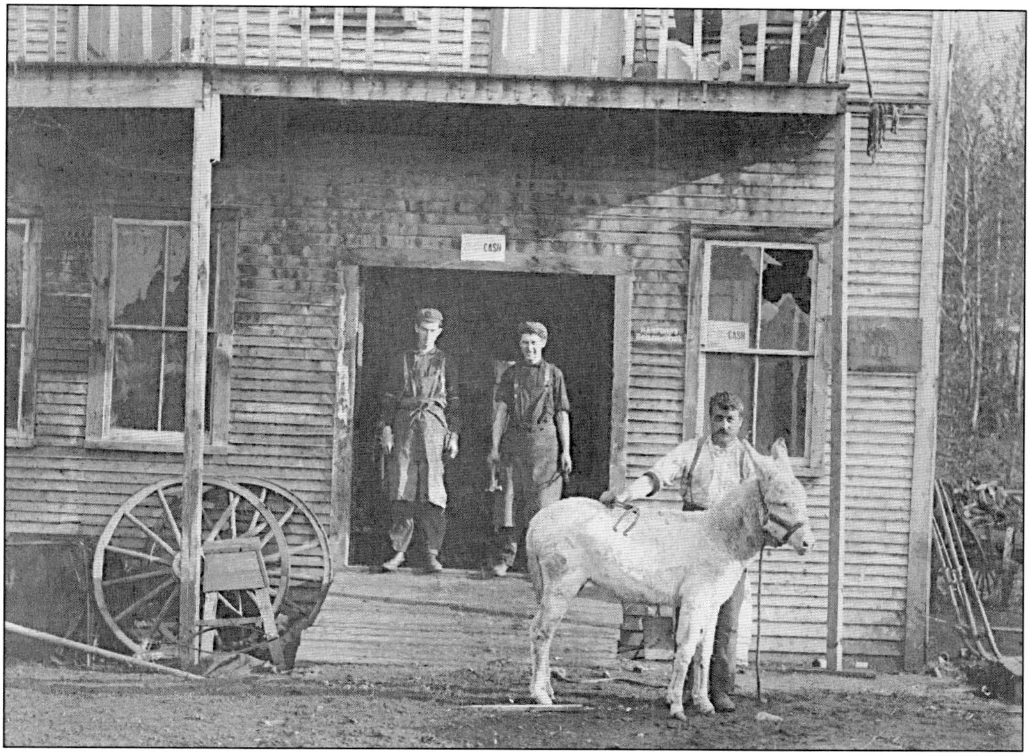

In an old *Tupper Lake Free Press*, a blacksmith was compared with an automotive mechanic: "The beauty of the old-fashioned blacksmith was that when you brought him your horse to be shod he didn't think of 40 other things that ought to be done to it." But times were changing, and the motorized vehicle won the day. By the 1950s, the craft had diminished to just a handful of local smiths. (Goff Nelson Library Collection.)

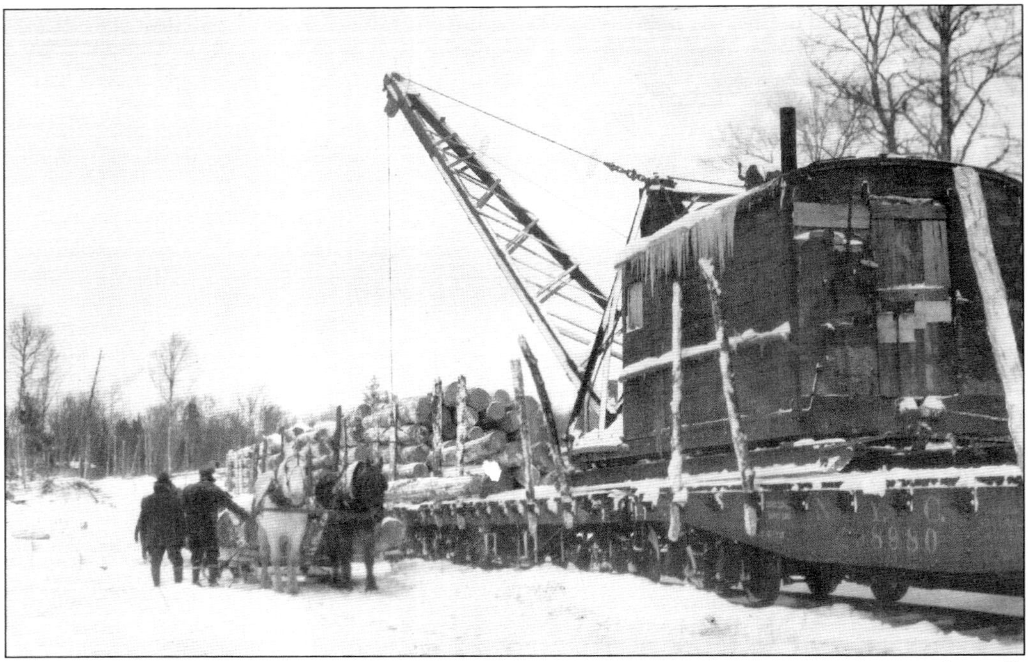

With the coming of the rails, there was less reliance on spring river drives to get logs to the mill. Horse teams pulled loaded sleds directly to the rail, where they were loaded by cranes and then shipped directly to the various mills for processing. (Goff Nelson Library Collection.)

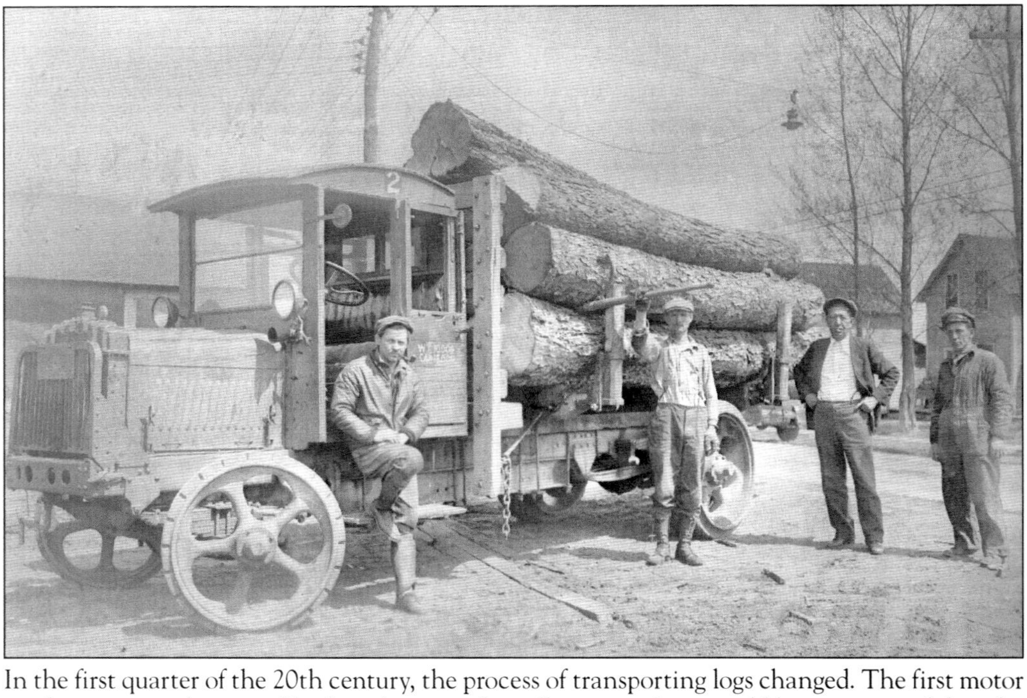

In the first quarter of the 20th century, the process of transporting logs changed. The first motor trucks were very basic and had steel tires and small engines. Logs could be transported, but the trucks could only endure the impact of a hard gravel road. While they were limited in the log length they could support, they were efficient in transporting logs from the rail yard to the mill. (Goff Nelson Library Collection.)

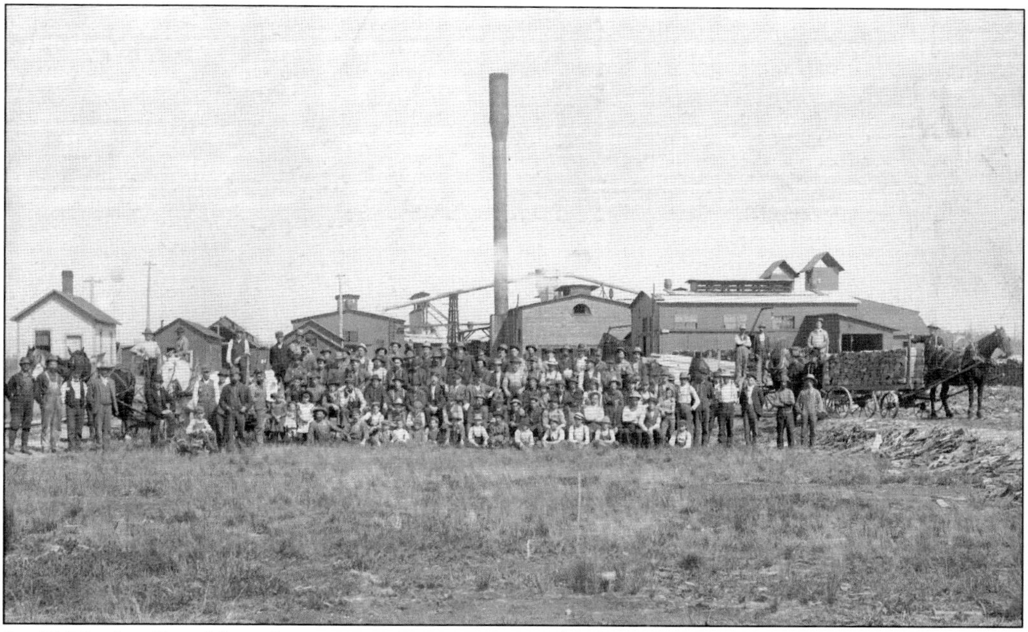

In 1900, the Brooklyn Cooperage Company, a subsidiary of the American Sugar Refining Company, erected a large barrel stave and heading mill below what is now McCarthy Street. A logging railroad was built from the plant to haul logs cut from a tract of land set aside by the state where Cornell University practiced experimental hardwood clear-cutting. The experiment failed after a gale blew down the remaining trees and fire roared through the picked-over forest. (Goff Nelson Library Collection.)

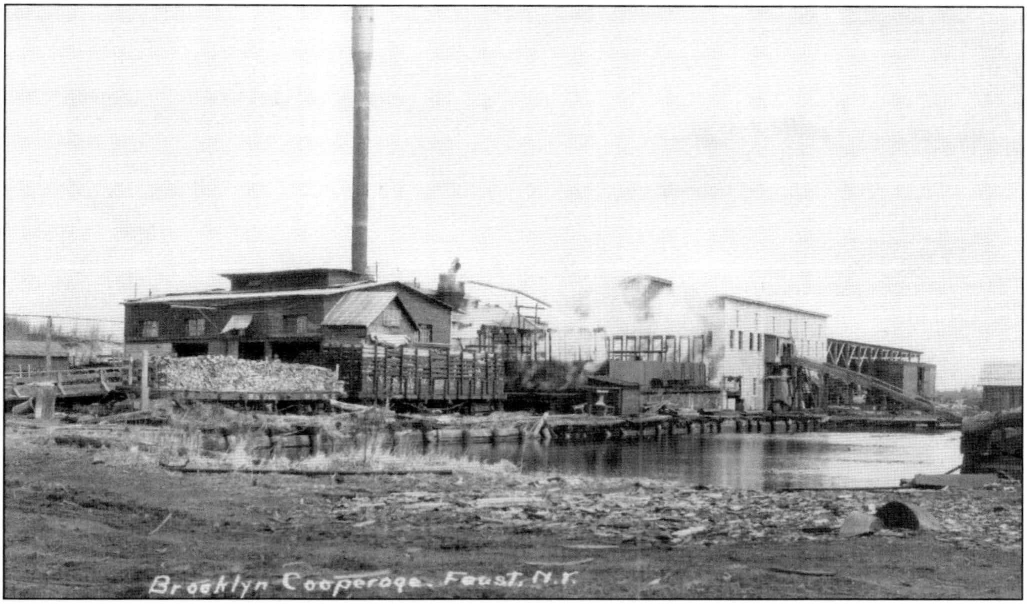

The smoke was thick enough to incite the fear of residents on nearby Upper Saranac Lake, who convinced the state legislature to shut down the program. In 1904, the courts prohibited further cutting on the 6,000-acre "College Tract." The railroad was abandoned, and the iron rails were sold for scrap. (Goff Nelson Library Collection.)

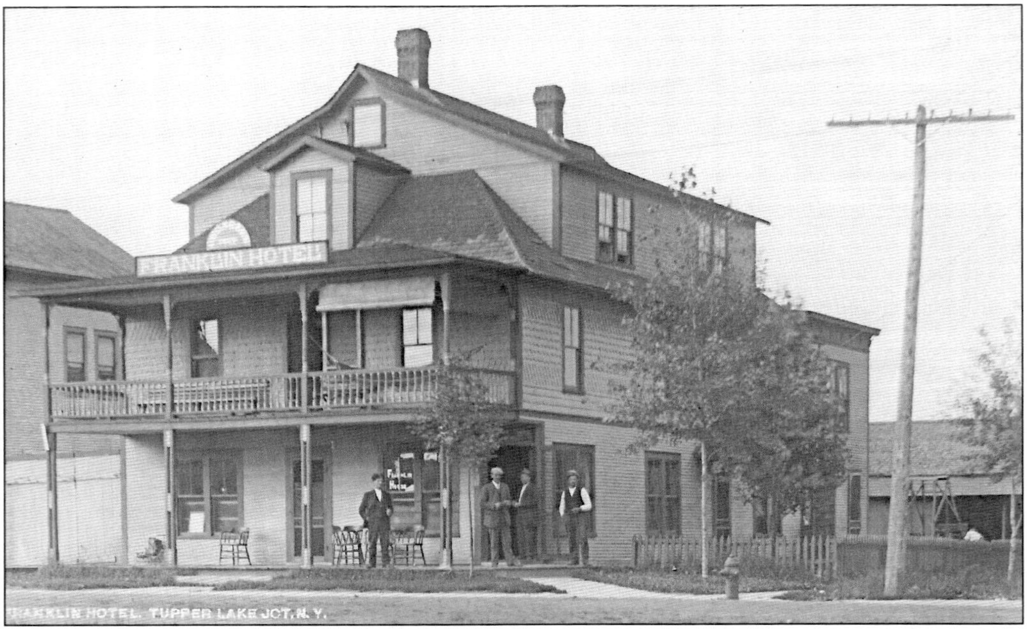

The Franklin Hotel was one of the many small hotels that catered to loggers during the slack times at the logging camps. The hotel stood at the corner of Main and Pine Streets in downtown Tupper Lake. In 1918, tragedy occurred when a meat cutter and a popular hockey player shot and killed their bartender for refusing to sell them alcohol. (Author's collection.)

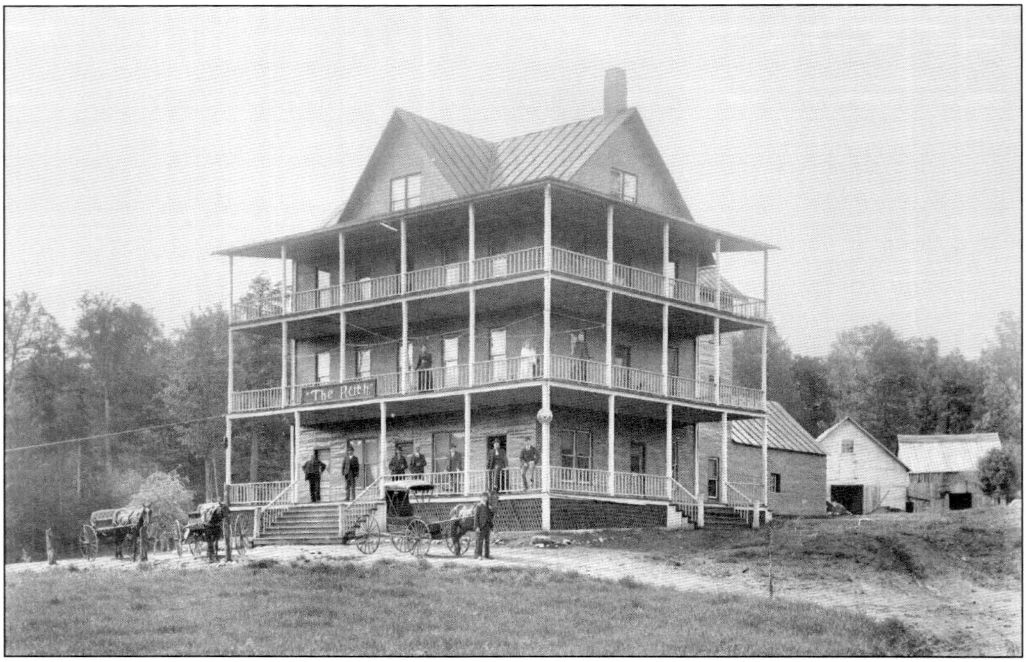

The Beechwood Inn was built in 1895 by Everest LeBoeuf, who served as Tupper Lake's village president in 1906, and was originally named the "The Ruth" in honor of LeBoeuf's daughter. In the old days, it took about an hour to drive a horse and buggy between Tupper Lake and Piercefield, and the inn, located at the halfway point, provided a nice rest to travelers. The inn had a large third-floor dance hall and a reputation for lively times. (Goff Nelson Library Collection.)

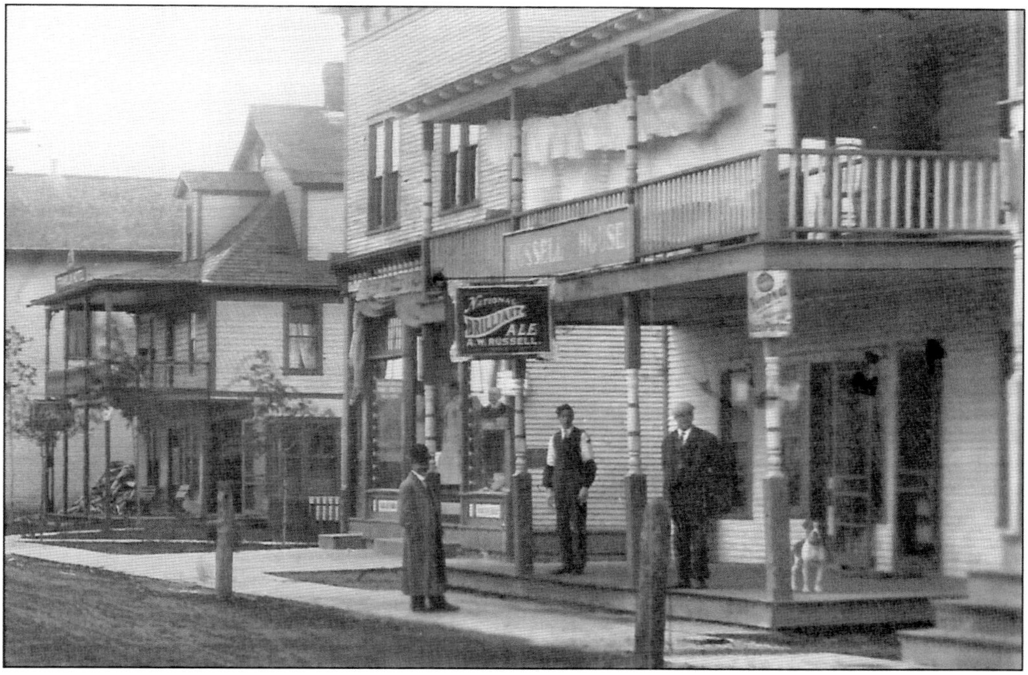

Most of Russell House's hotel business came from itinerant woodsmen who worked the seasonal logging operations. At the time of this photograph, Allen W. Russell was the proprietor of the hotel, but in 1914, he gave the hotel over to John Tobin. Russell went on to purchase Saranac Lake House, one of the oldest hotels in the area. (Author's collection.)

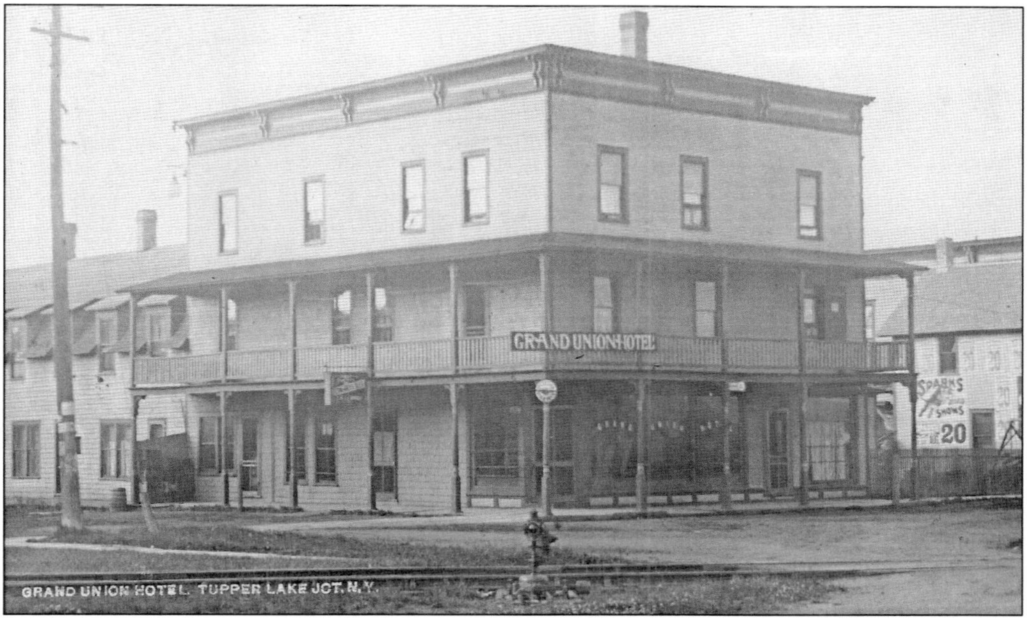

Travelers would step off the train and walk across the street to the Grand Union Hotel for a room and beverage. Located opposite the train depot, the Grand Union, built in 1896, still operates under the same name. Judge John Black erected the hotel and added the five-family tenement section seen at the back of the hotel. At one time, there was a store in the hotel to aid the needs of the tremendous influx of newcomers. (Author's collection.)

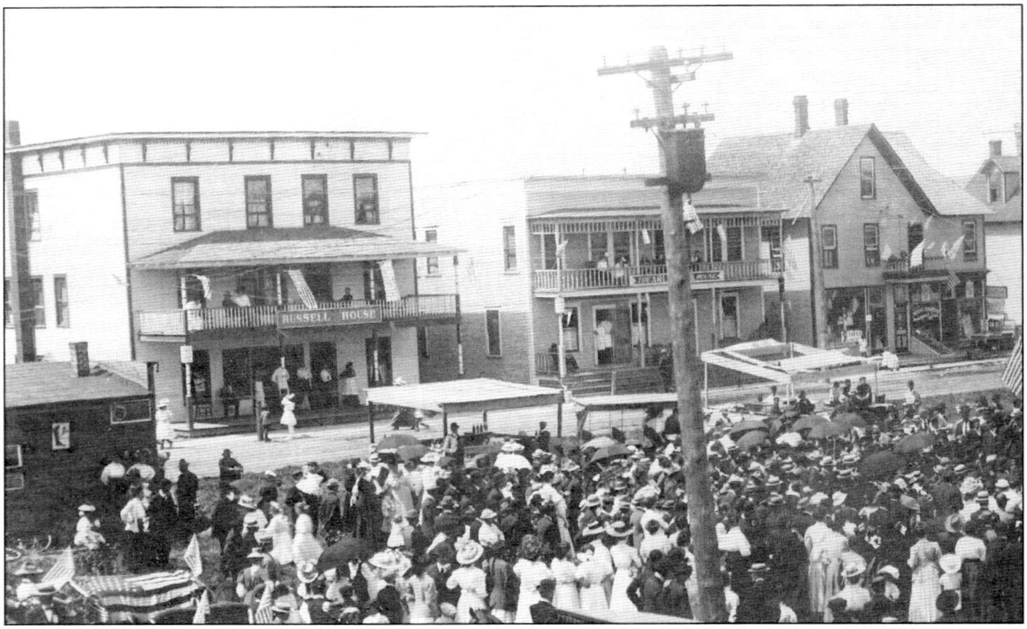

The downtown Faust area was bustling with activity at this 1908 junction revival celebration where Charles Evans Hughes, the governor of New York, was the guest speaker. The crowd was gathered in the lot of what is today Larkin Enterprises. Two early hotels are seen here as well, the Russell House (left) and the Arlington House. (Goff Nelson Library Collection.)

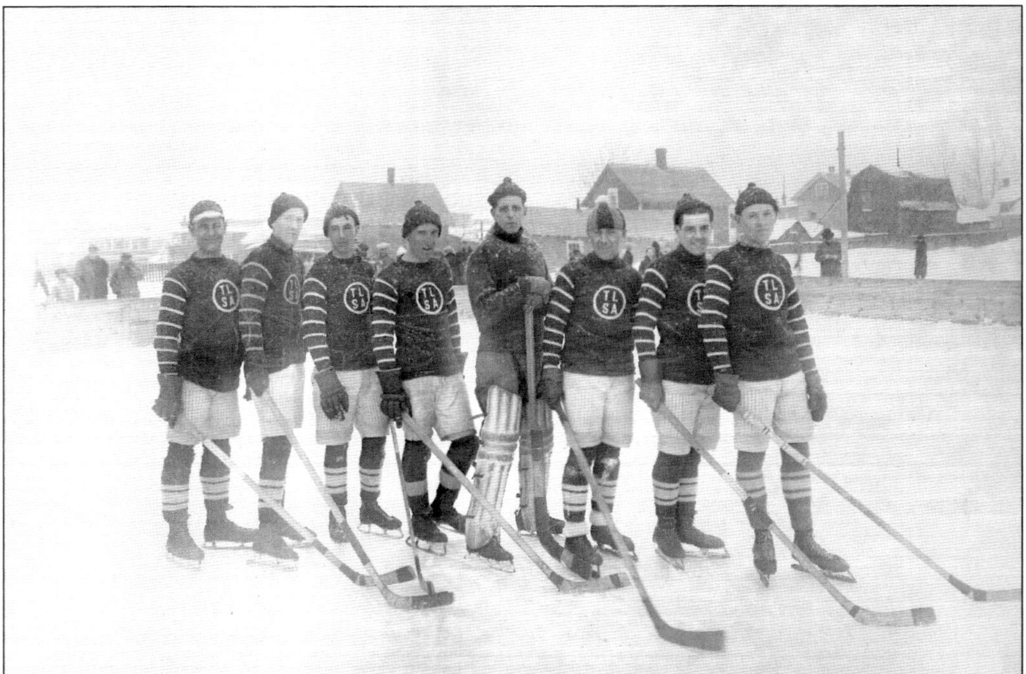

Ice hockey was an important part of life for Tupper Lake residents. Teams often traveled as far away as Canada, and rivalries could foster street brawls and hot-fisted rink action. (Goff Nelson Library Collection.)

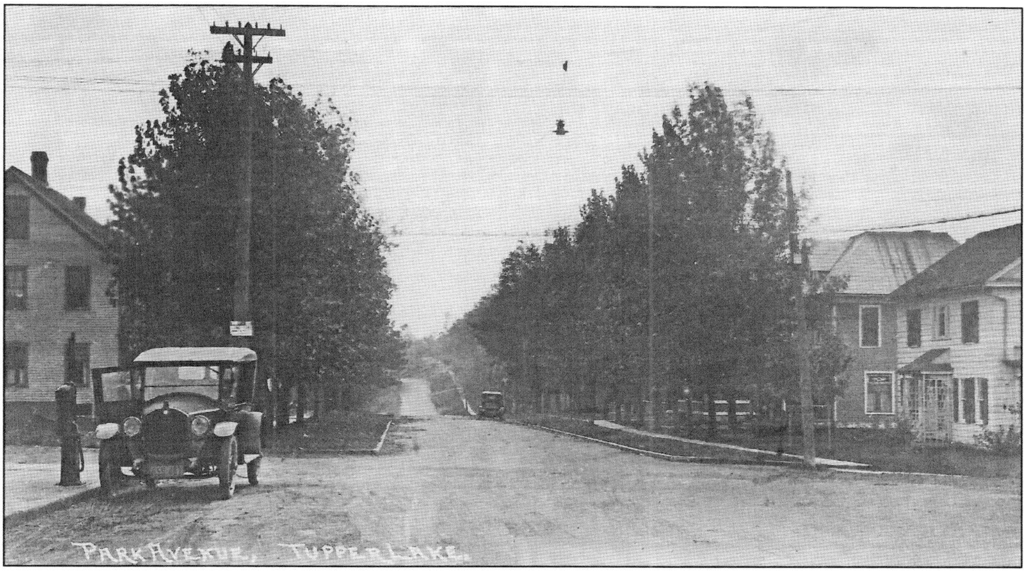

A very early automobile stops to fill up at one of the first gas pumps in town at the corner of Park Street and Wawbeek Avenue. Just a drum buried in the ground with a hand pump, the gas pump sits in front of what is today Tip Top Sport Shop. (Author's collection.)

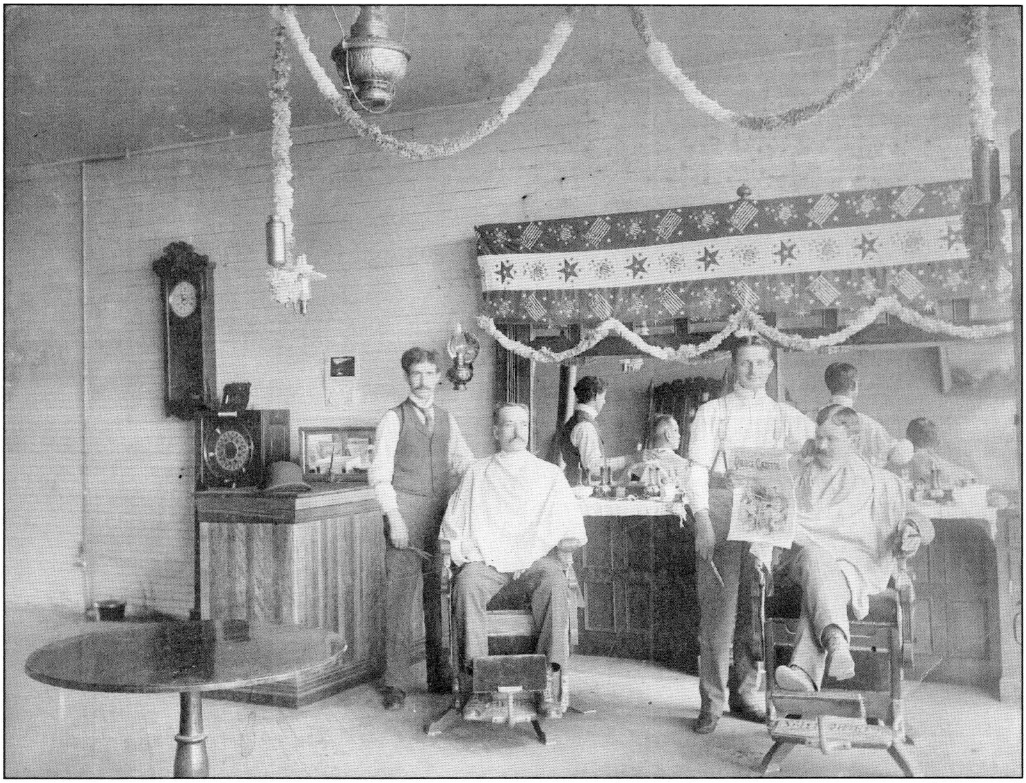

John Pervonga's barbershop, pictured here in 1914, was located at 96 Park Street and sported pool tables and bowling lanes. Pervonga gave out 5¢ tickets to young boys who came to him for a haircut, good for a free pass to the Palace Theater. (Goff Nelson Library Collection.)

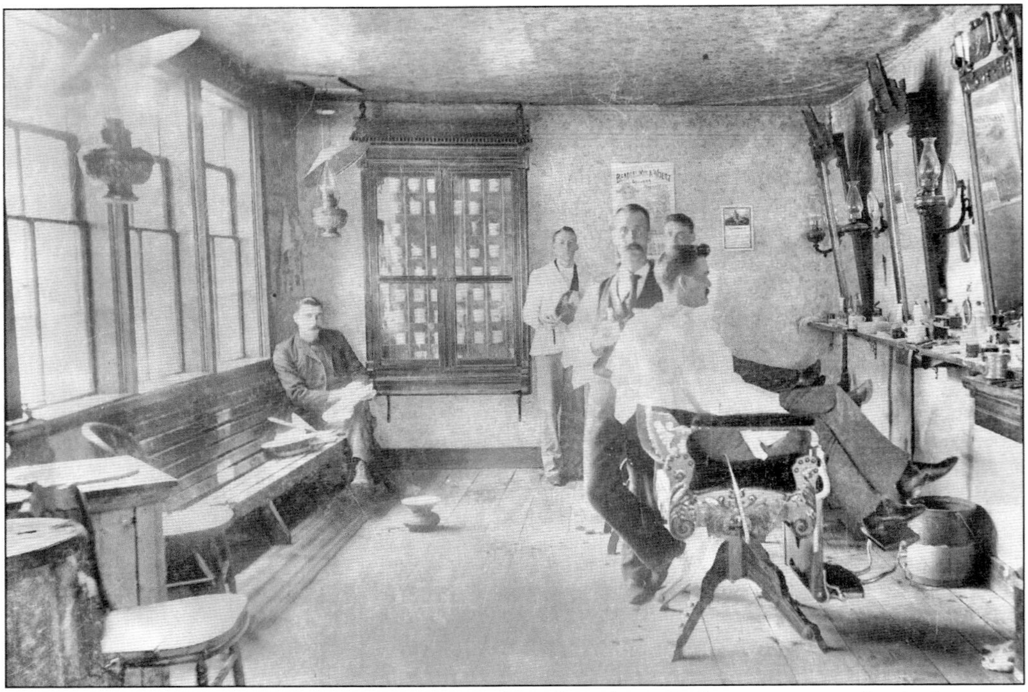

Tupper's early barbershops were places to meet friends and get the latest news on the day's events. There was no electricity in this shop, where Eastlake mirrors and oil lamps lined the walls. (Goff Nelson Library Collection.)

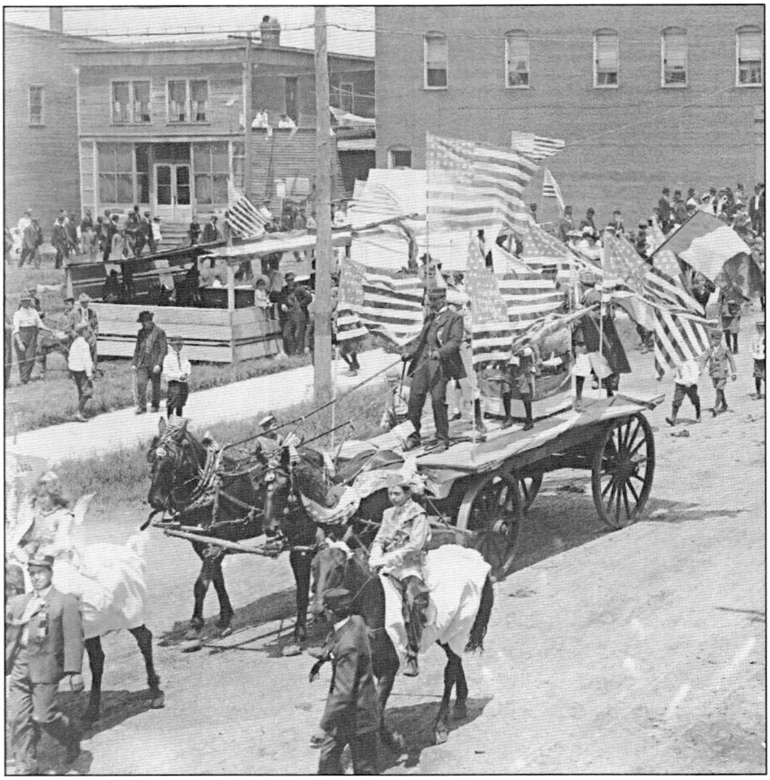

During celebrations, vendors and civic groups would set up in the empty lot opposite the Goldberg and Ginsberg store, which would soon be the site of the Tupper Lake National Bank. The bank, under new management, still stands today. (Goff Nelson Library Collection.)

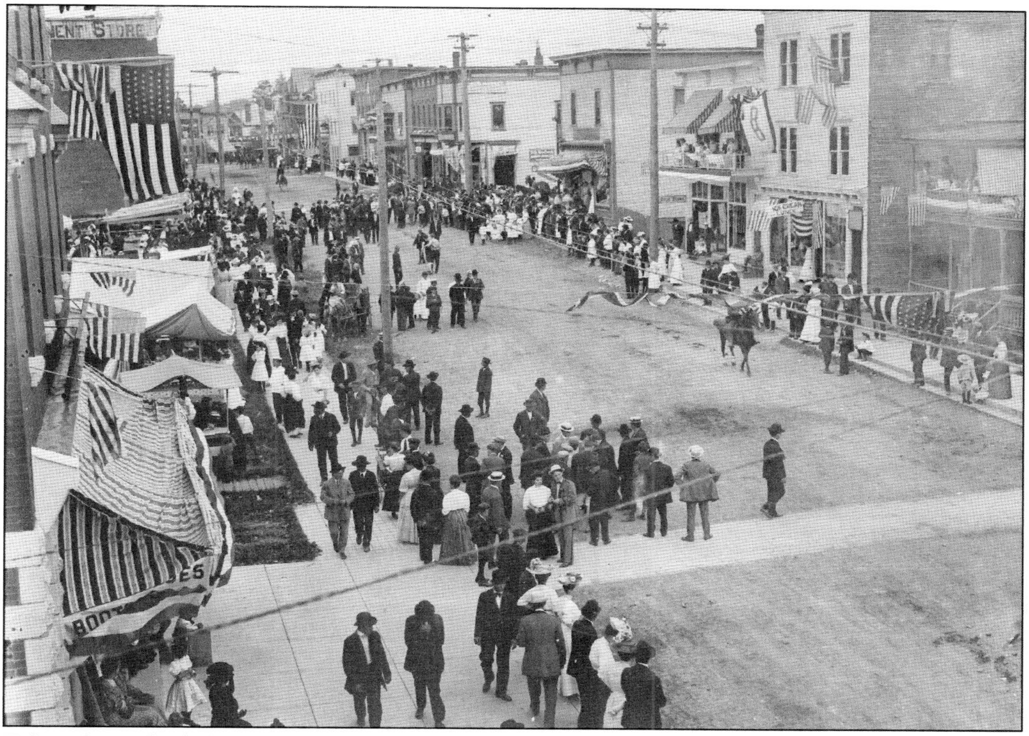

Taken from the balcony of the Altamont Hotel, this view looks up Park Street towards L.C. Maid's pharmacy in the distance on the corner of Cliff Street. Concrete walkways were built to give pedestrians solid footing to cross what was often a muddy slosh to the other side. (Goff Nelson Library Collection.)

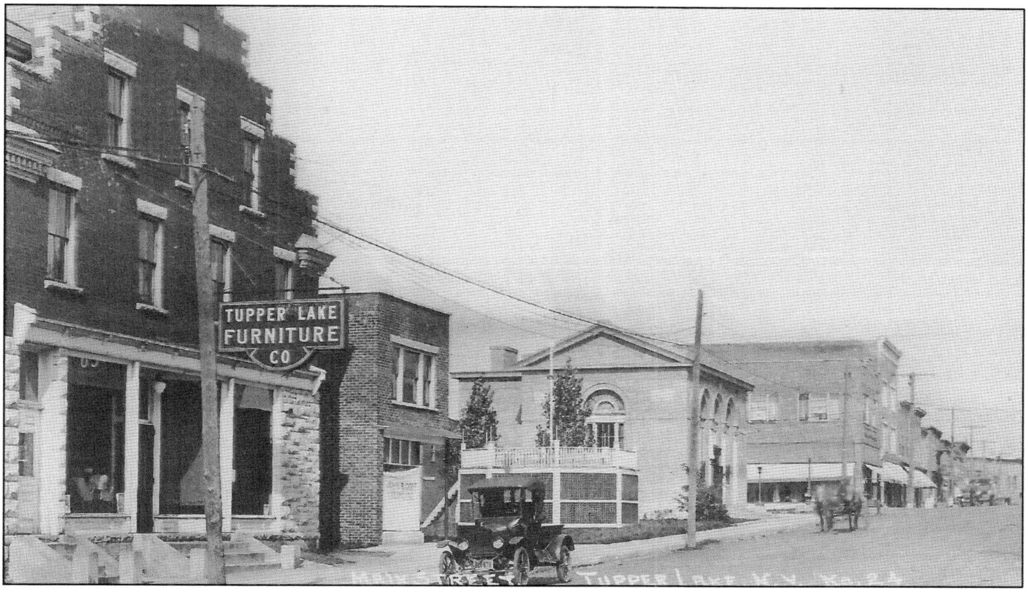

Both horses and automobiles drive Main Street in front of Tupper Lake Bank and the Tupper Lake Furniture Company. The furniture company is no more, and the building now houses village offices. Horses and automobiles occupied the street when this photograph was taken. (Author's collection.)

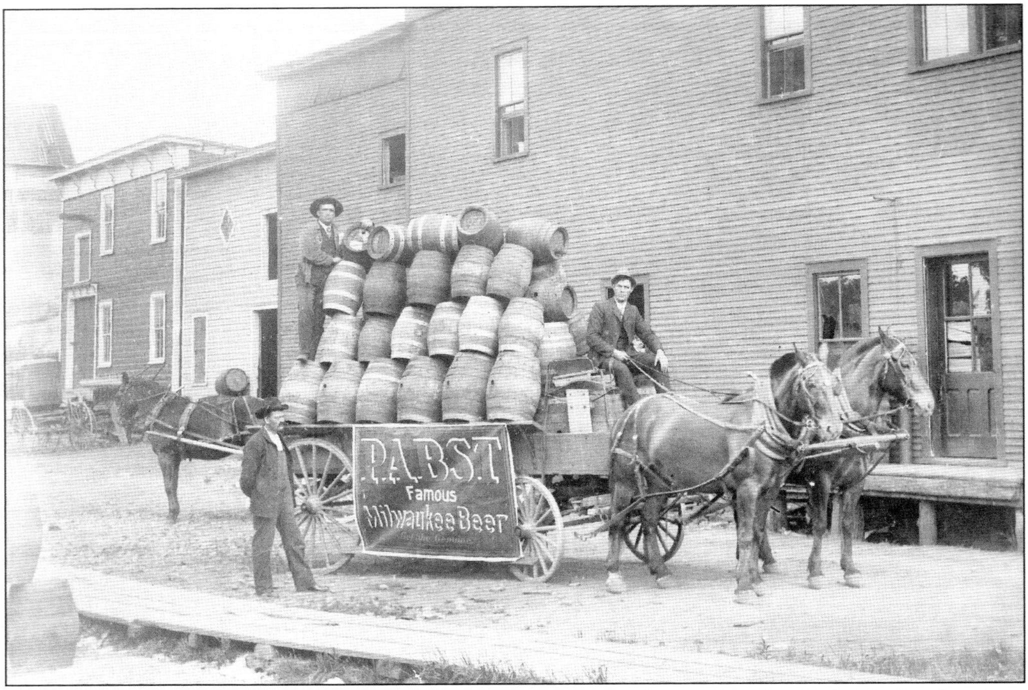

This 1912 photograph shows Joseph Potvin on the wagon in front of the Fred McCloskey bottling works. This High Street location was more recently the Frenette Brothers property. (Goff Nelson Library Collection.)

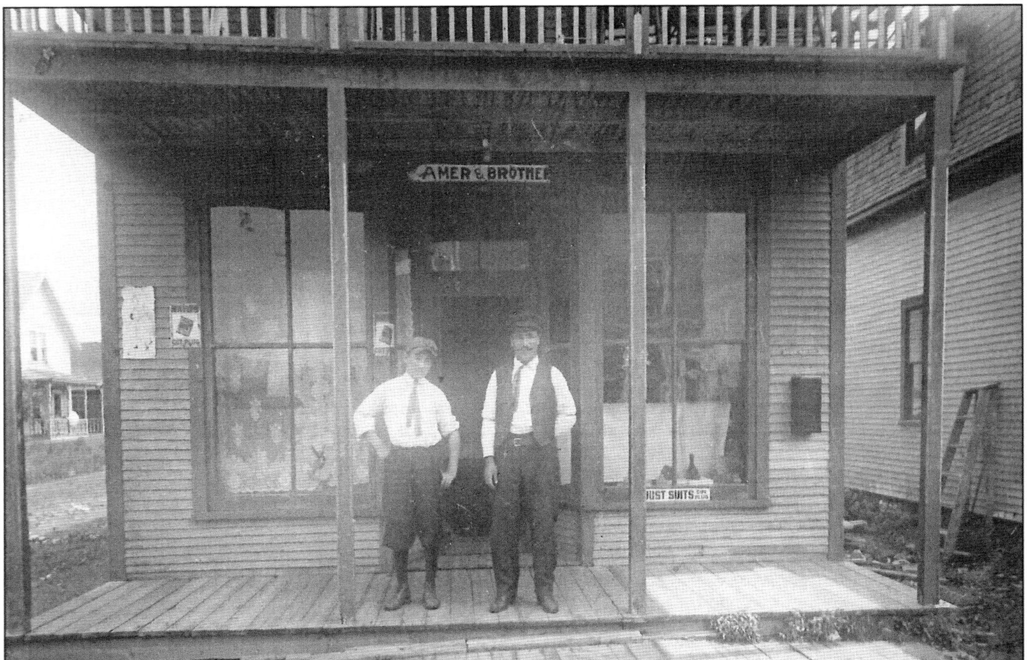

John Maroun (left) and his brother Amer Maroun stand in front of their dry goods store on Main Street in 1937. The store was in the heart of downtown Tupper Lake's Faust district. (Camille and Ellen Maroon.)

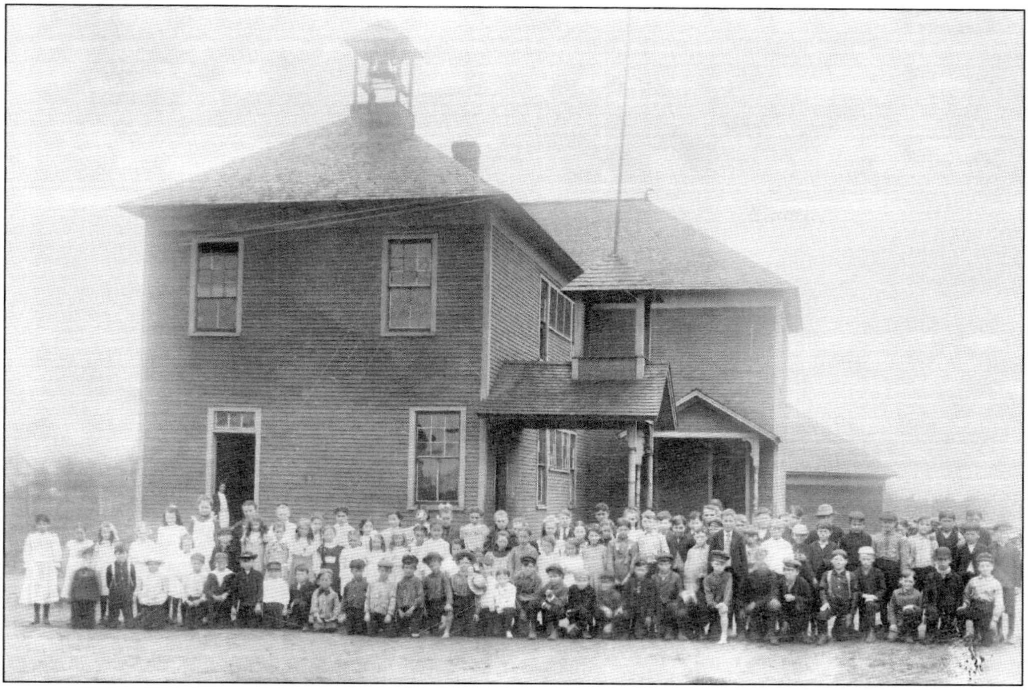

The original Faust Grammar School was a two-room frame structure built before 1900 opposite the food pantry on Demars Boulevard. In about 1906, the school moved to this location on Cedar Street. (Goff Nelson Library Collection.)

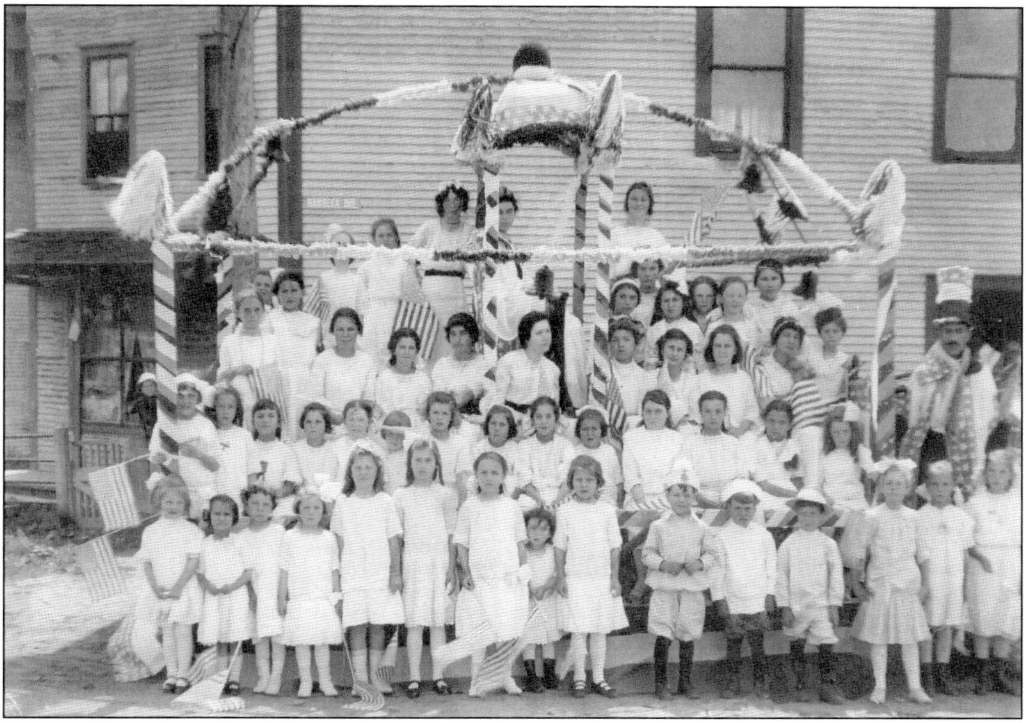

These young ladies, perhaps from the local Catholic school near where this picture was taken on Wawbeek Avenue, pose on their float before a Fourth of July celebration. (Author's collection.)

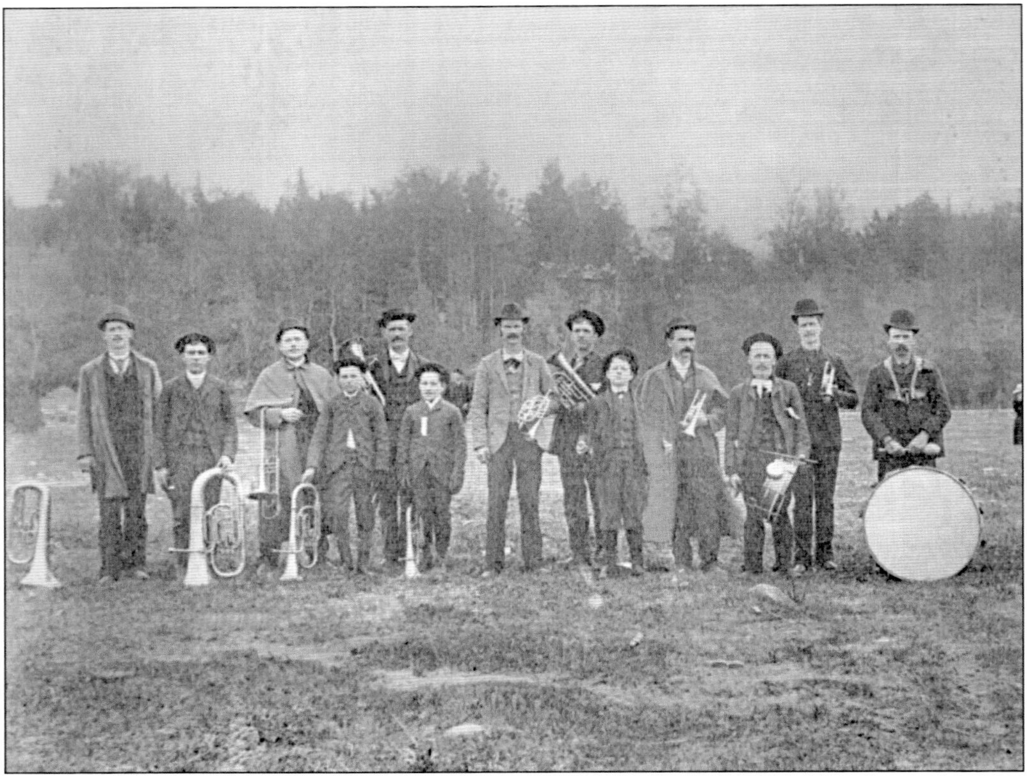

This is perhaps the oldest photograph of a Tupper Lake band, probably taken in the late 1890s. (Goff Nelson Library Collection.)

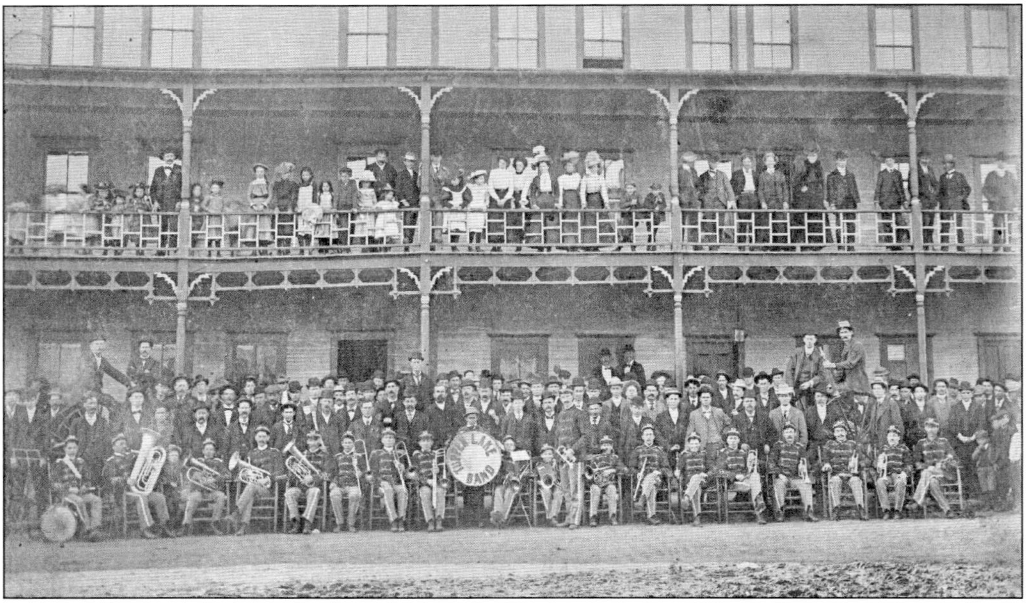

Early pioneers and members of the Tupper Lake Band pose in front of the Altamont Hotel. The band played at numerous celebrations throughout the Adirondacks. Two early band members were Mose H. Ginsberg and Don Delosh, who were both important, longtime residents of the community. (Goff Nelson Library Collection.)

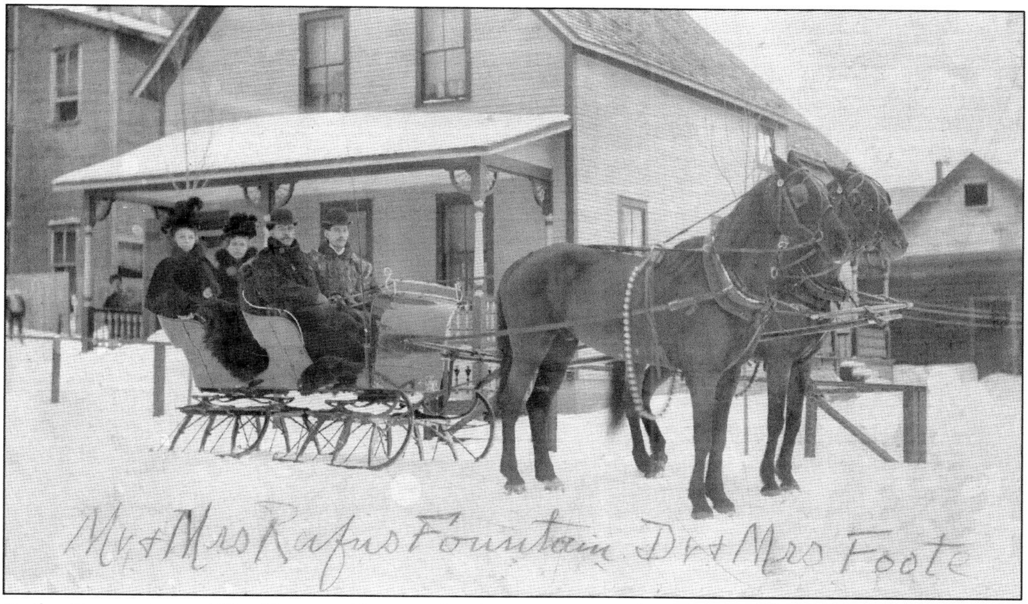

Rufus Fountain and Dr. Newton Foote take their wives out for a snowy sleigh ride. Dr. Foote was a graduate of Franklin Academy in Malone and the University of Maryland, School of Dentistry, and came to Tupper Lake from Constable as a pioneer dentist, establishing his practice in 1897. (Goff Nelson Library Collection.)

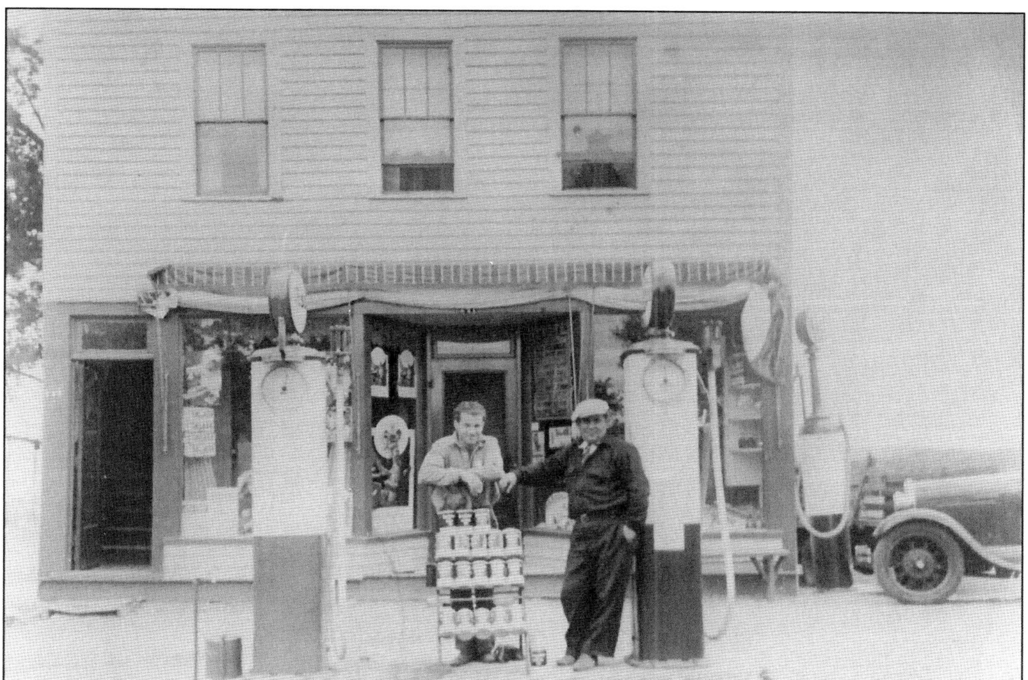

John Salamy (left) stands with Edward Younis in front of his grocery store, located on the corner of Park Street and Boyer Avenue. (Camille and Ellen Maroon.)

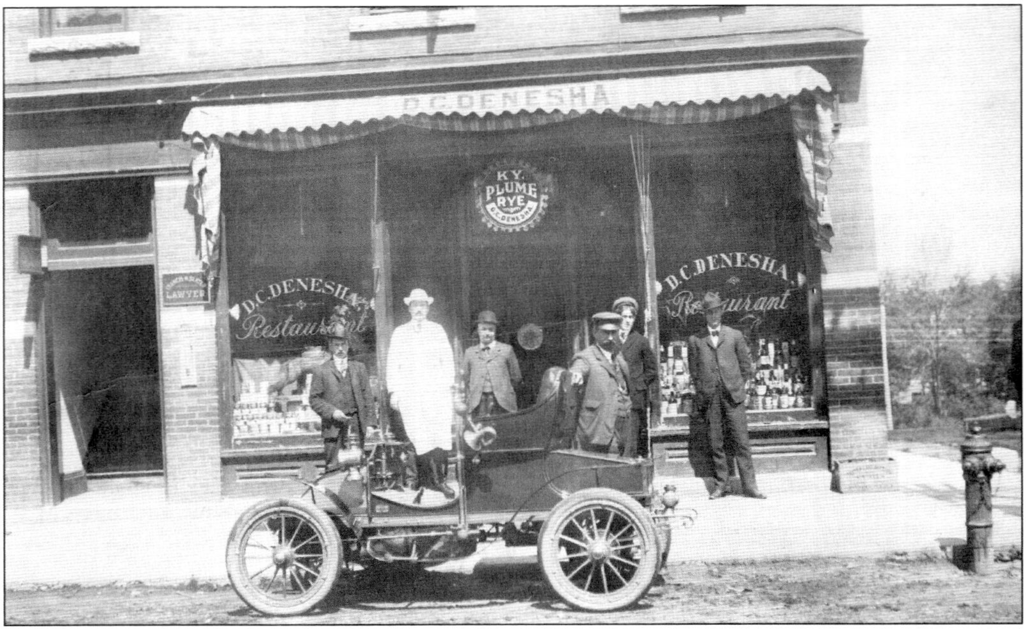

A group of early Tupper Lakers poses in front of Dave Denesha's restaurant at what is now 127 Park Street, below Francis Slater's second-floor law office. The gentleman in the derby is Art Cluett, and Fred Lang is in the duster. Lang owned the first automobile in Tupper Lake and operated a garage downtown at what eventually became the Gladd and Leaper property. (Goff Nelson Library Collection.)

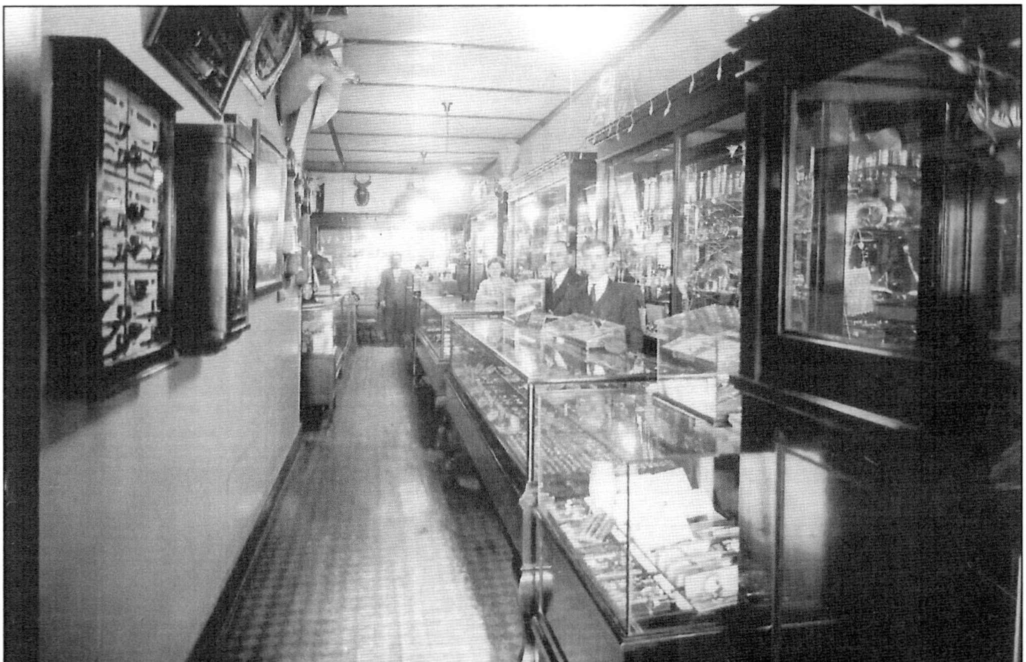

Alfred A. Asel (closest to the camera) poses in his jewelry store in the Park Street business district with friends, from right to left, George Fayad, employee Julia LaForest, and a Mr. Hajas. (Camille and Ellen Maroon.)

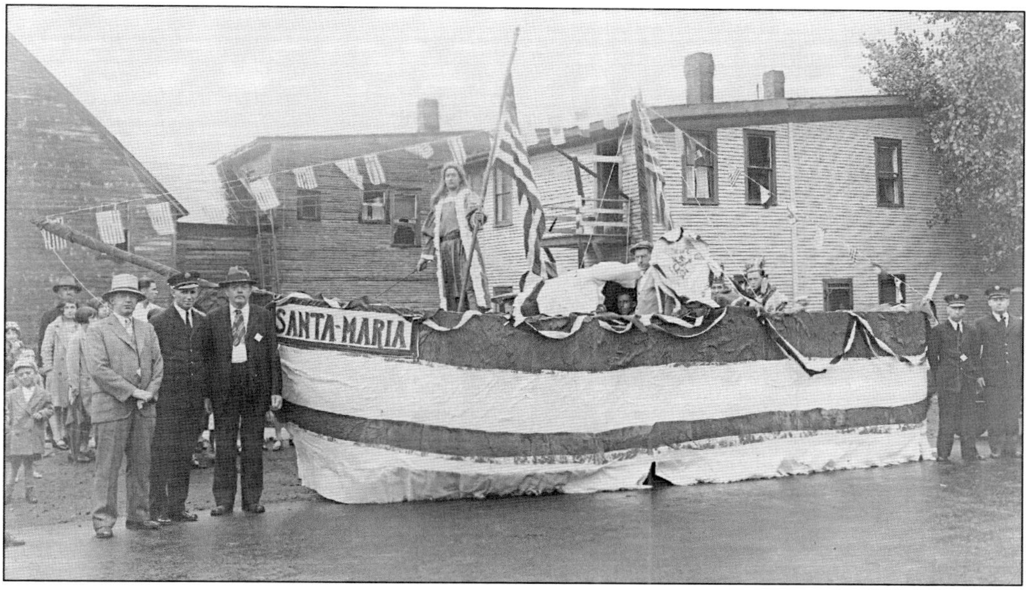

The good ship *Santa Maria* was dry-docked on High Street opposite the Methodist parsonage. At the far left in the hat is L.P. Quinn. The float was built by the late Octave Frechette for a parade, presumably for the Fourth of July. The structure at right, behind the *Santa Maria*, has been considerably enlarged and modernized and is now the Knights of Columbus building. (Goff Nelson Library Collection.)

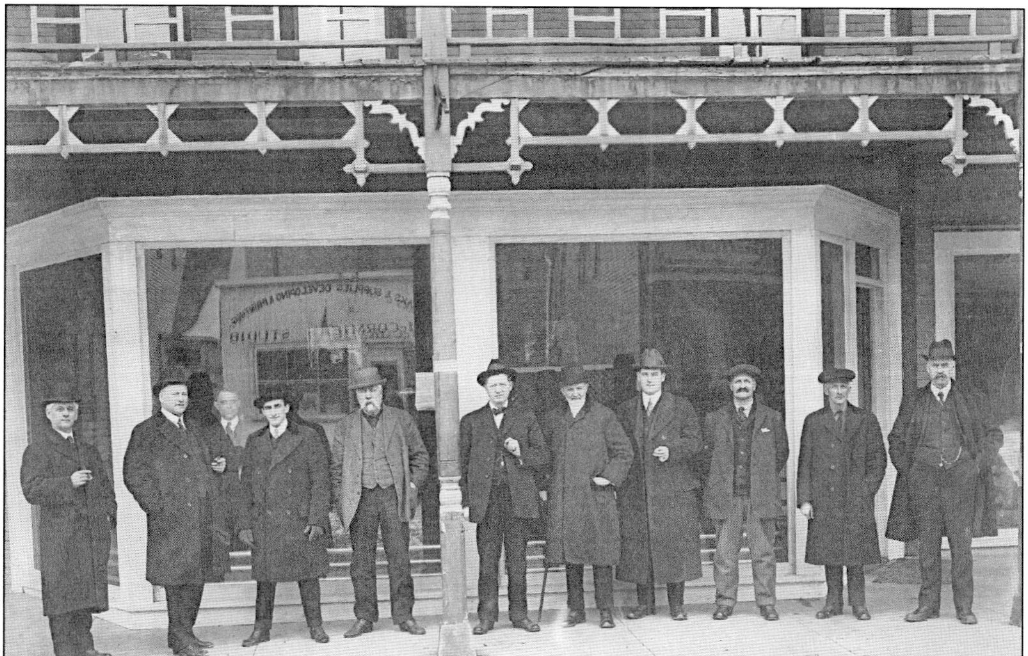

The arrow points at Wales Chaney, the early landowner who was credited by Tupper Lake's first mayor, Charles Sisson, as the man who built the "town upon the hill." Chaney grew wealthy supplying horses to the Union army and purchased large tracts of cutover lands from pioneer lumberman John Snell, which he then resold to new settlers. (Goff Nelson Library Collection.)

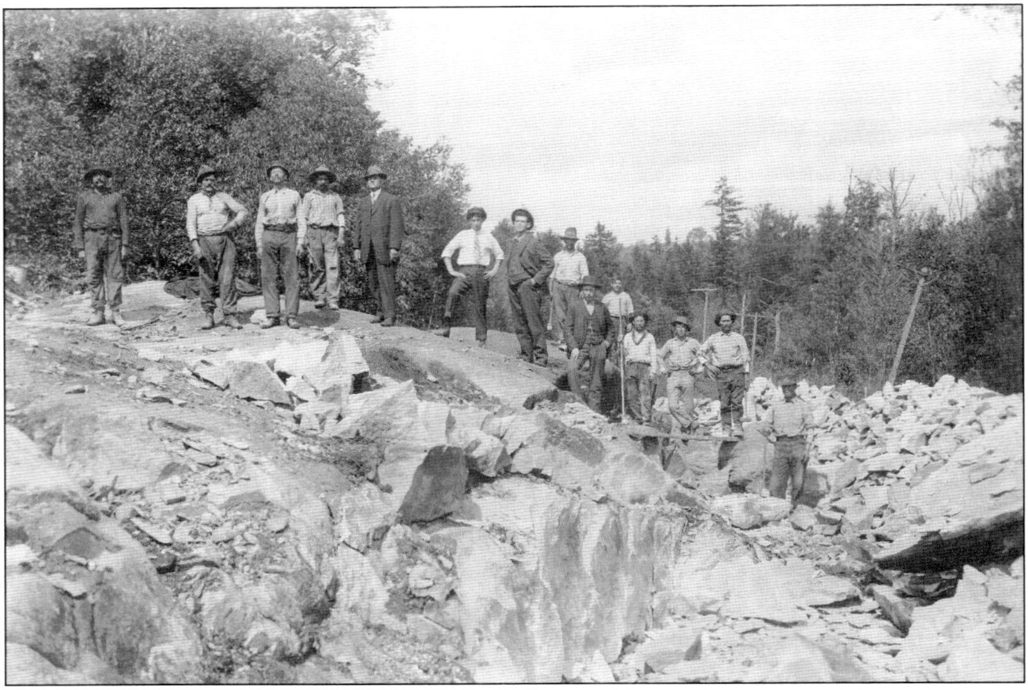

Local road contractors blast through granite rock to build a road connecting Tupper Lake and Long Lake. Better roads were needed to service the continuous expansion of motorized travel. (Goff Nelson Library Collection.)

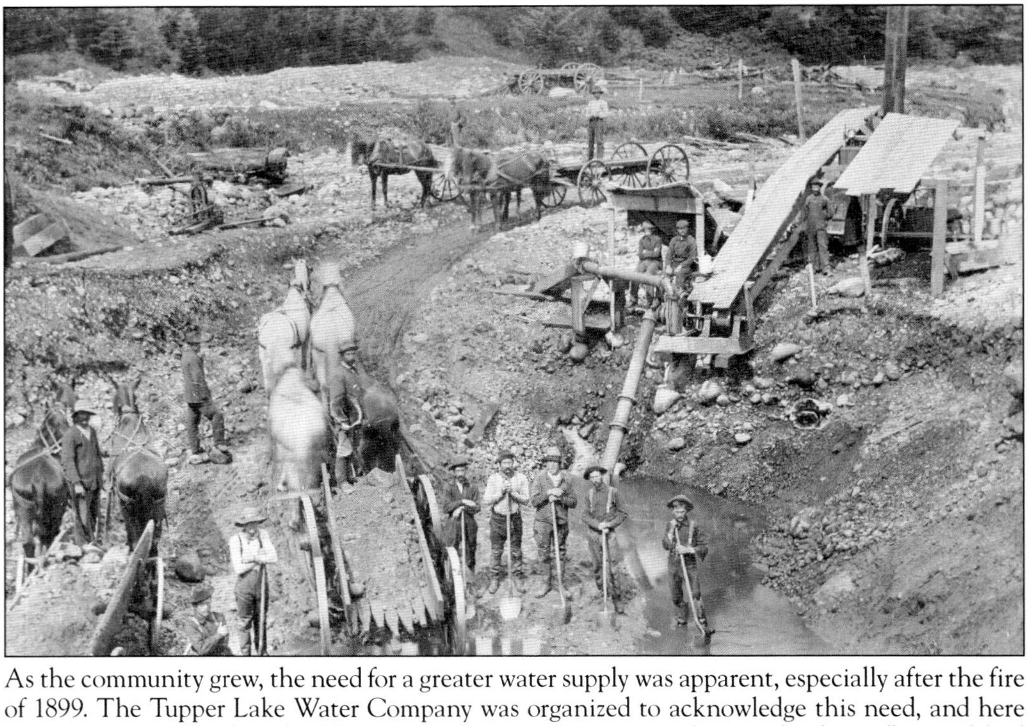

As the community grew, the need for a greater water supply was apparent, especially after the fire of 1899. The Tupper Lake Water Company was organized to acknowledge this need, and here local contractors work on building an auxiliary reservoir to supplement the direct flow and feed from the local water resource at Cranberry Pond. (Goff Nelson Library Collection.)

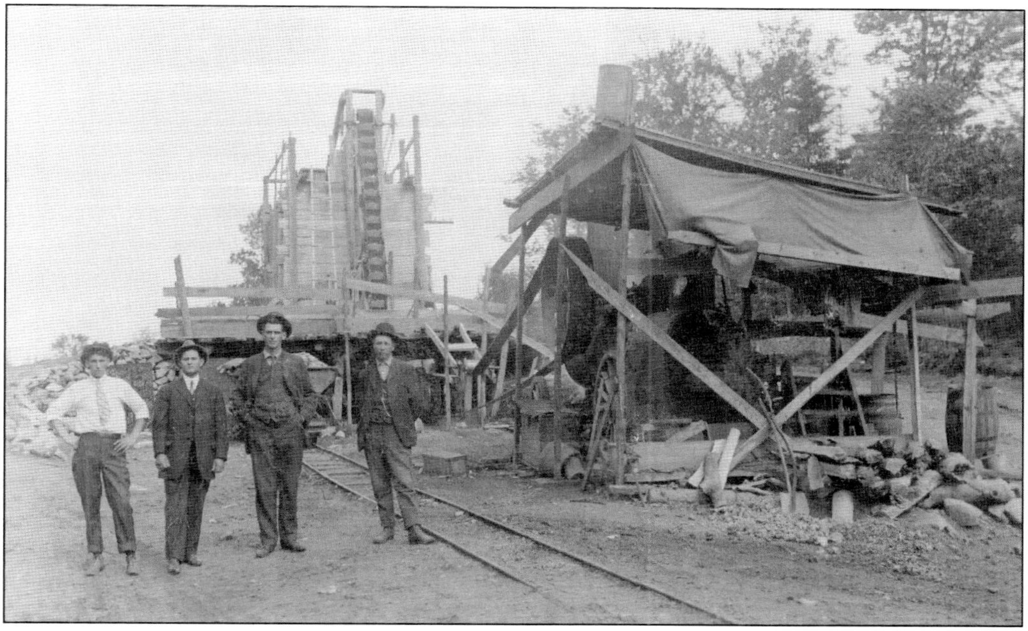

With the coming of automobiles and the need for better streets, the town created a stone crusher in a quarry at the end of Park Street. So close to the village, this high-elevation granite bluff provided the ideal location. In early years, there was a cry to make a scenic vista to lure tourists, Cliff Park. But that never happened, and today it is the location of Rock Ridge condominiums. (Goff Nelson Library Collection.)

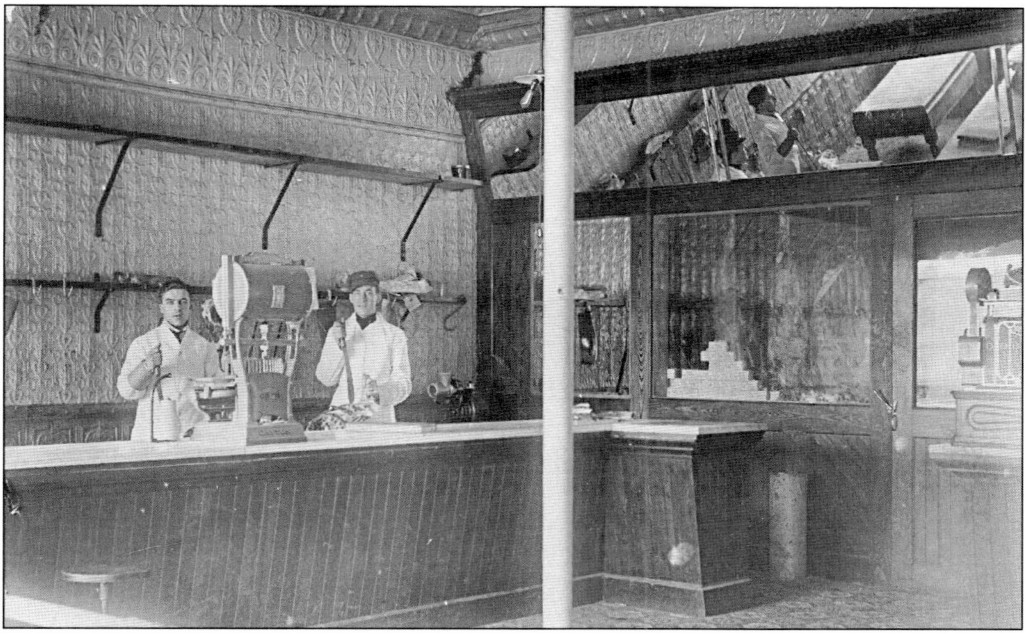

In 1925, the *Free Press* wrote about "The Store for Thrifty People" saying, "The grocery and meat business conducted by D.J. & F.J. McCarthy for three years in the Guiney block has been transferred to the new store, which they purchased two months ago from Mrs. Paul Malio, The store is one of the finest and best equipped markets in Northern New York and will be a credit to the Town and the enterprise and business ability of the two young men." (Goff Nelson Library Collection.)

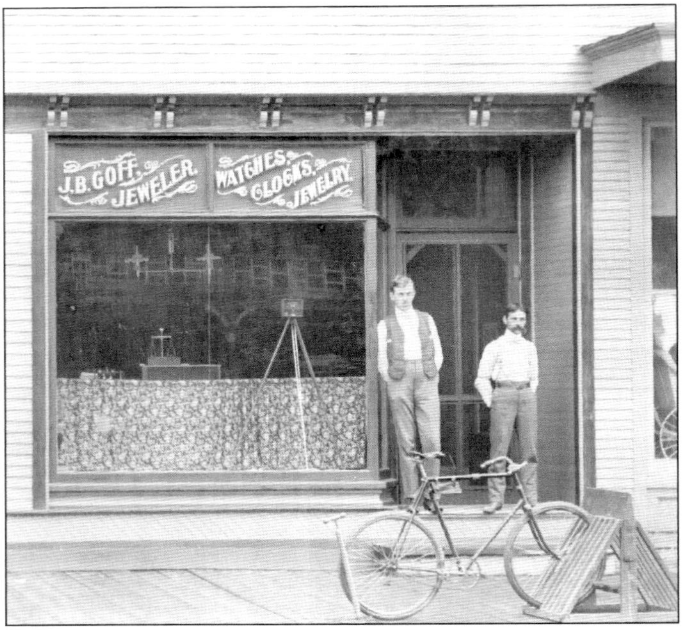

John B. Goff (left) stands in front of his store on Park Street opposite the Hotel Altamont. In addition to being a jeweler and specializing in watch and clock repair, he was also an optometrist. The bicycle stand served peddling customers who were able to cruise on the wooden boardwalks. (Goff Nelson Library Collection.)

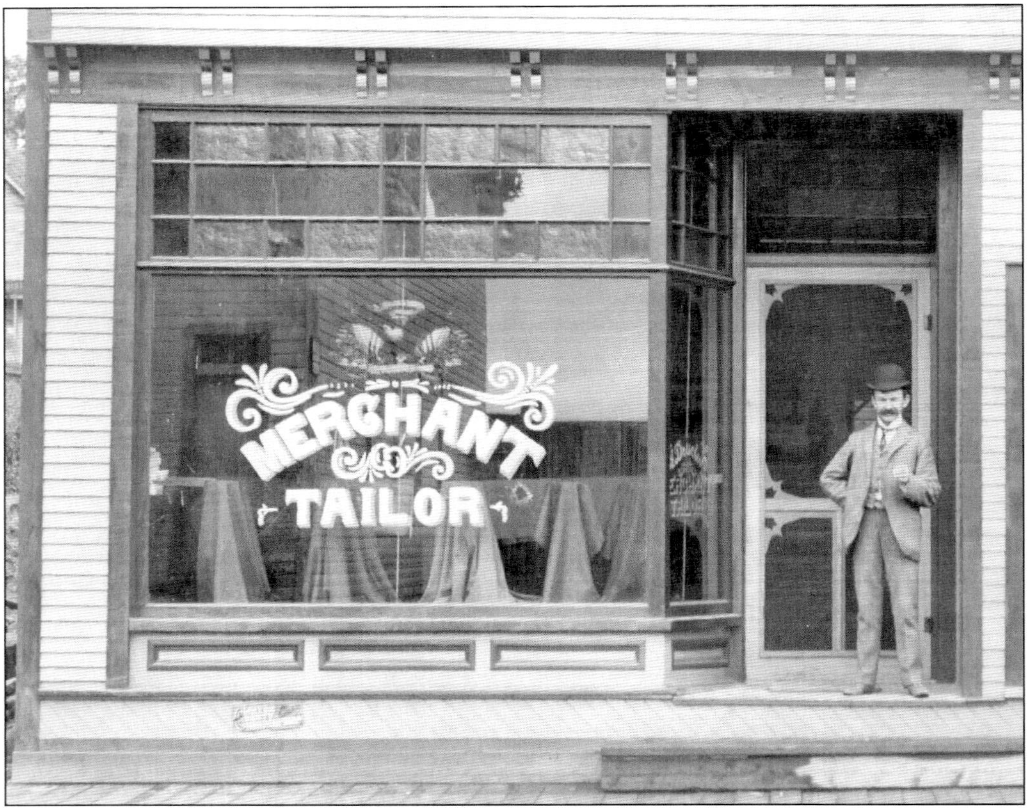

Tony Drescher stands in the doorway of his tailor shop on Park Street. Drescher was a merchant tailor, a clothier who traded textiles. In Tupper Lake's early years, people not only grew their own food on subsistence farms, they also made their own clothes or had them made by the local tailor. (Goff Nelson Library Collection.)

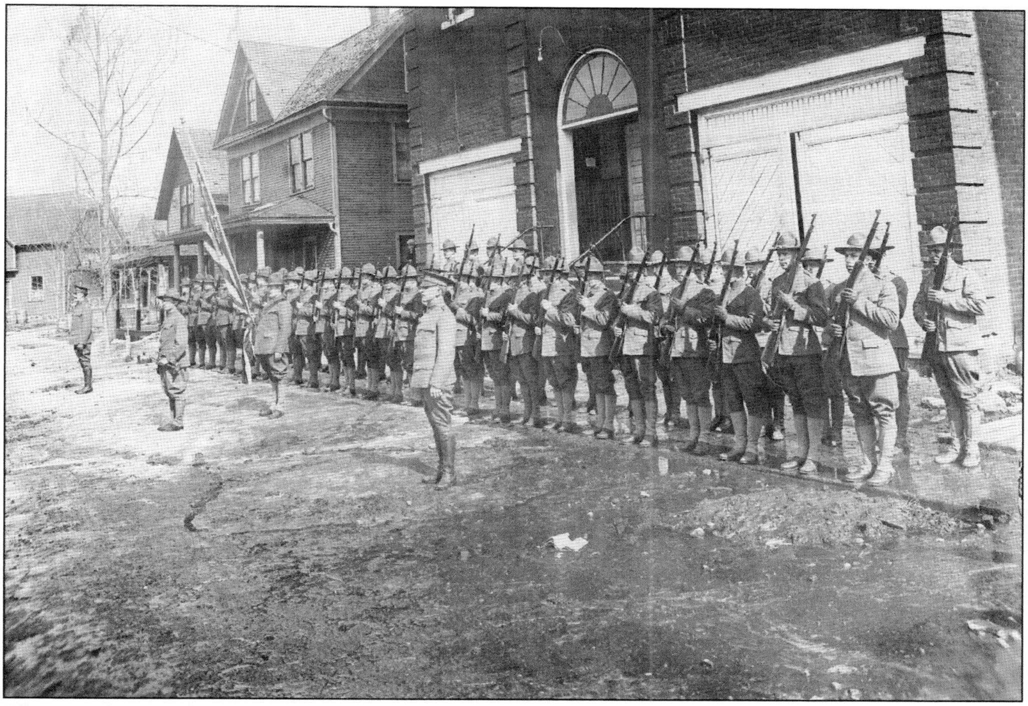

The guardsmen of Company A line up in front of the old town hall, which was the headquarters for the fire department from 1901 on. The building, rich with the memories and history of this village for over 40 years, was destroyed by fire on March 14, 1942. (Goff Nelson Library Collection.)

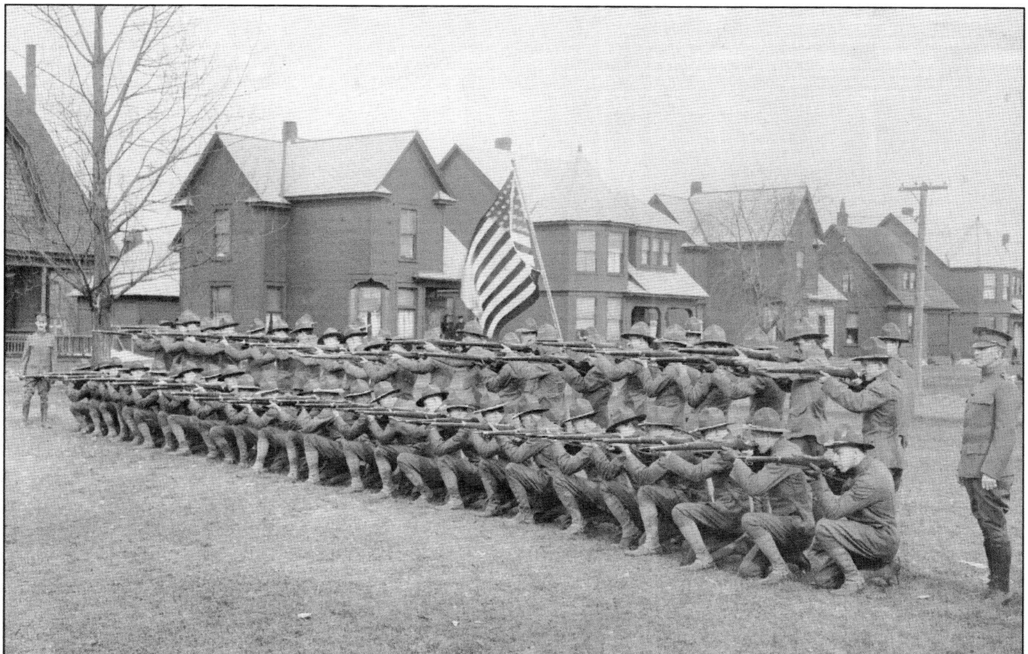

The same group of guardsmen line up for a photograph on Webb Row, adjacent to the New York Central Railroad station. The row was named in honor of Dr. Seward Webb, who was so instrumental in bringing the rail and industry to Tupper Lake. (Goff Nelson Library Collection.)

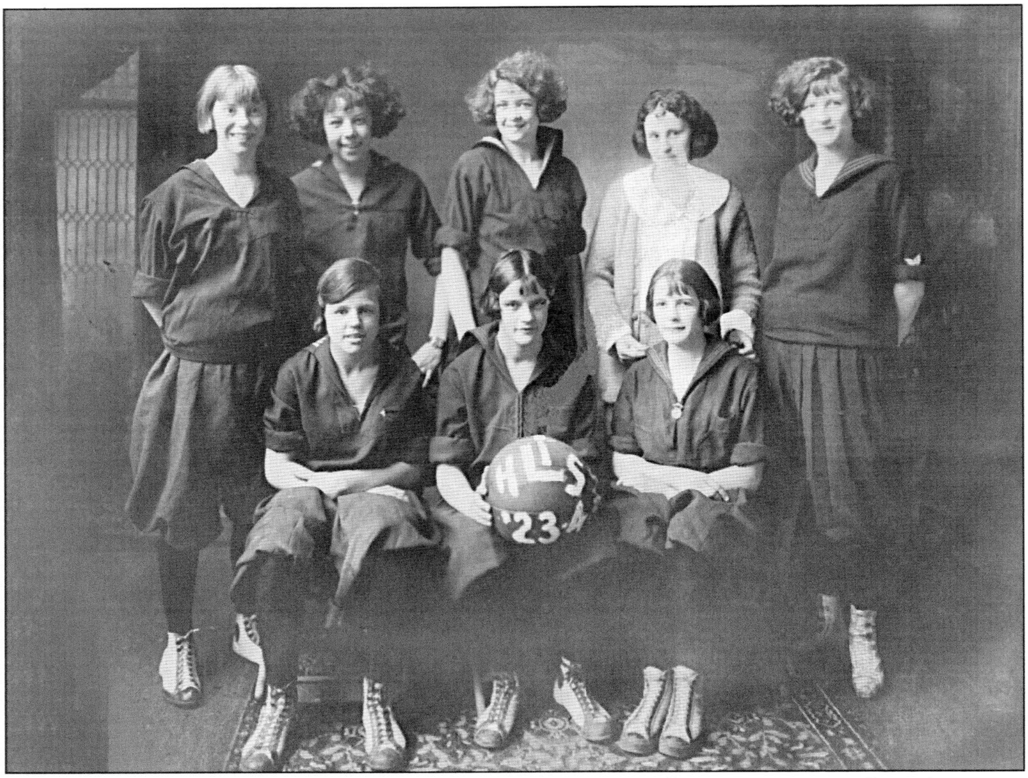

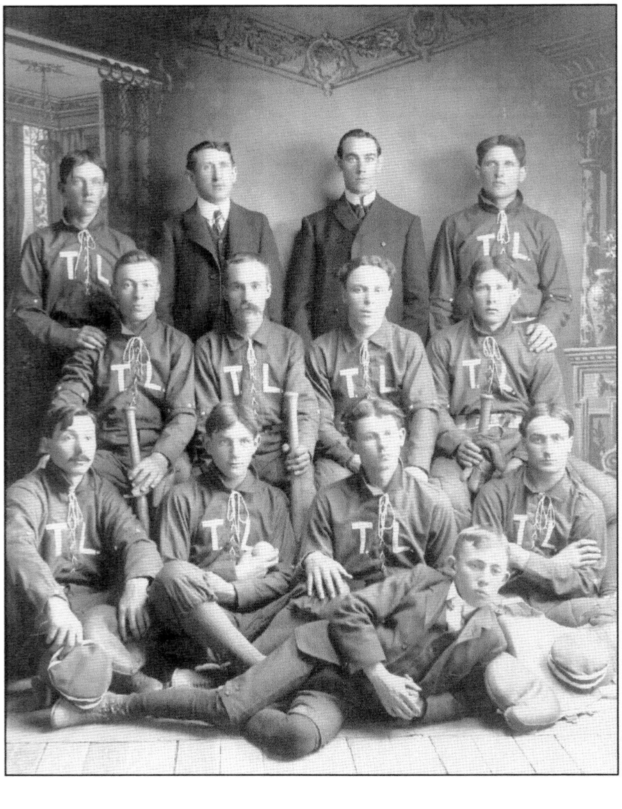

The 1923 Tupper Lake girls basketball team included (first row, from left to right) Jacqueline Proulx, Agnes Cheverette, and Helen McCormick; (second row, in no particular order) Beatrice Clark, Muriel Ginsberg, Mary Hayes (the coach's wife), Laura Paiment, and unidentified. (Goff Nelson Library Collection.)

This early Tupper Lake baseball team included, with some names missing and in no particular order, (first row) Jim Reynolds, Jim Stowes, Del Delosh, and Ed Darvey; (second row) William Delair, George Rafferty, and Phil Derouchie; (third row) Lawrence C. Maid and Art Trudeau. (Goff Nelson Library Collection.)

Four

The Future Unfolds

Indispensable to the local Tupper Lake economy, Sunmount Veterans Hospital had a constant employment level of approximately 475 people, a payroll in the millions, and created hundreds of thousands of dollars of purchases made at local businesses. Approximately 95 percent of the employees resided in the immediate area and had above-average earnings and higher purchasing power, adding diversity of industry from the logging industry.

The Oval Wood Dish Corporation introduced the "Ritespoon" and "Ritefork" in 1937, and they proved to be great successes. By 1940, Oval Wood Dish employed 539 workers in Tupper Lake. They also manufactured clothespins, bowling pins, tongue depressors, furniture pieces, commercial veneer, hardwood flooring, ice cream, and Popsicle sticks.

More and more women entered the workforce, and Oval Wood Dish made a point of reaching out to them, advertising that "Tupper Lake Girls Do Better Here." Female workers were offered "light pleasant work . . . the factory is clean, light, well ventilated, and warm in winter."

By 1930, the growth of the Tupper Lake area had reached a plateau, where it remained until the 1950s, when sawmills began to close as wood products were being replaced by plastics. Hurd's Northern Adirondack Railroad was long since gone, and the New York Central had stopped passenger service in 1965 and freight by 1972. Manufacturing industries moved offshore, and the small hometown retail businesses were out-competed by larger malls and shopping centers.

In 1965, the federal government closed the veteran's hospital only to have the institution transferred to the New York State Department of Mental Hygiene. Today, it runs as a development center and is still the major employer for Tupper Lake.

The town's current population is about 4,000, and the pioneer spirit still lives on. Efforts are under way to revitalize the economy of Tupper Lake with the building of the Natural History Museum of the Adirondacks, better known as the Wild Center, as well as a reopening of the Big Tupper ski slope by the partners of the Adirondack Club and Resort. The old train station has been rebuilt, and hopes are high about restoring rail service and creating a recreational trail.

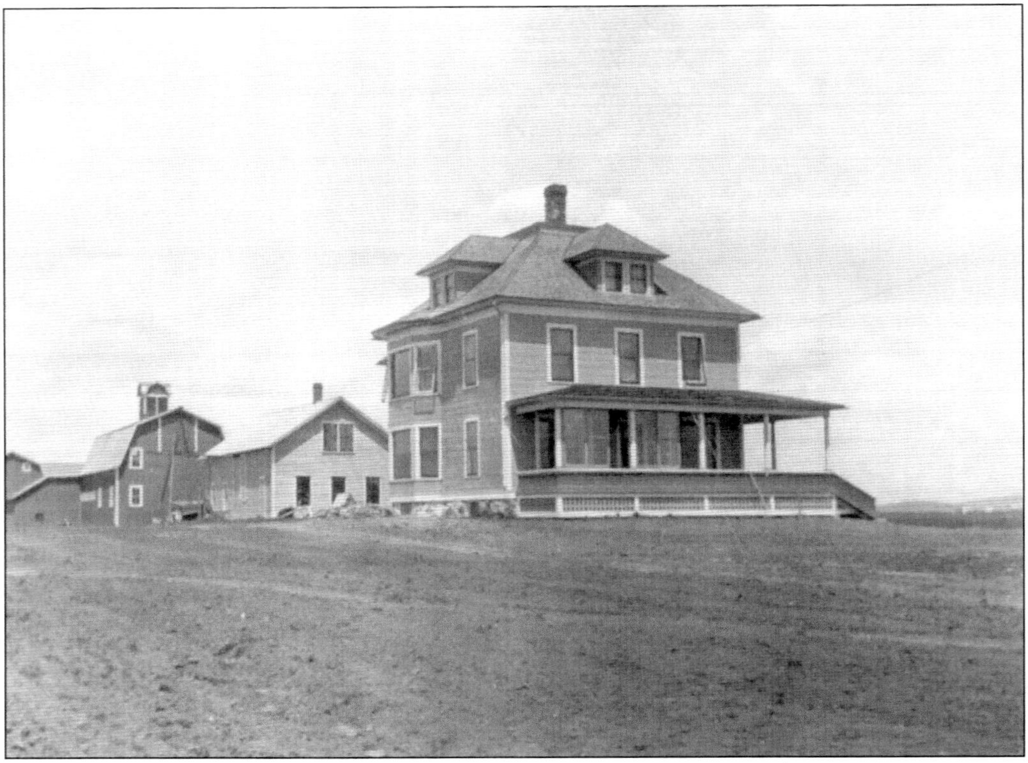

With an amazing display of community spirit, the growing village raised $20,000 dollars in 1922 to purchase the 160-acre Hosley farm and build Sunmount Veterans Hospital. (Goff Nelson Library Collection.)

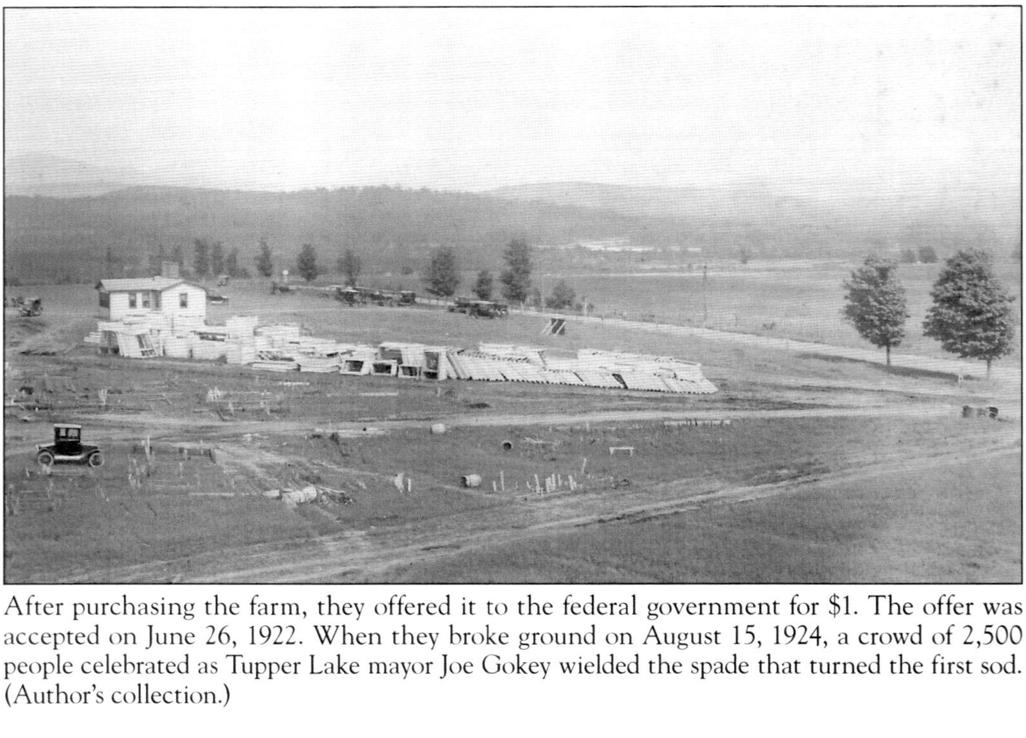

After purchasing the farm, they offered it to the federal government for $1. The offer was accepted on June 26, 1922. When they broke ground on August 15, 1924, a crowd of 2,500 people celebrated as Tupper Lake mayor Joe Gokey wielded the spade that turned the first sod. (Author's collection.)

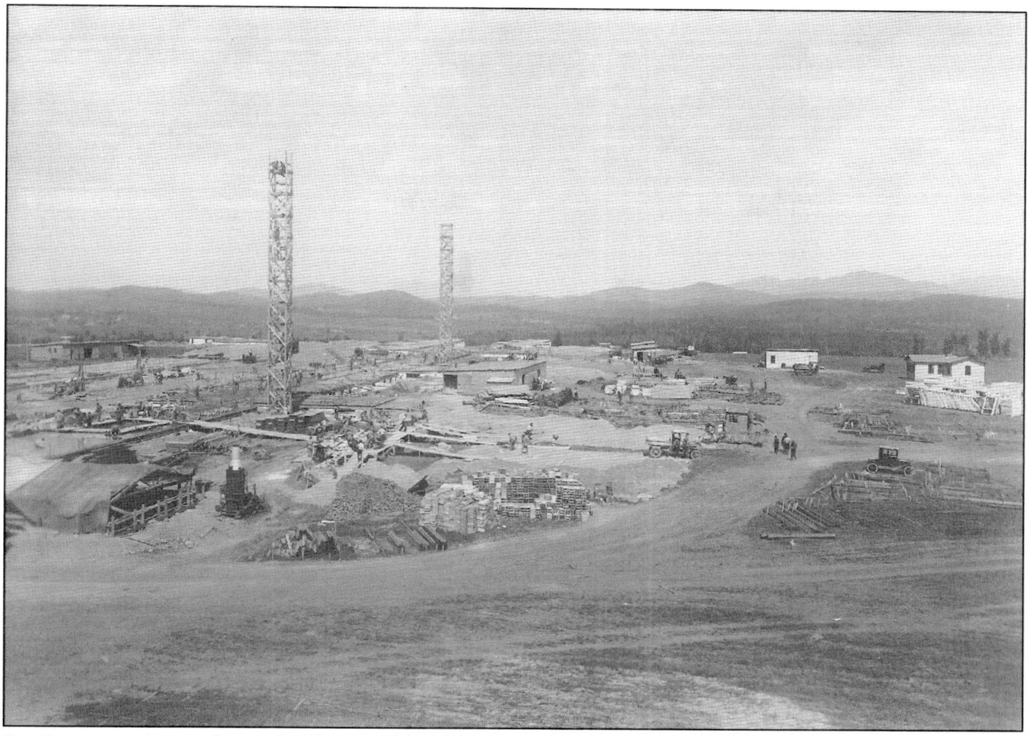

Looking southeast from the hospital building site is the old McCarthy farm. A section of the Raquette River known to the community as the "Oxbow" is visible in the distance. At that time, there were still no houses on Park Street. (Author's collection.)

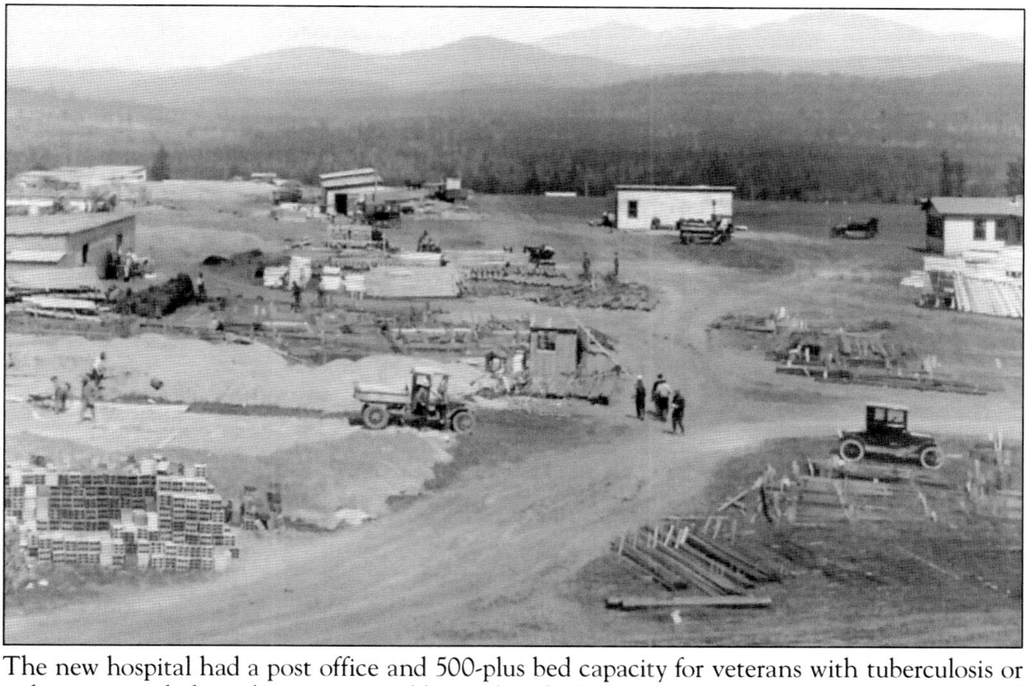

The new hospital had a post office and 500-plus bed capacity for veterans with tuberculosis or pulmonary and chest diseases. An additional 26 beds were set aside for general medical and surgical care. (Author's collection.)

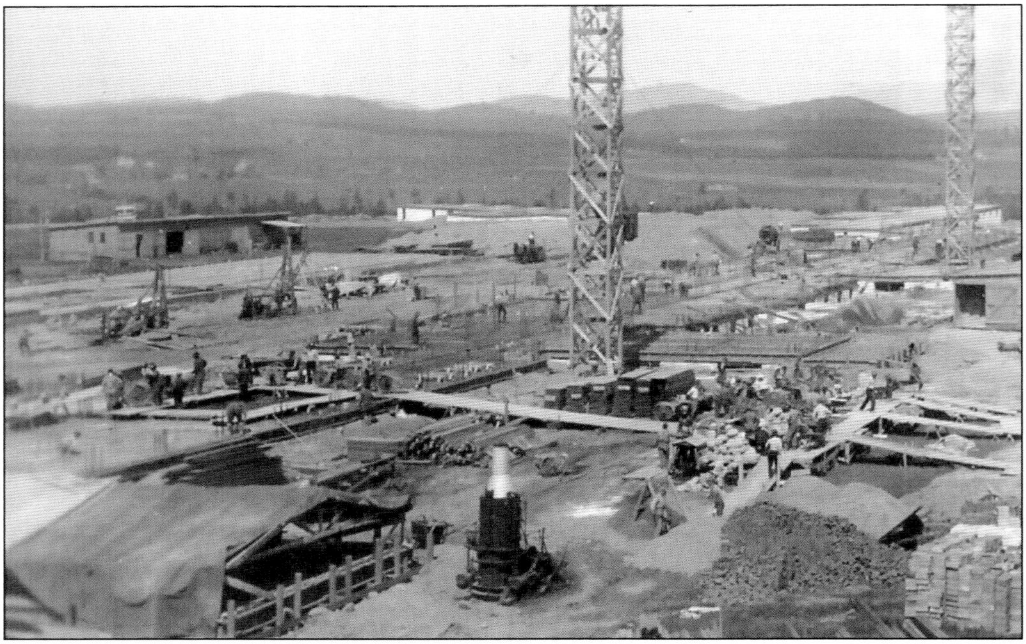

This view of the construction site looks to the northeast. In the distance, the vast expanse is full of farms along old Wawbeek Avenue. (Goff Nelson Library Collection.)

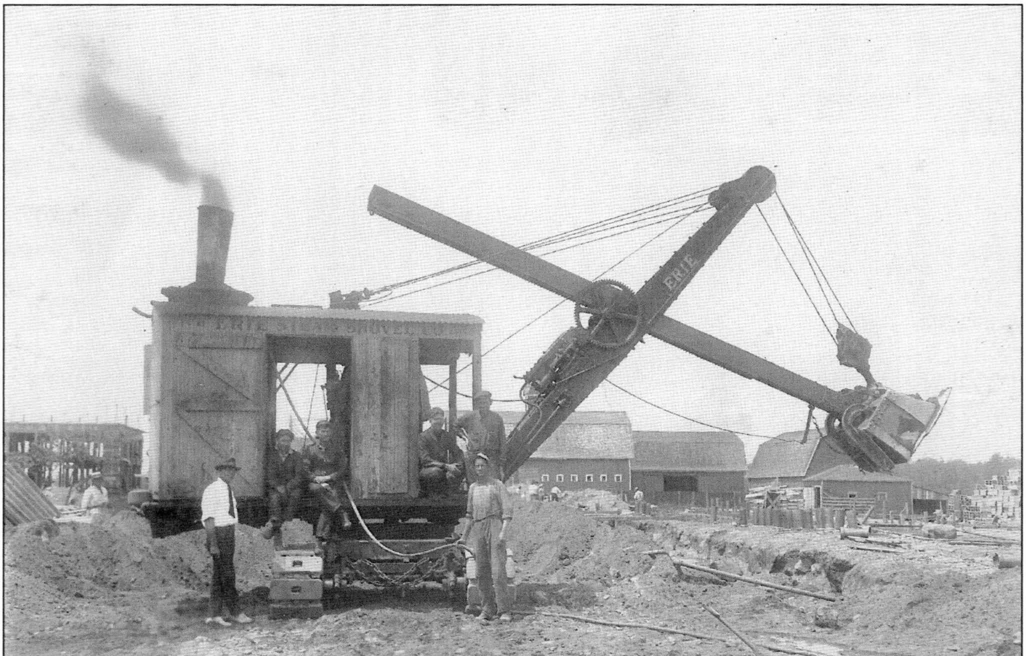

The Erie Steam Shovel was a large steam-powered excavating machine popular when steam shovels came in vogue in the 1920s. Thousands of miles of state highways were built in this time period as well as new factories and institutions like Sunmount. The development of simpler, cheaper, diesel-powered shovels caused steam shovels to fall out of use in the 1930s. (Goff Nelson Library Collection.)

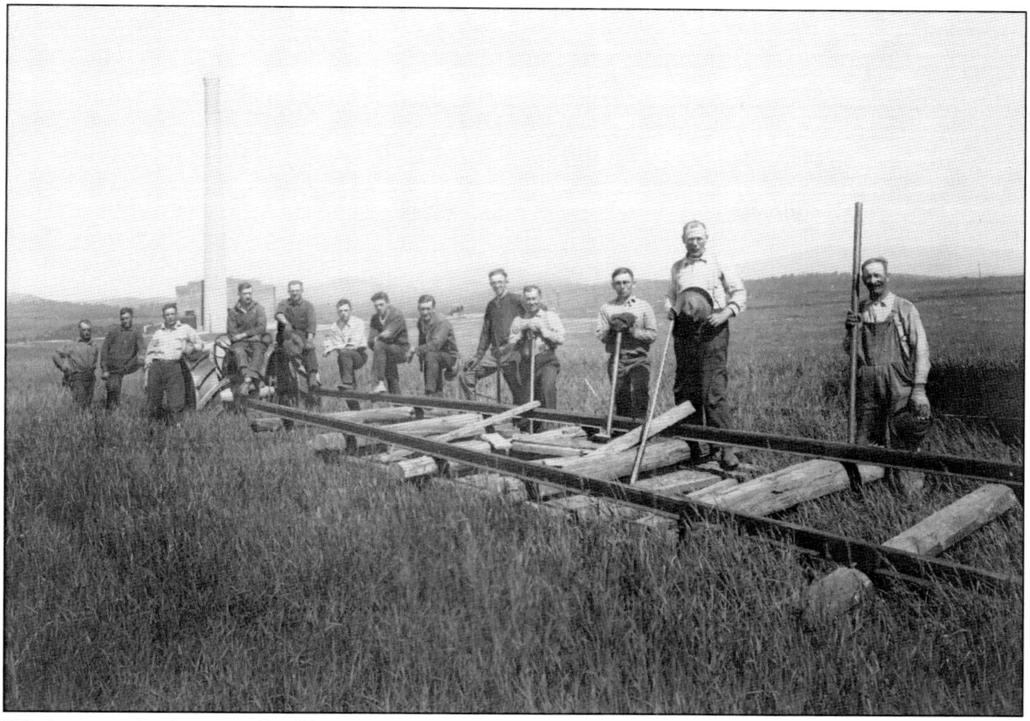

Workers at the hospital building site construct a temporary rail to clear old farm structures out of the way. (Goff Nelson Library Collection.)

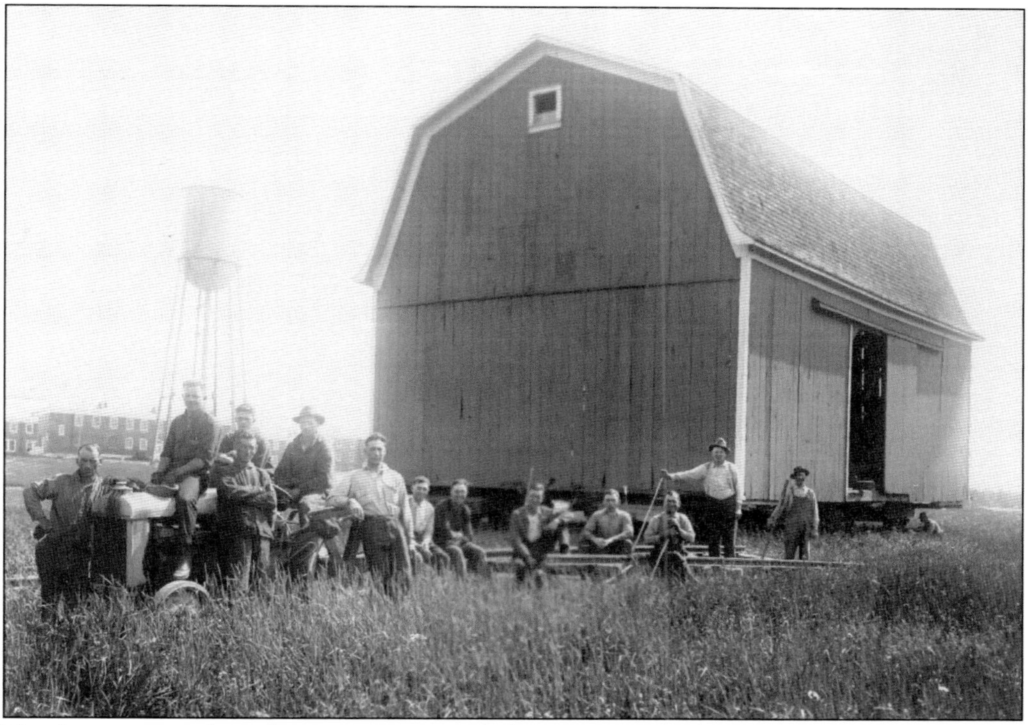

This happy crew takes a few minutes to pose before returning to the task of relocating this barn. (Goff Nelson Library Collection.)

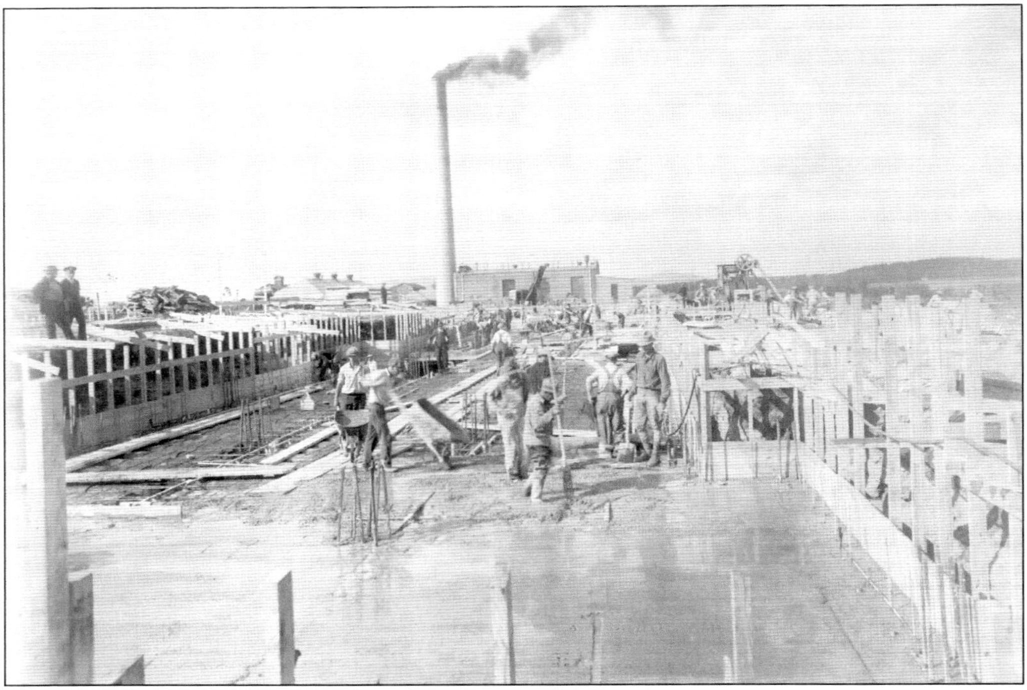

Workers pour the cement floor of one of the buildings in the new hospital. Today, this building is used for visitors and living space for employees. (Goff Nelson Library Collection.)

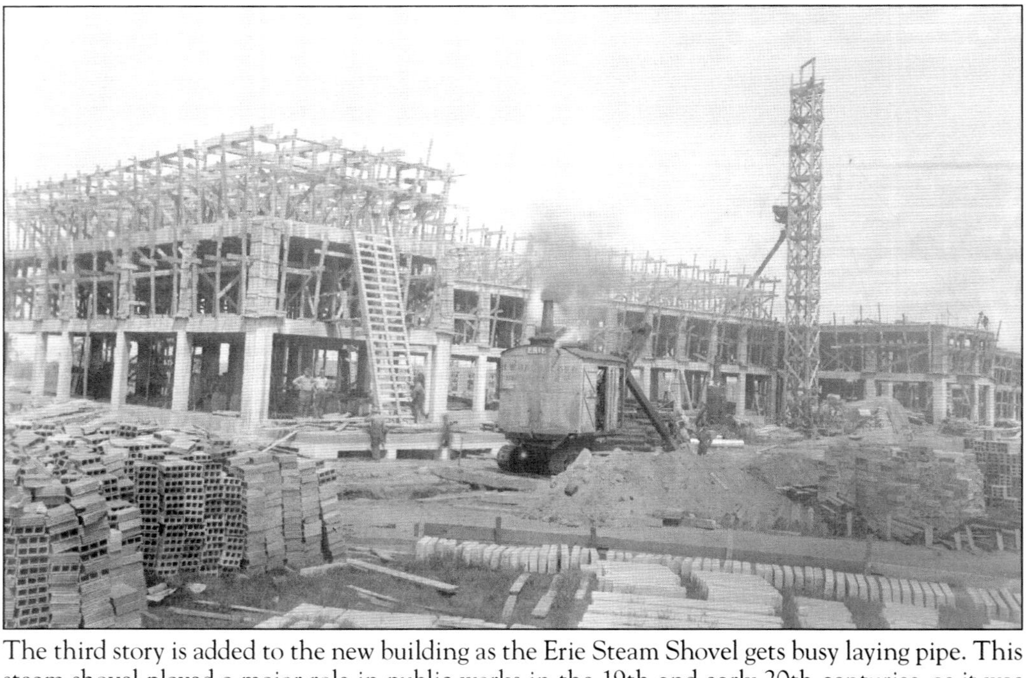

The third story is added to the new building as the Erie Steam Shovel gets busy laying pipe. This steam shovel played a major role in public works in the 19th and early 20th centuries, as it was key to the construction of railroads and the Panama Canal. (Goff Nelson Library Collection.)

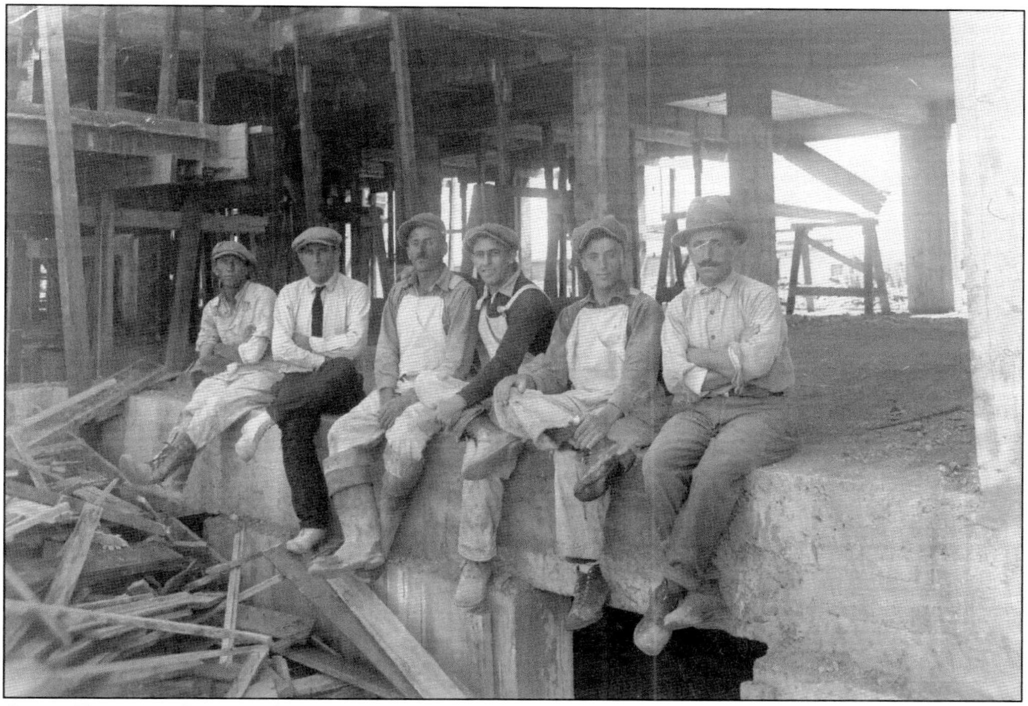

A small group of men take a break from the day's work. When the building was constructed, the equipment inserted was the most modern assembled by any institution of the day and was fireproof throughout. (Goff Nelson Library Collection.)

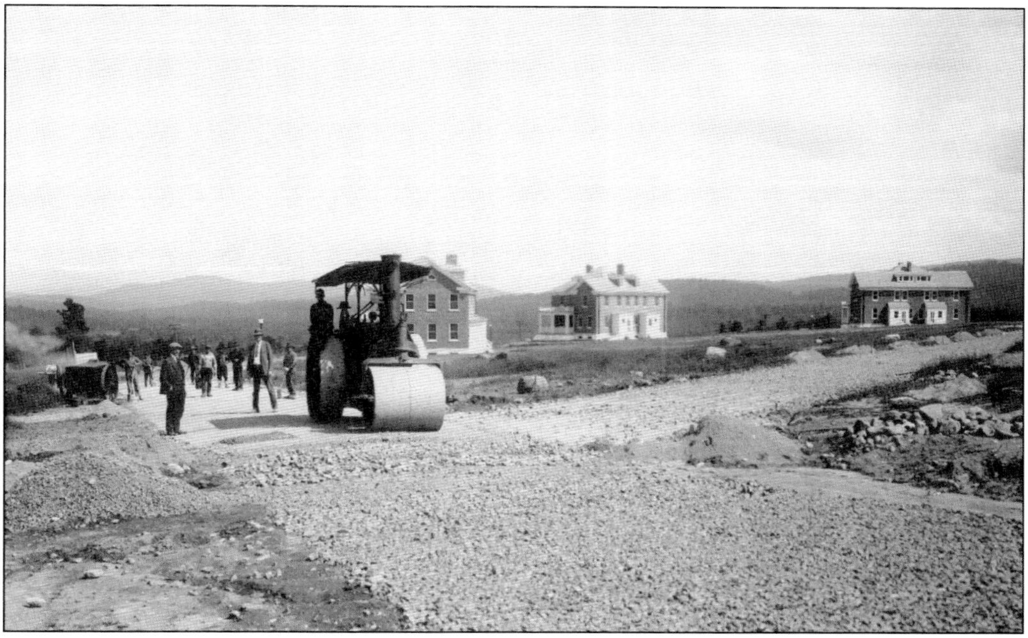

A large steamroller puts the finishing touches on one of the institution's new roads soon before the first patient was admitted. The doctors' residences can be seen in the background. (Goff Nelson Library Collection.)

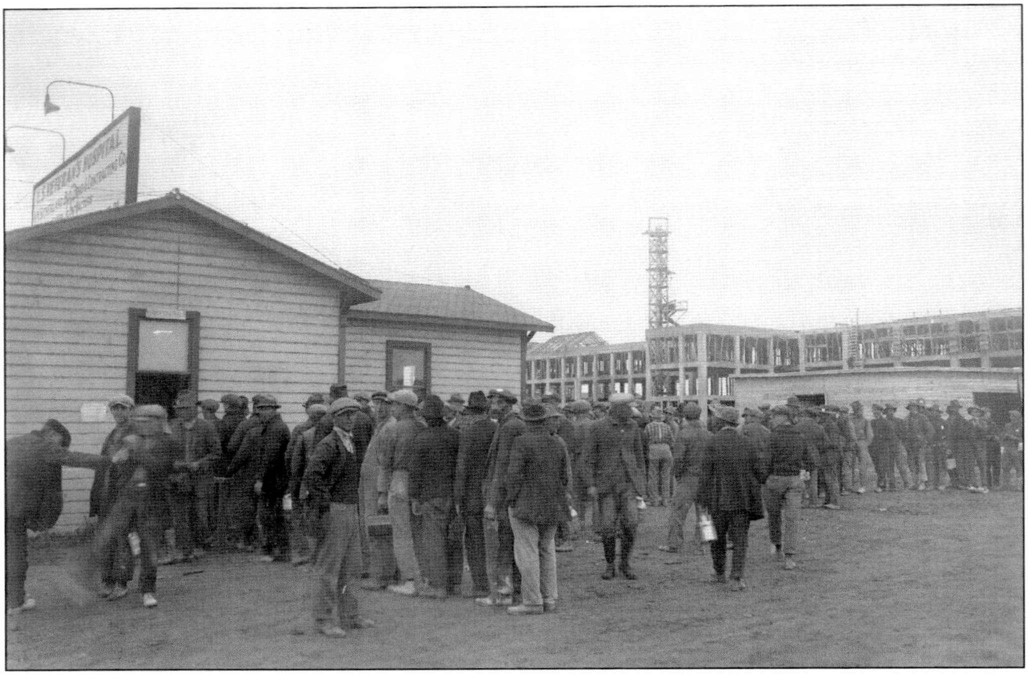

The carpenter's pay window featured a lot of smiling faces on this day. Over 70 men waited in line at Southerland Building and Construction. After the project ended, many men stayed on to work as carpenters for the new hospital. (Goff Nelson Library Collection.)

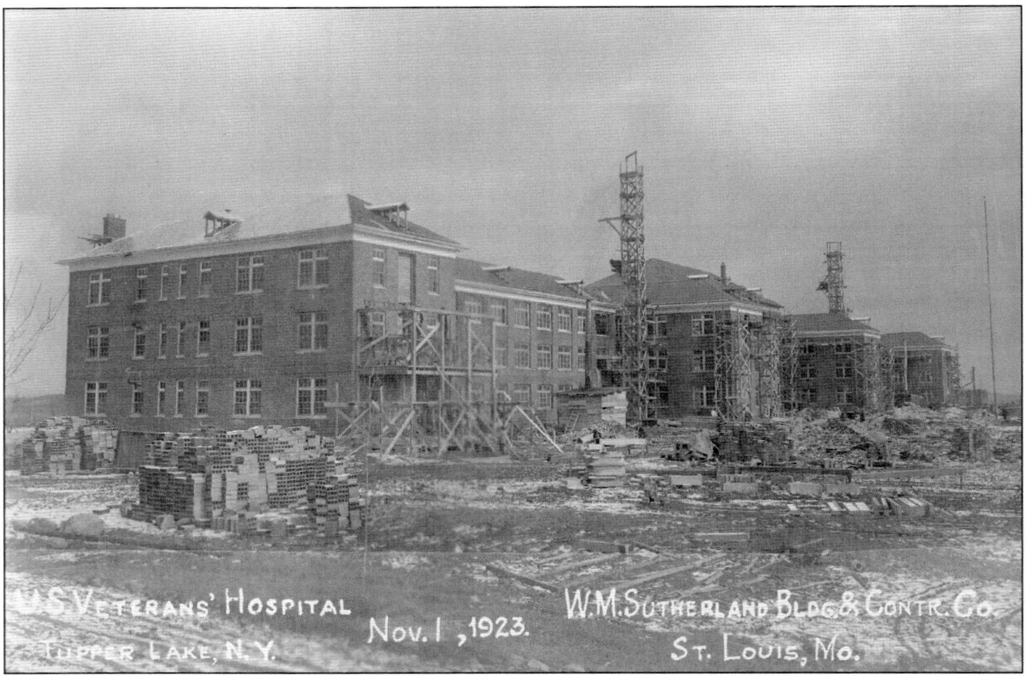

The hospital was well on its way to completion when this photograph was taken on November 1, 1923. It was to be the largest construction project ever built in Franklin County, with 700,000 square feet of floor space and more than three-quarters of a mile of covered walks and underground passages. (Goff Nelson Library Collection.)

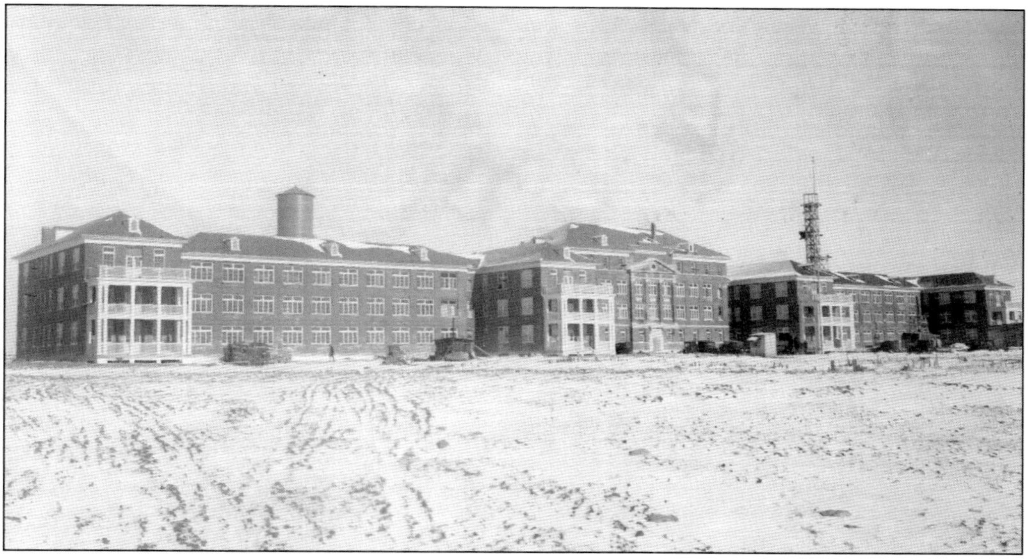

After years of work on the 130-acre site at the old Hosley farm, workers finally completed the sprawling complex. A crowd of 2,500 people packed the area in front of the infirmary building to hear a speech from Gen. Frank T. Hines, the director of the Veterans Administration. The facility did not have a name then, only a number. It was listed as Federal Hospital No. 96 but was soon known as Sunmount. (Goff Nelson Library Collection.)

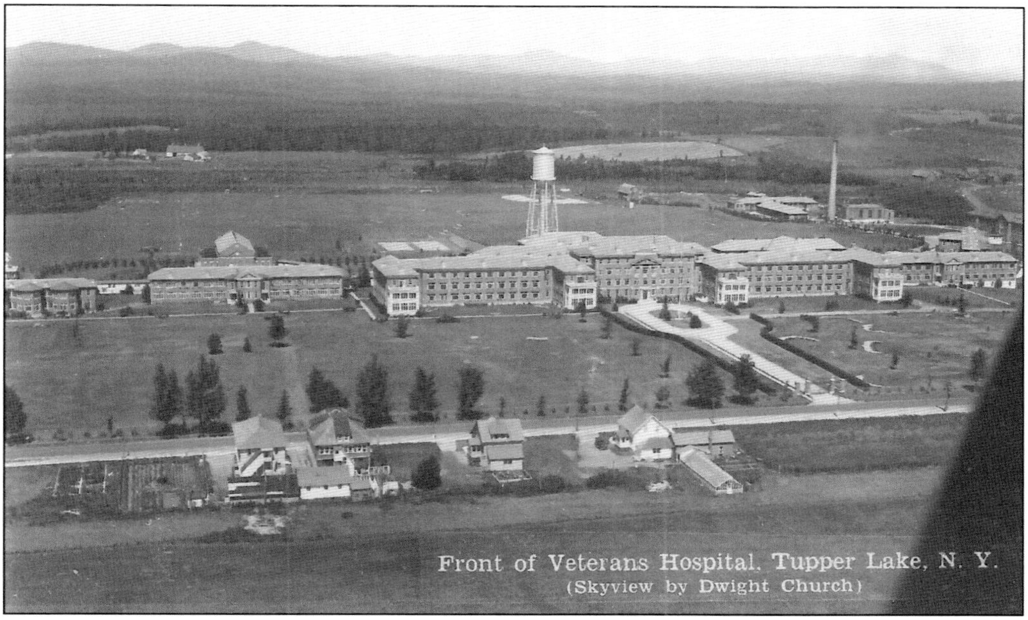

Dwight Church took this aerial photograph around 1950, showing the massive complex years after it was built. On August 11, 1965, after 41 years of service to ailing veterans, director John J. Whalen announced that the hospital was closing its doors. It was a sad day but not the end of the story. Sunmount exists today as a development center and is still the lifeblood of the community. (Goff Nelson Library Collection.)

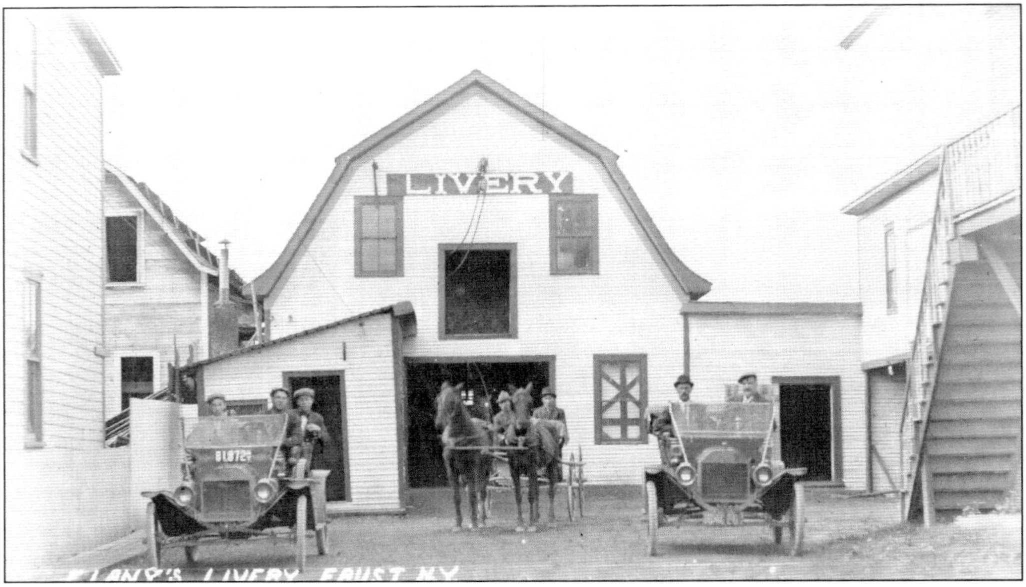

The first livery in Tupper Lake was established by the late William Sabin in 1892 and owned by several different people through the years, including Hewitt & Waddell of Long Lake, John McDonald, and Louis Badger, who moved it to the site adjoining Cohn's Pharmacy. In that location, it was acquired by Fred Lang and became the nucleus of the prosperous garage business he developed as the automobile gained in popularity over the horse. (Author's collection.)

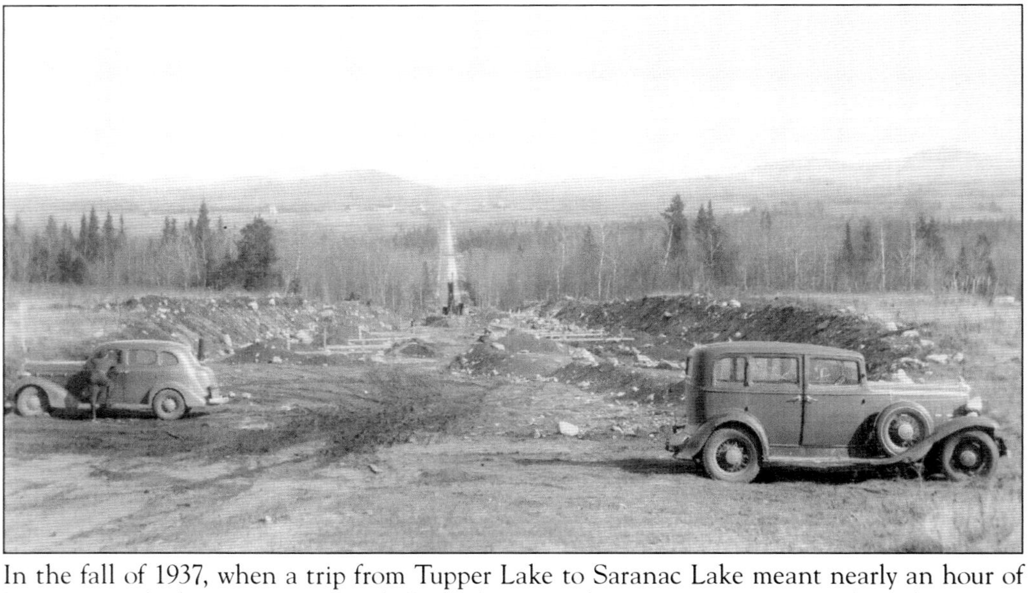

In the fall of 1937, when a trip from Tupper Lake to Saranac Lake meant nearly an hour of bouncing and jolting over curving, hilly, broken macadam, construction crews from the Belmar Construction Company of Troy push to complete a 20-foot-wide concrete highway between the two villages. (Goff Nelson Library Collection.)

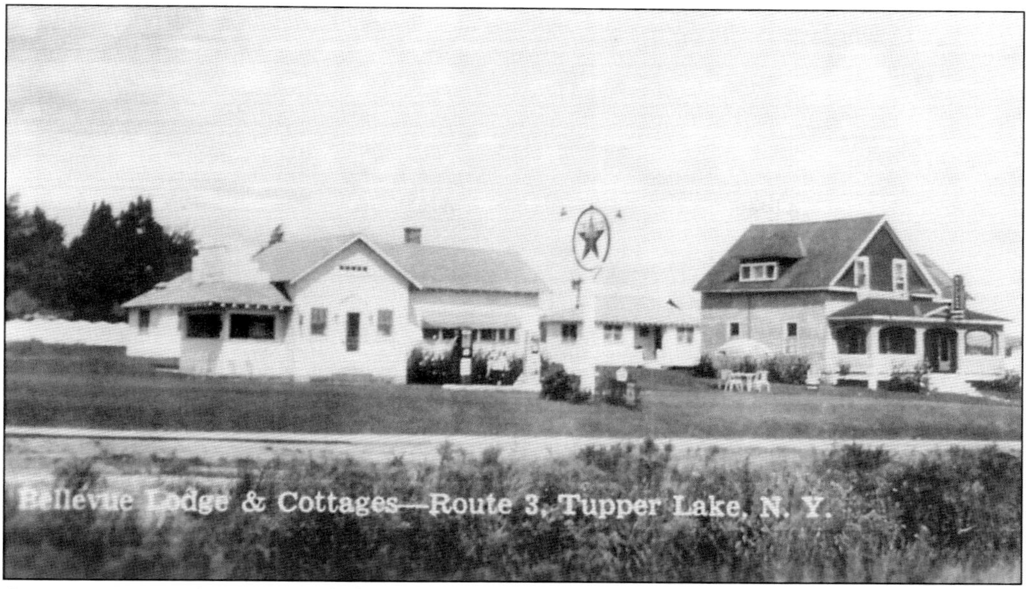

A new cottage industry, "Roadside America," was spawned with the advent of better roads and the use of the automobile. Roadside residents built cottages for overnight stays and some installed gas pumps. Many cottages cropped up along the major roads coming in and out of Tupper Lake. Amos LaBarge ran the Bellevue Cottages. He also served many years on the local school board and was an assessor for the town of Altamont. (Author's collection.)

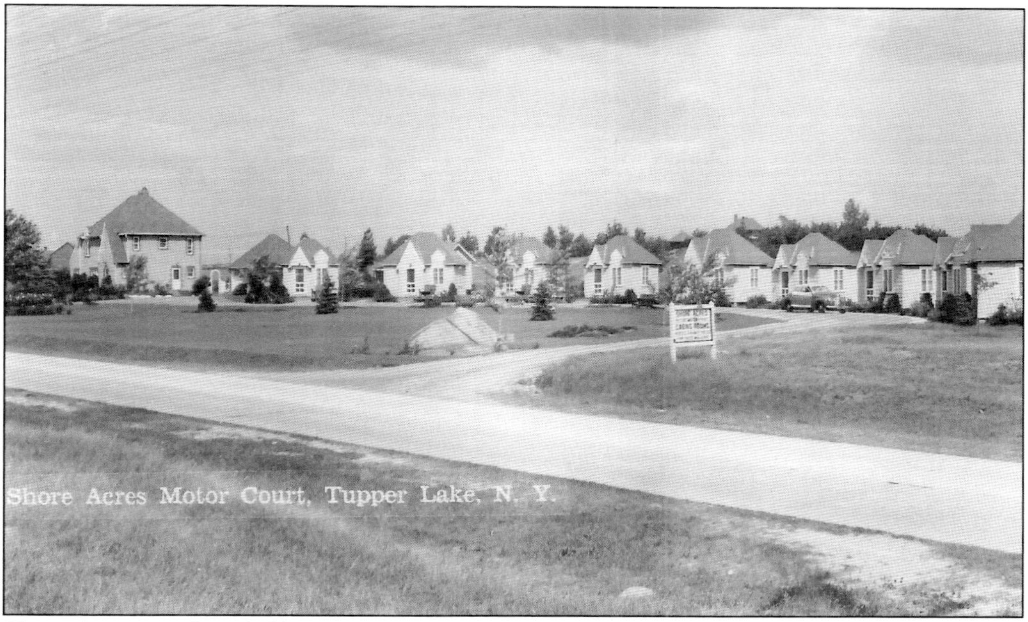

Shore Acres was founded by Frank and Mary Dinet. Dinet was born in Syracuse on November 18, 1893, and conducted a wholesale candy business. In the early 1930s, he began the Shore Acres tourist cabins. Today, it houses the Skyline ice cream stand. (Author's collection.)

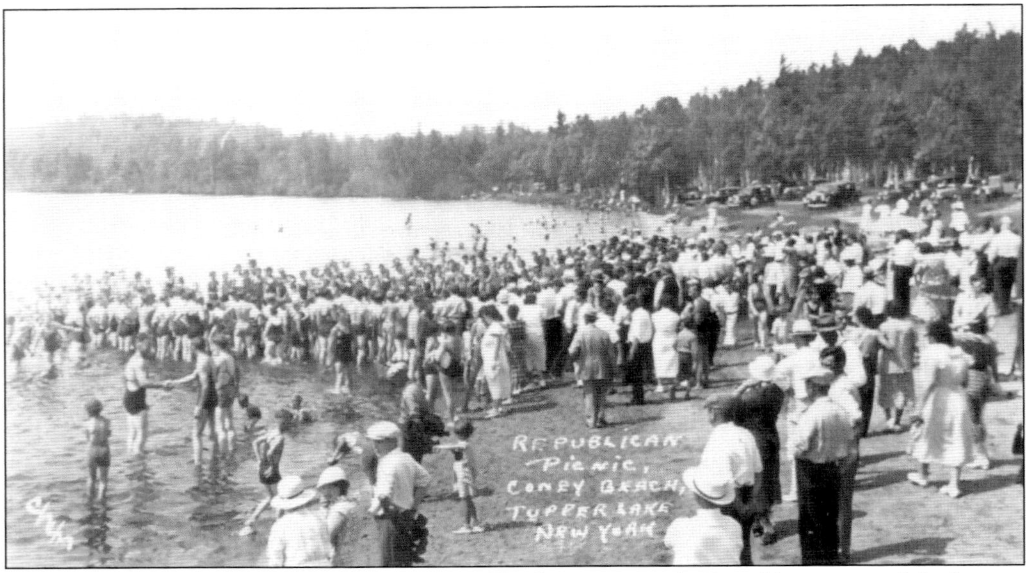

On July 20, 1935, at Coney Beach on Little Wolf Lake, Tupper Lake Republicans staged the biggest GOP gathering of the year. The open-air gathering was followed by a dance. Charles Bellows and Harold E. Bellows took charge of the music, Chester Young arranged a program of athletic stunts, and Vilas Chalmers and Melvin Bruce were in charge of the barbecue. (Author's collection.)

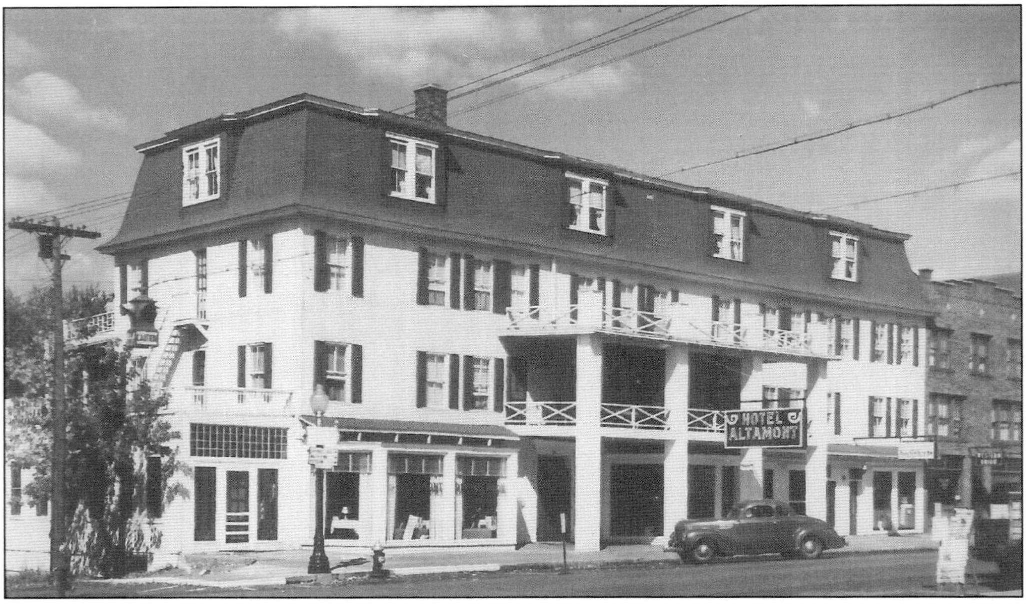

The Altamont Hotel was extensively renovated and modernized in 1946 by Hugh A. Beaton, who added the attractive "Mountain Room." In 1951, it was purchased by William Snider, who was its last owner. It stood empty and forlorn in the mid-1950s before it was sold to Grand Union Co. It was razed in 1957. (Author's collection.)

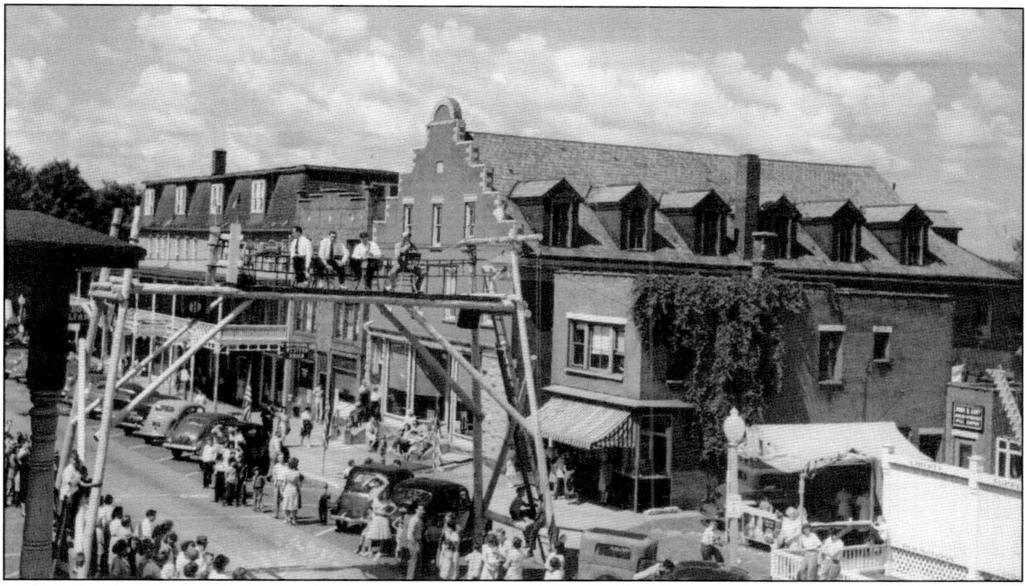

Judges and parade announcers eagerly await the beginning of the woodsmen's parade. Displays and vendors set up in the vacant lot nearby. The building with the Flemish roof today houses the village offices. For years, John B. Goff ran his business in the back of the old chamber of commerce building. (Goff Nelson Library Collection.)

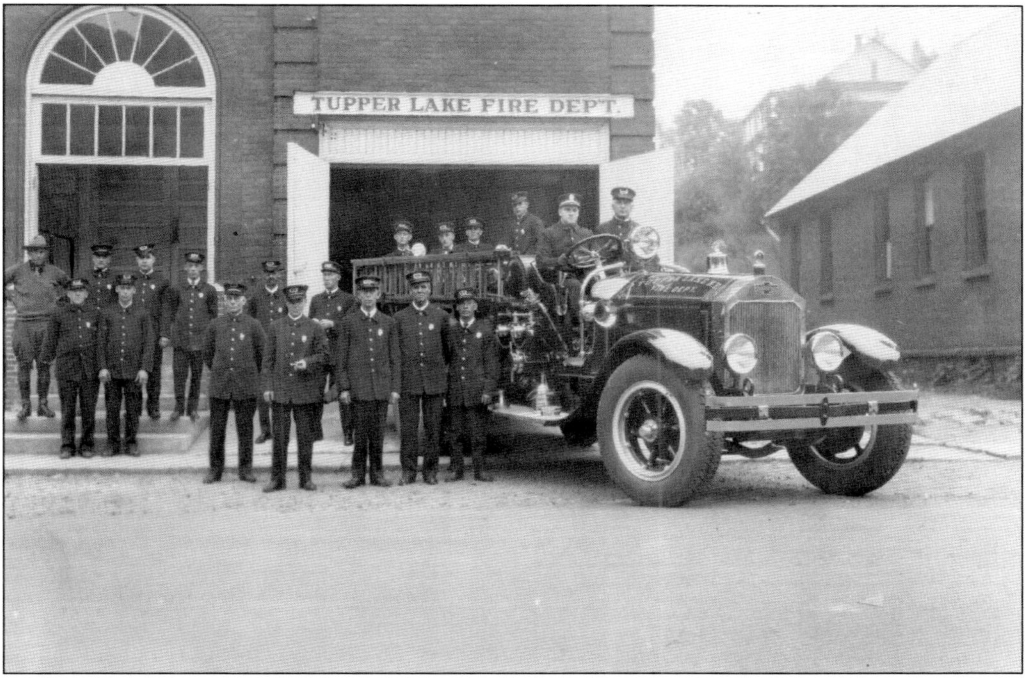

The disastrous fire of 1899 motivated citizens to establish the Tupper Lake Fire Hose Company in 1900. By the end of 1902, two more companies were added, with 59 charter members. Over the years, the fire departments matured as many proud men answered the call to protect the community. Although equipment was scarce in the early years, the men stand proudly around their sleek hook and ladder truck. (Goff Nelson Library Collection.)

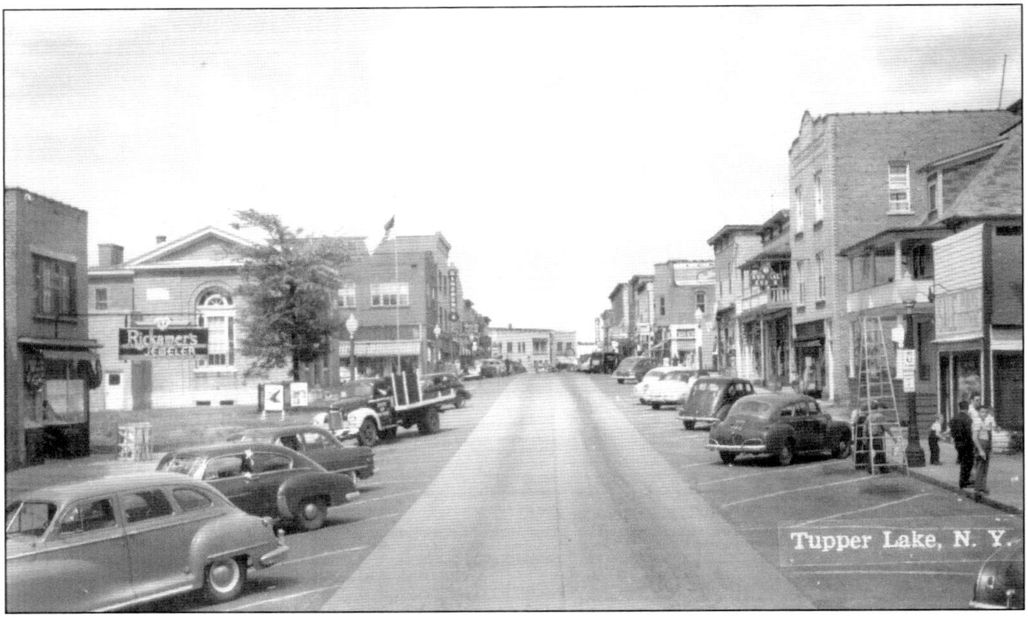

By the 1940s, the street began taking on a modern appearance, with diagonal parking and a paved concrete road. At that point, businesses were well established and the local economy had diversified with the building of Sunmount Veterans Hospital. (Author's collection.)

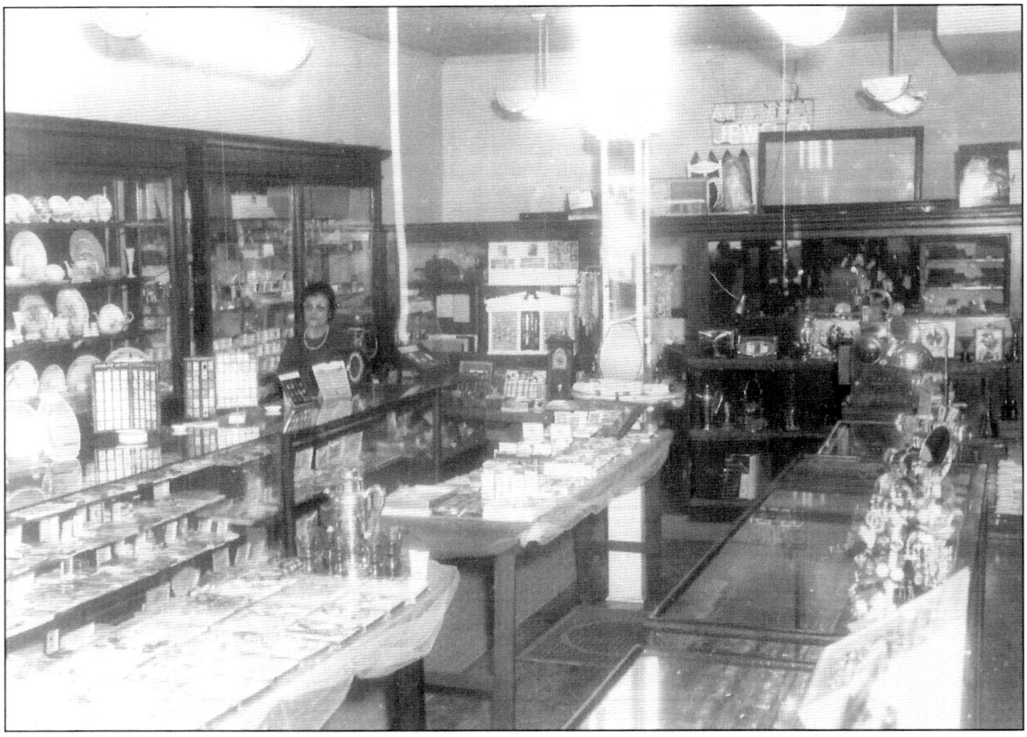

In 1903, Alfred A. Asel started out as an itinerant peddler, going from house to house and tramping back to the woods to serve the lumber camps. He opened his first store in St. Regis Falls and moved it to Tupper Lake in 1922. He married his wife, Fadwa, in 1930. Many a young couple cemented their dreams at Asel's Jewelry's on Park Street. (Camil and Ellen Maroon.)

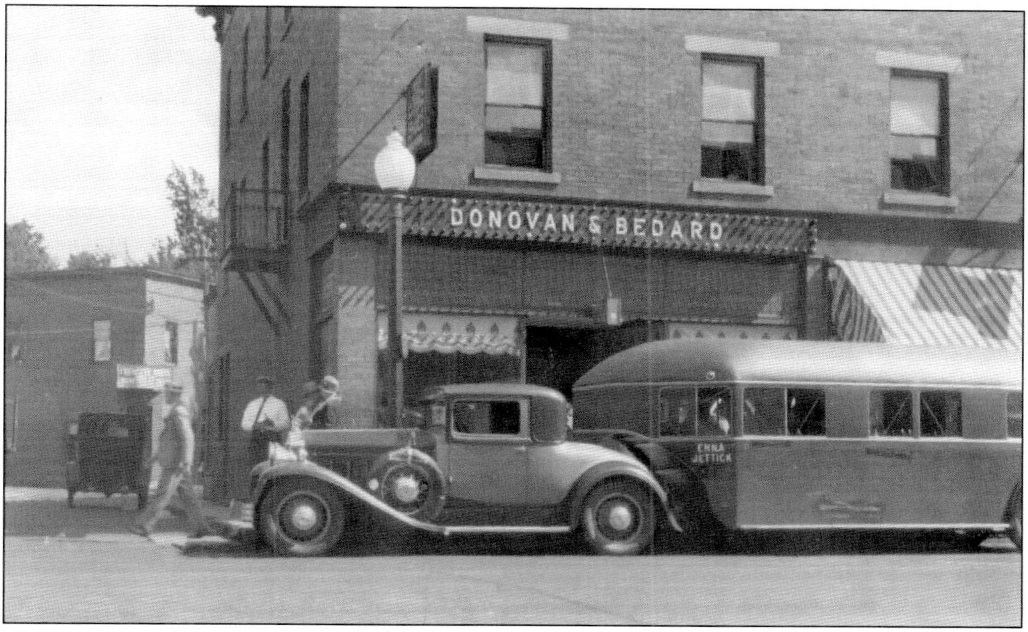

The Enna Jettick "aerocar" is parked on Park Street in front of the Donovan & Bedard clothing store. In the 1930s, Enna Jettick shoes were a quality line of women's shoes, manufactured in Auburn, New York; they were selling for $5 and $6 a pair. The company's slogan was "You need no longer be told you have an expensive foot." The aerocar, of interest in itself, was designed by the famous aviator Glenn Curtiss. (Author's collection.)

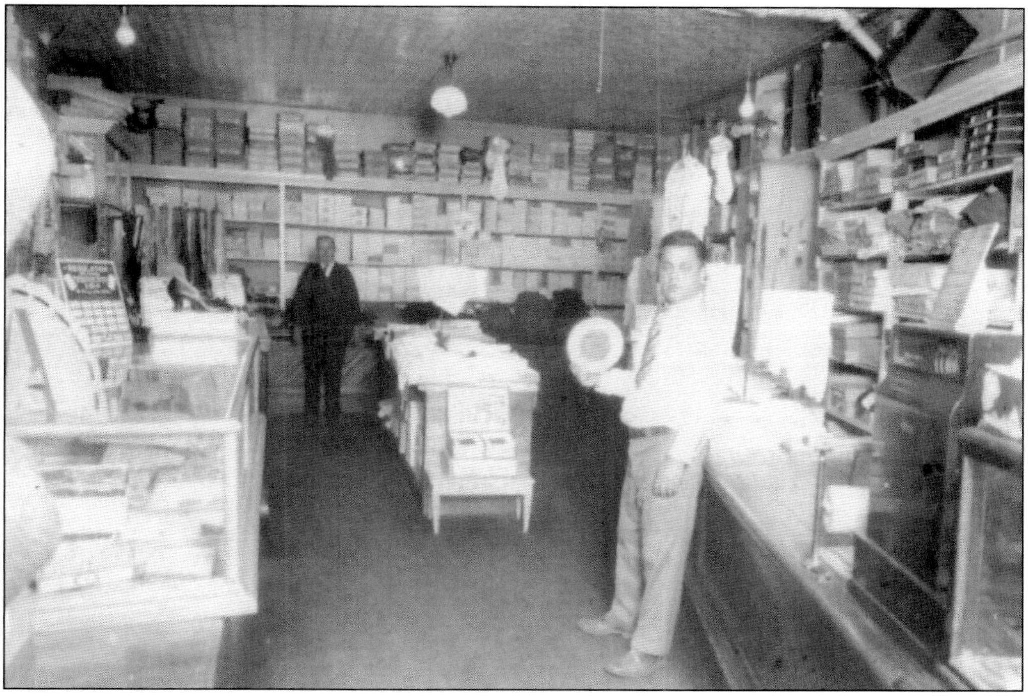

Camil A. Maroon stands with his hat in hand at the counter of his well-stocked dry goods store. The store was located at 75 Wawbeek Avenue, on the corner of Broad Street. (Camil and Ellen Maroon.)

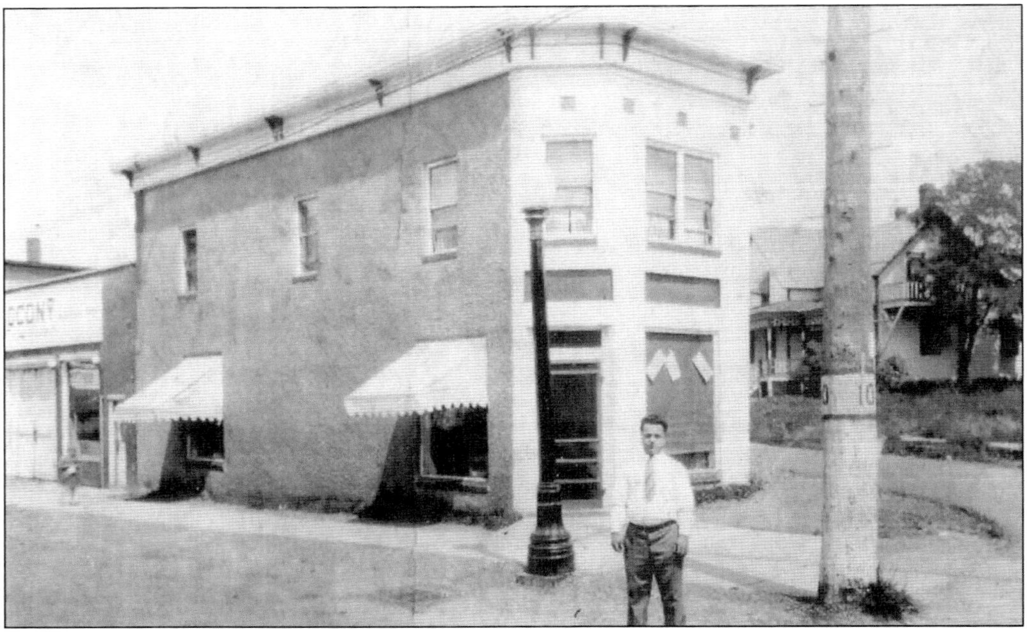

This is the Camil A. Maroon store from the outside. In later years, this was the Gwen Whallen antique shop. Gwen Whallen was famous in the antique world for her fabulous Victorian fan collection. (Camil and Ellen Maroon.)

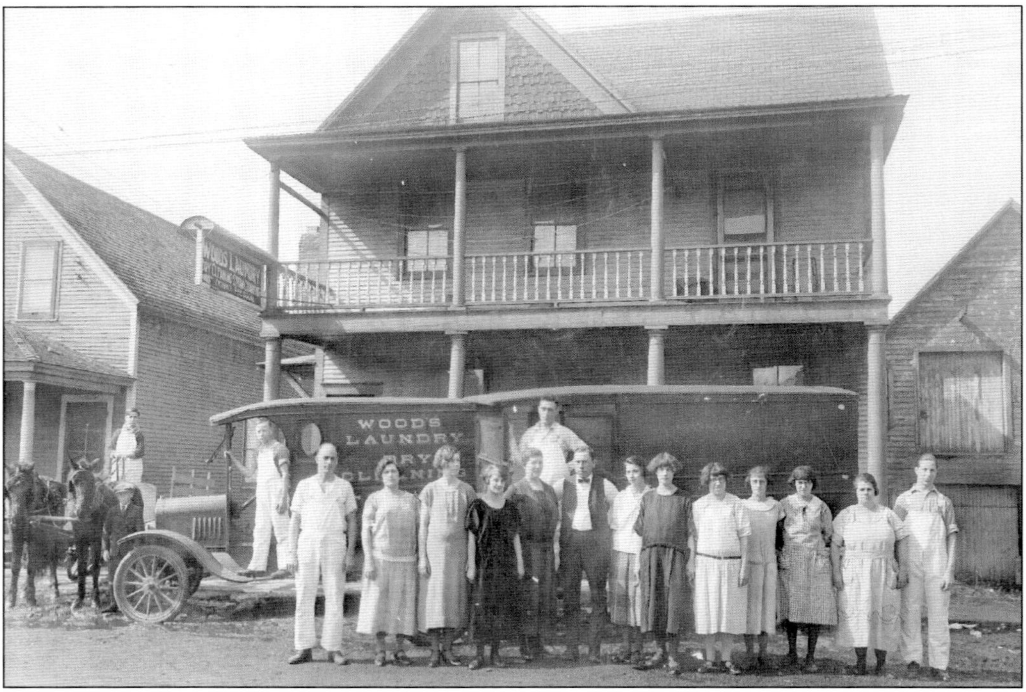

By 1925, Tupper Lake was large enough to establish a substantial laundry business, Wood's Laundry. Driving the horse is Larry Wood, and standing by the horse is Ernie Wood. On the truck's running boards are Red Gilbert (left) and Ernest Trudeau. Standing in front are Ernest Reando, Edith (Scanlon) Johnson, Ida Wood, Frank Wood, Gert Ellis, Aldea Reando, Leo Wood, and five unidentified people. (Goff Nelson Library Collection.)

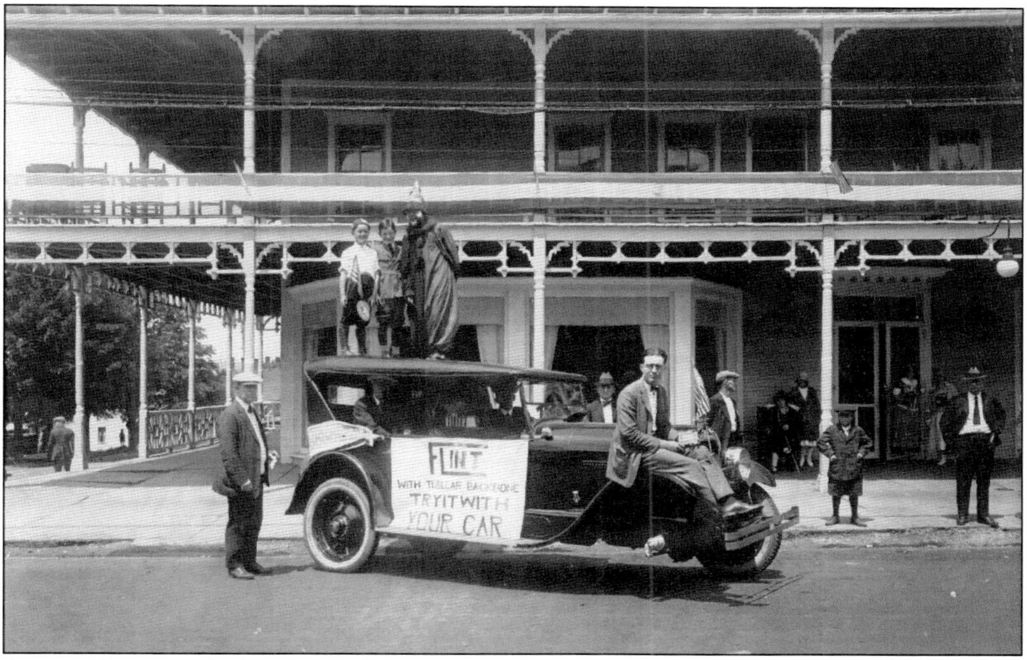

A new Flint is parked in front of the Altamont Hotel. The Flint was assembled by the Flint Motors Division in Flint, Michigan, starting in 1923. The Flint was priced to compete with Buick; however, following financial troubles, the Flint was discontinued in 1927. (Goff Nelson Library Collection.)

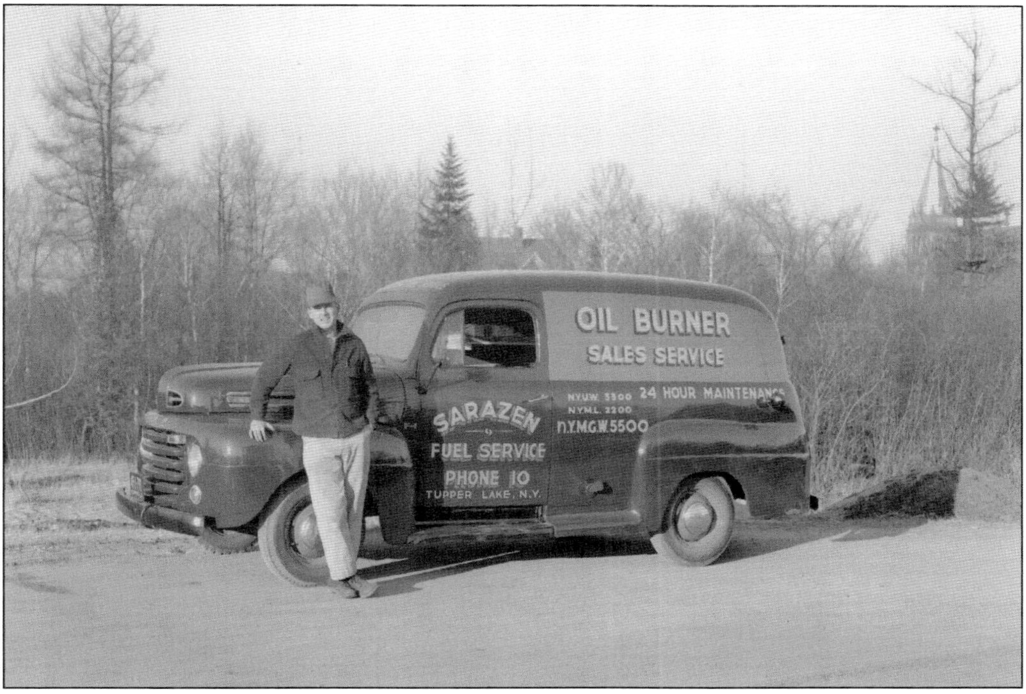

As Tupper Lake approached the 1950s, wood and coal stoves began to make way for the cleaner, more modern oil burner. The Sarazen Fuel Service was there to take care of residents' burners and supply the fuel needed for the winter. (Author's collection.)

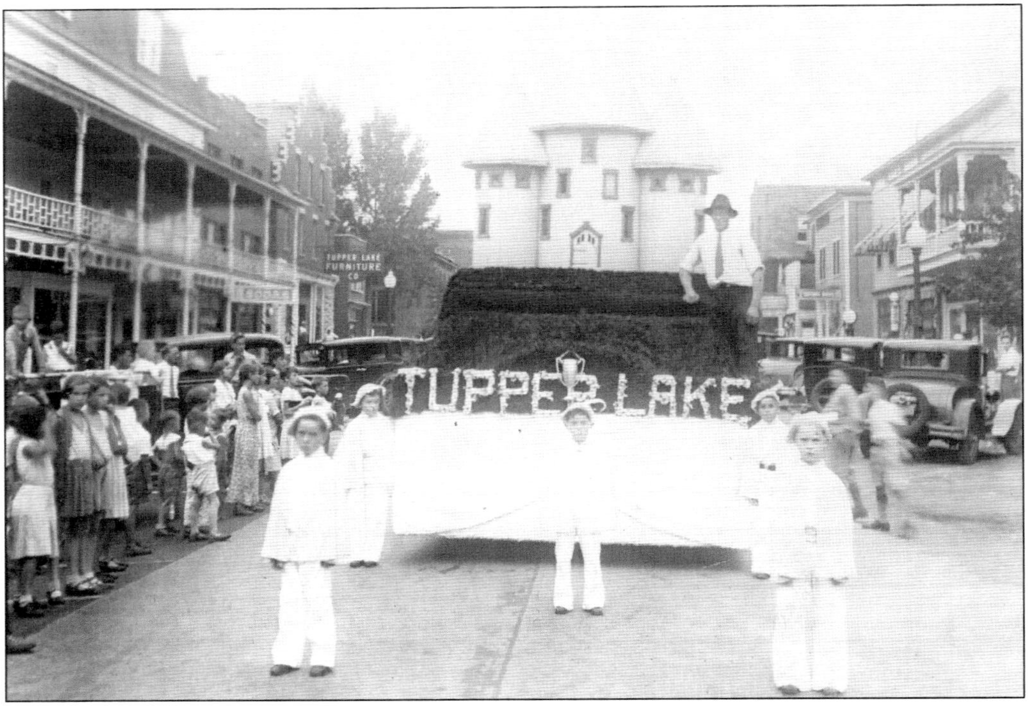

This 1932 float was entered to represent Tupper in a big parade at Saranac Lake and took top prize honors. The triple-towered castle was an appropriate setting for the nursery rhyme characters celebrating in front of the Altamont Hotel. (Goff Nelson Library Collection.)

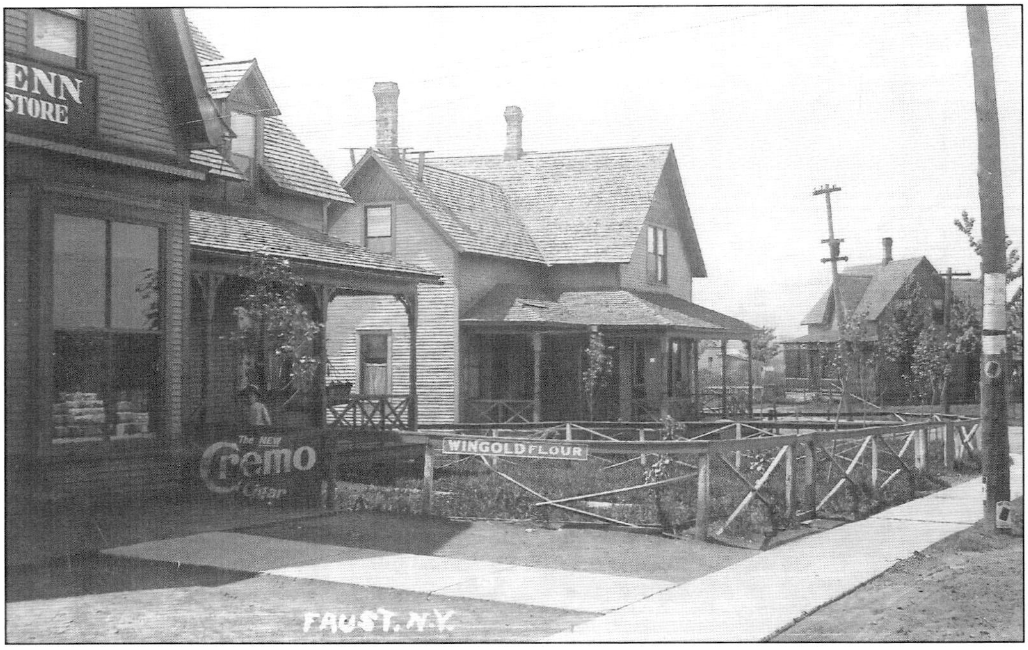

Fred W. and Cora Fenn moved to Tupper Lake in 1902, when Fred, in partnership with James Bliss, opened a grocery store on the present site of the Grand Union Hotel. In 1905, he established Fenn's Grocery at 79 Main Street and operated there for the next 38 years. Today, the Main Street Restaurant is in that space. (Author's collection.)

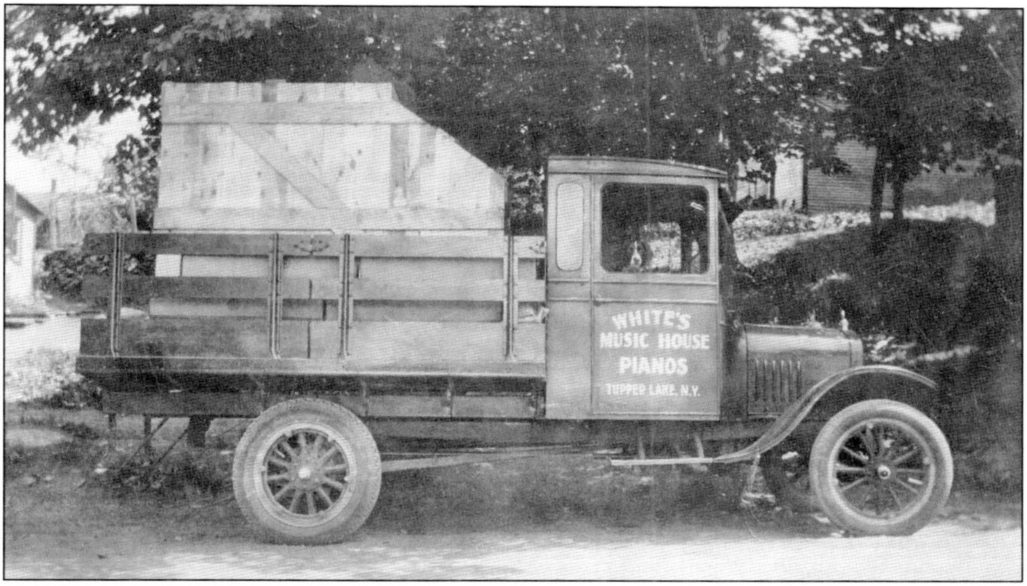

William H. White's dog looks out the window of an early truck. White opened his music store in Tupper Lake around 1924, initially running it out of the Hotel Iroquois before moving to 123 Park Street. He expanded and renamed his store White's Music & Electric, taking on General Electric in 1927. (Goff Nelson Library Collection.)

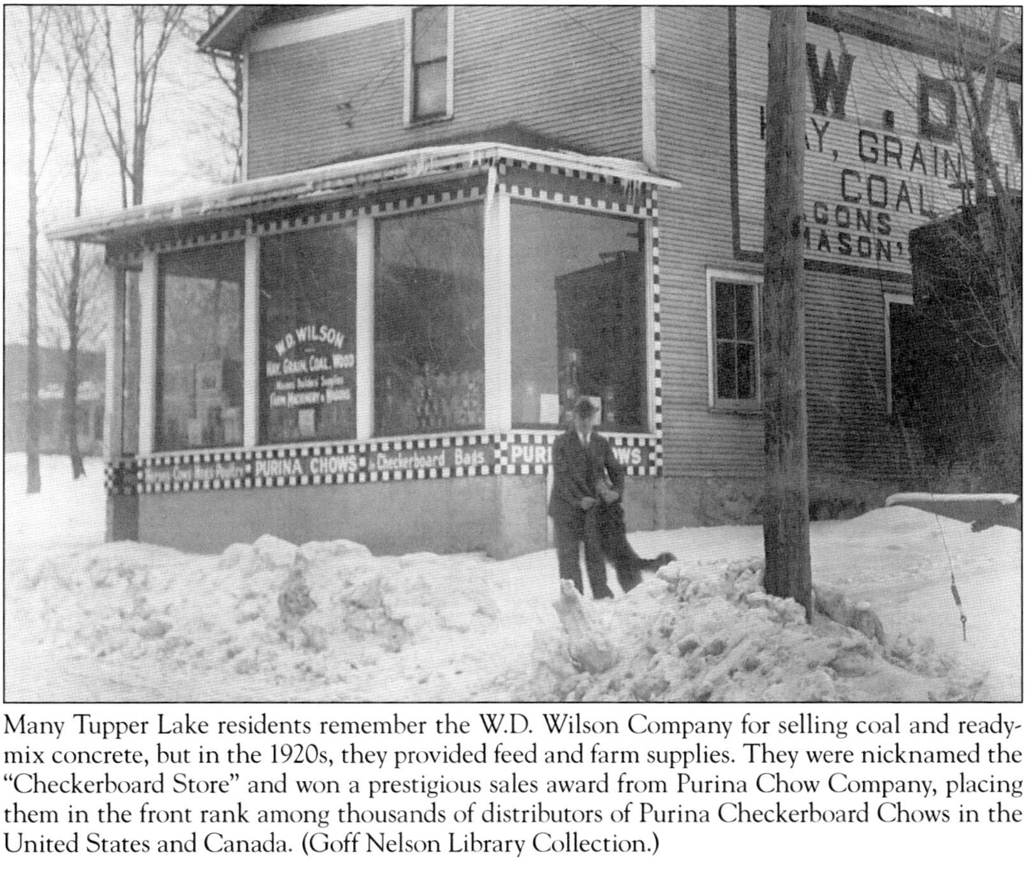

Many Tupper Lake residents remember the W.D. Wilson Company for selling coal and ready-mix concrete, but in the 1920s, they provided feed and farm supplies. They were nicknamed the "Checkerboard Store" and won a prestigious sales award from Purina Chow Company, placing them in the front rank among thousands of distributors of Purina Checkerboard Chows in the United States and Canada. (Goff Nelson Library Collection.)

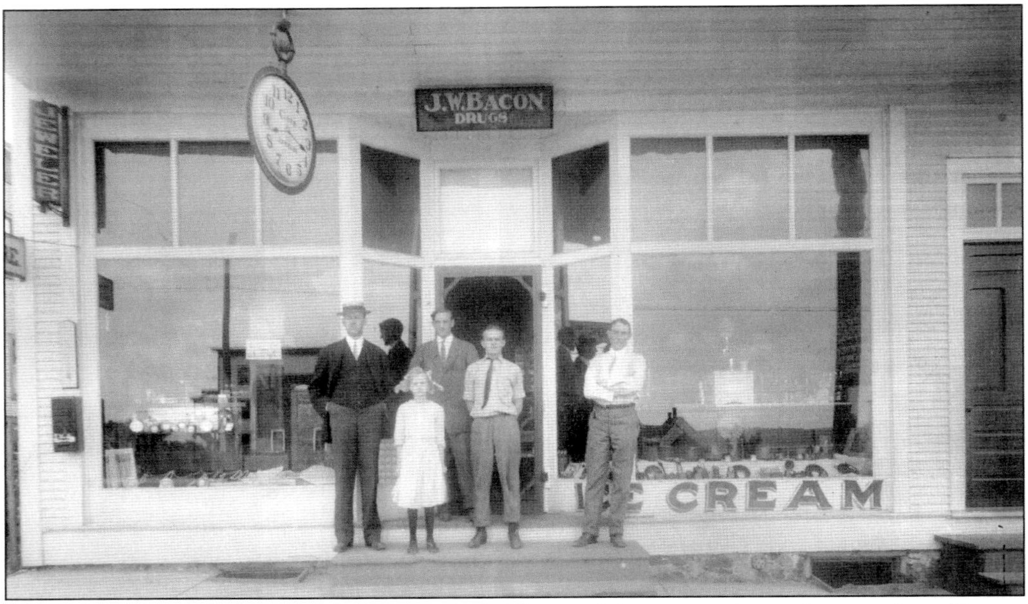

Employees of the J.W. Bacon drugstore pose in front of their store, located across from Tupper Lake National Bank at 80 Park Street. (Goff Nelson Library Collection.)

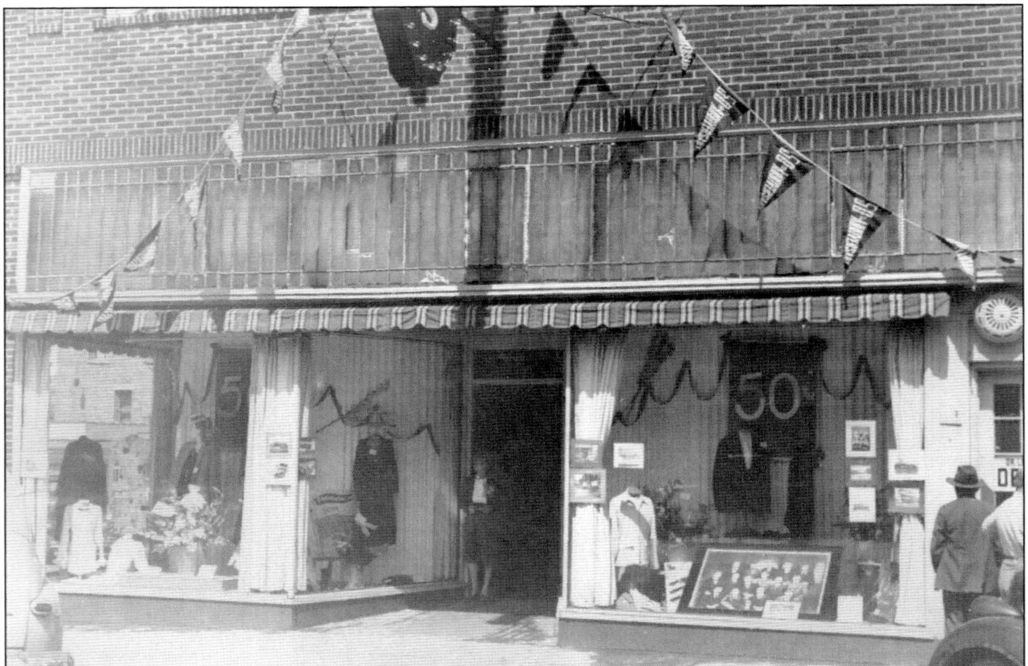

Moses "Mose" Ginsberg was a determined businessman who began his career as a peddler before opening his own department store, the Ginsberg Store. He famously said, "He who serves best, profits most. You've got to work, and do something for someone else." With the help of his determination and ideals, the Ginsberg Store grew into a thriving business, eventually reaching lofty status as one of the largest and longest lasting department stores in the entire United States. Mose lived to be 95, and at the time of this writing, his daughter Muriel, Tupper Lake's grande dame, is still alive and more than 100 years old. (Camille and Ellen Maroon.)

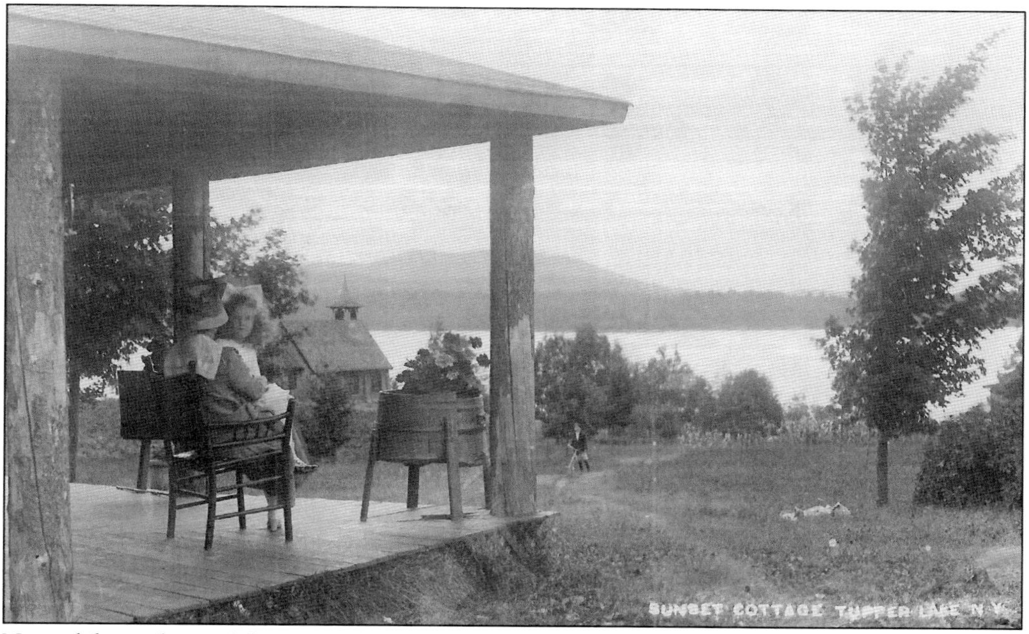

Named for its beautiful sunsets, Sunset Cottage was run by James and Rachel Cameron. The Camerons first came to Tupper Lake in 1898 and ran the small river-driver lodge at Bog River Falls, Camp Welcome. As business dried up, they sold the camp and purchased the Sunset Cottage property in Moody. They ran the business from 1906 well into the 1930s and were in a key location on the road from Long Lake to Tupper. (Goff Nelson Library Collection.)

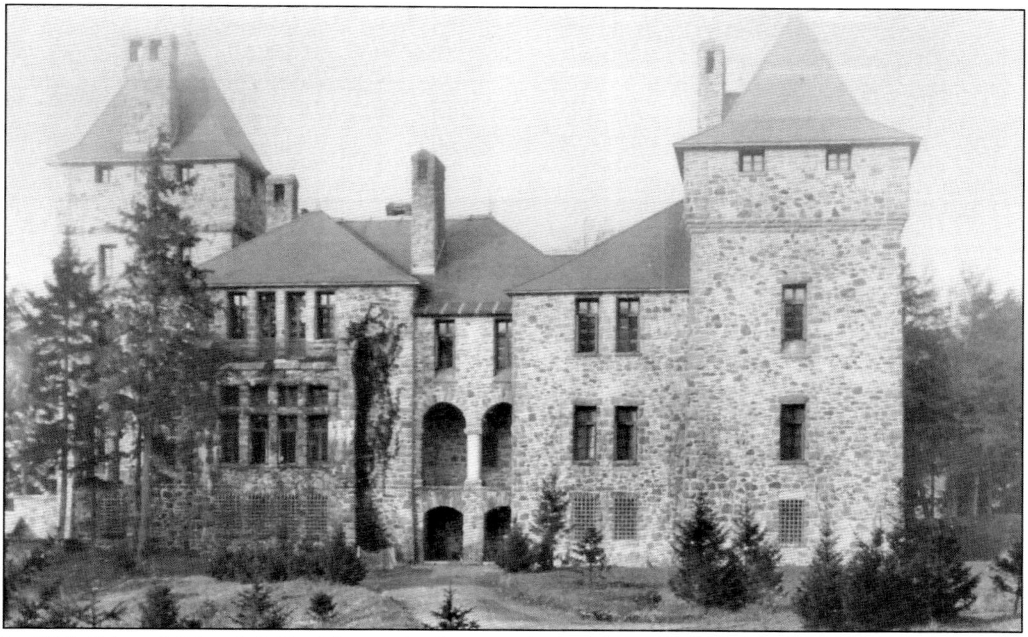

In 1893, Edward S. Litchfield of Katonah, the president of the Litchfield Park Corporation, acquired what was soon hailed as the most extensive game preserve in this country. In 1910, utilizing a force of 600 stonemasons, he began quarrying native granite and erected this spectacular castle on the shore of Lake Madeleine, formerly Jenkins Pond. The castle still stands today. (Goff Nelson Library Collection.)

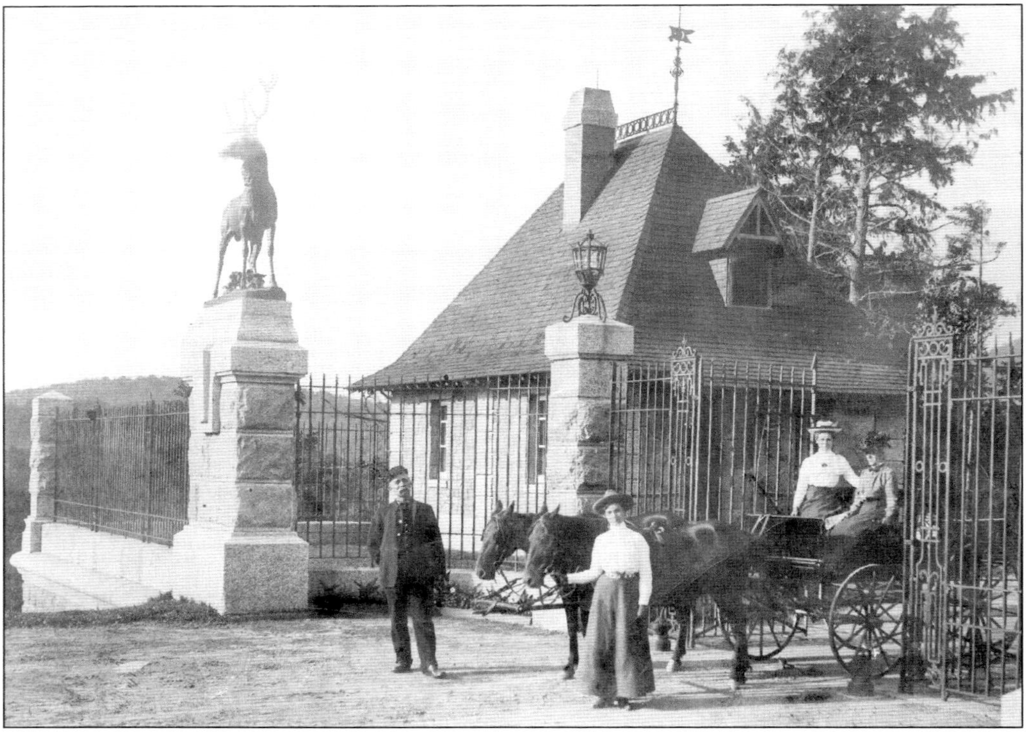

At the entrance gate, atop large granite spires, two bronze figures stand majestically and overlook the grounds. One is an American elk, the other an English stag. The gatekeeper's house is made of native granite quarried on the property. (Goff Nelson Library Collection.)

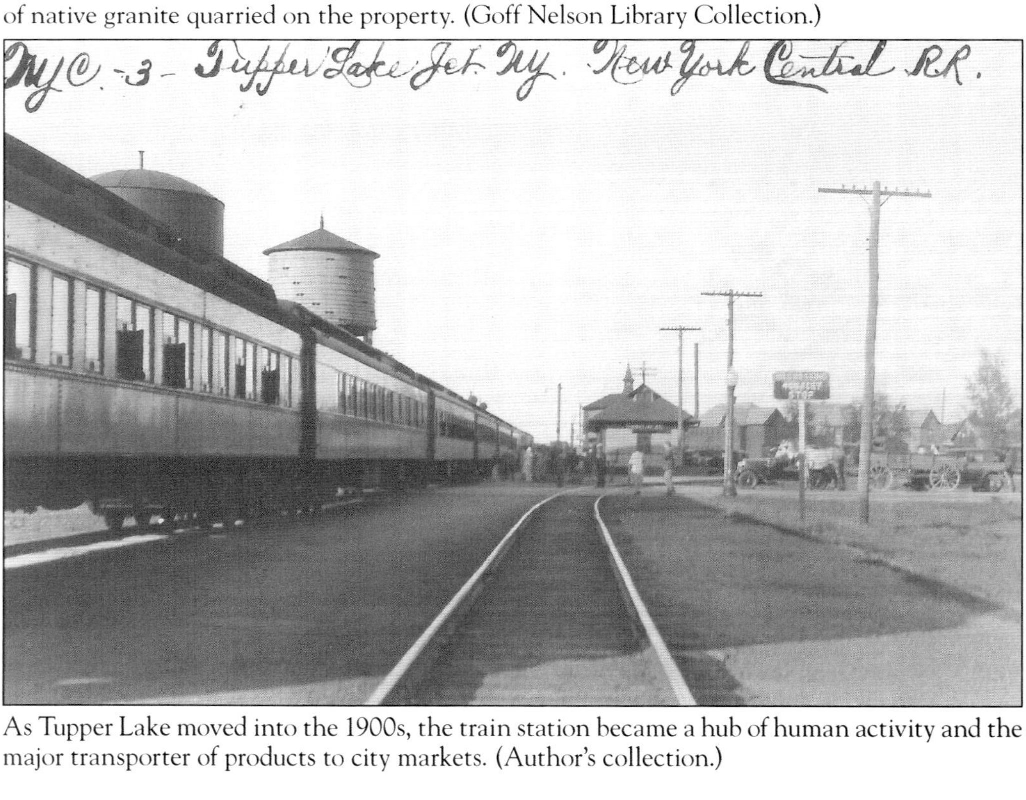

As Tupper Lake moved into the 1900s, the train station became a hub of human activity and the major transporter of products to city markets. (Author's collection.)

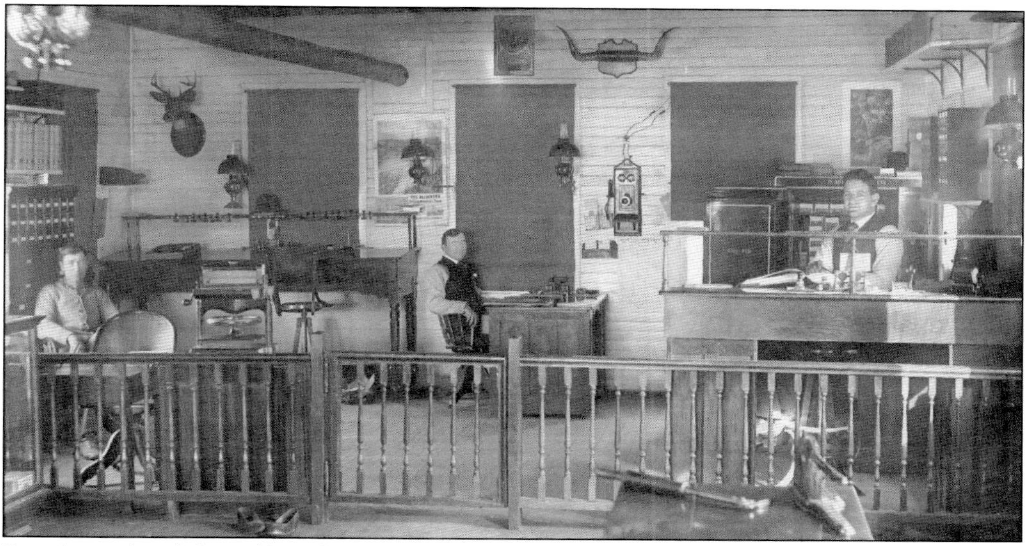

Rayo lamps lined the walls and a small printing press sat on the table inside the New York Central train station in Faust before electricity was installed. The man at the desk is most likely the telegraph man and the man at the window the ticket agent. (Goff Nelson Library Collection.)

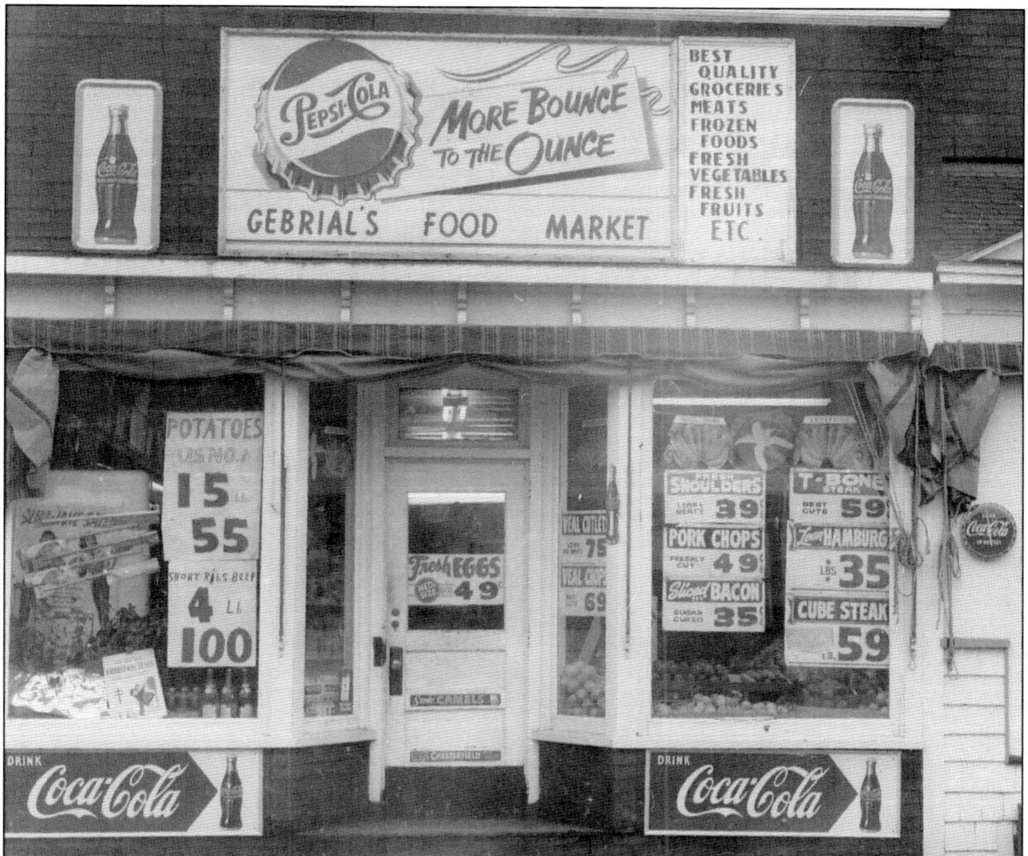

Gabriel's Food, located at 28 Main Street, was a typical corner grocery, of which there were so many in the community. (Camille and Ellen Maroon.)

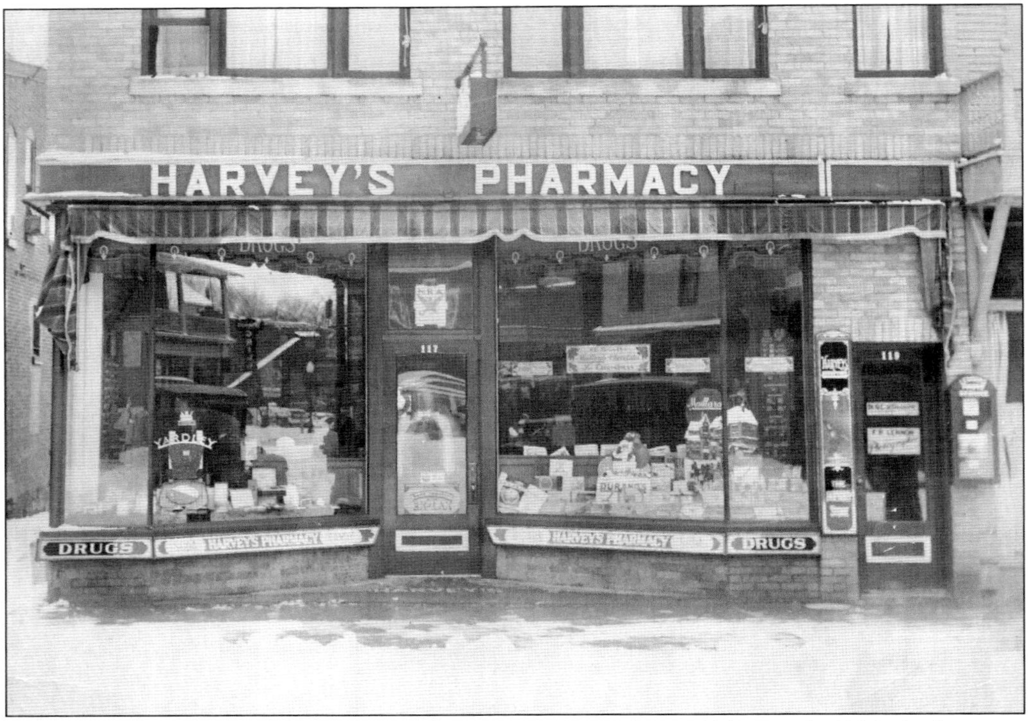

Harvey's Pharmacy was destroyed by a devastating winter fire on February 3, 1956. At the time, it was run by Reginald Hawkins, who purchased the pharmacy in the 1930s and continued to operate the business under that name until its destruction. Thereafter, he was the pharmacist with Mercy General Hospital until his retirement in 1965. (Goff Nelson Library Collection.)

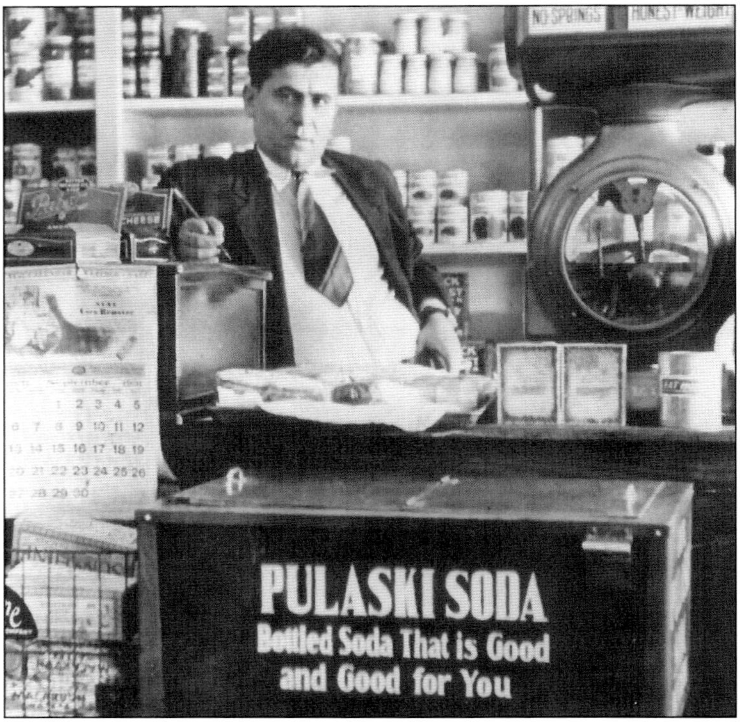

John "Monsour" Salamy works the register of his grocery store at the corner of Park Street and Boyer Avenue. (Camil and Ellen Maroon.)

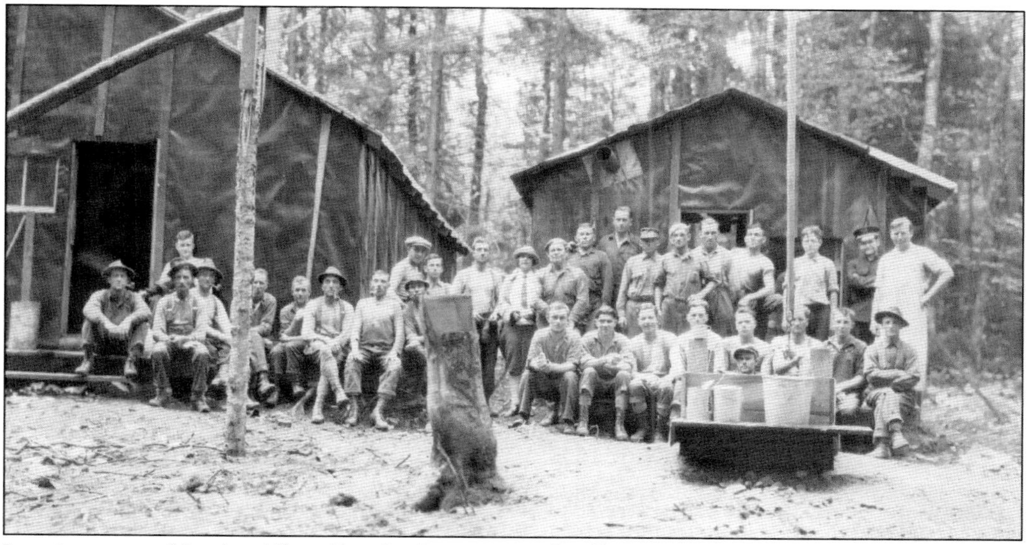

Logging camps like the Albert Brooks Camp existed well into the 1950s, looking much the same as they did in 1900. Tar paper and shingles replaced bark roofs and sidings, and a few camps still used horses even though tractors and skidders eventually replaced them. Still, horse teams found a home on a few of the select jobs because it was thought that they did much less damage to the wood lot during the logging operation. (Goff Nelson Library Collection.)

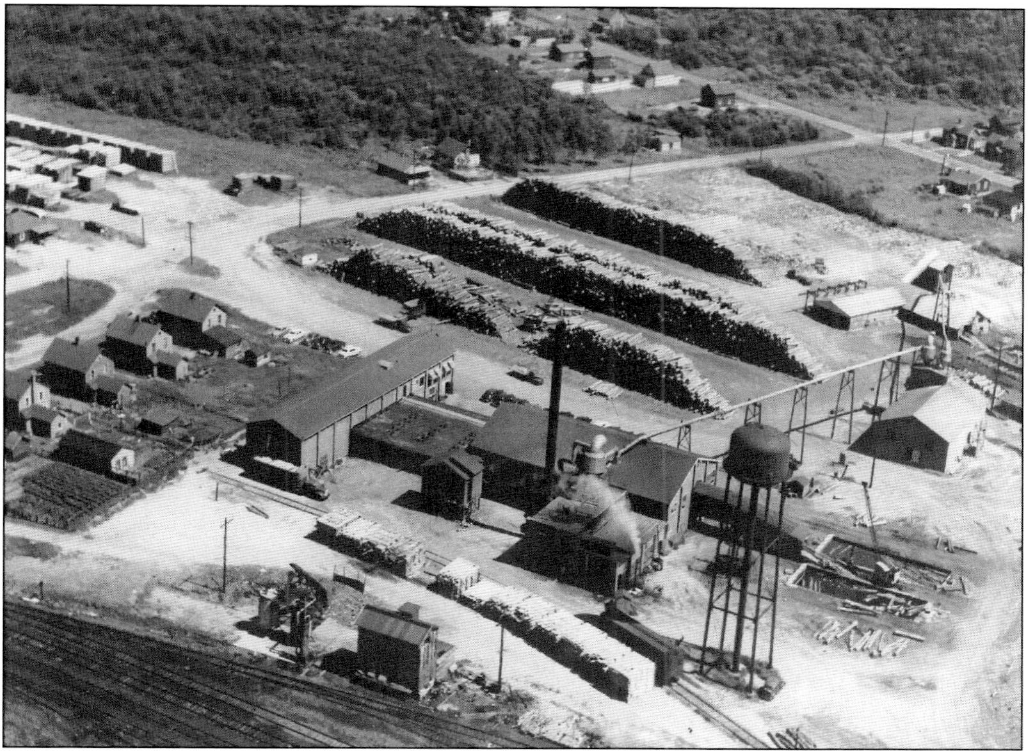

The United States Bobbin & Shuttle Company plant was a modern bobbin roughing plant erected in 1948 at a reported cost of $465,000. It was closed in 1963. Wooded bobbins, long used in shuttle looms, were soon replaced by plastics. The Draper Mill, which made the same product, closed its doors about 10 years later. (Author's collection.)

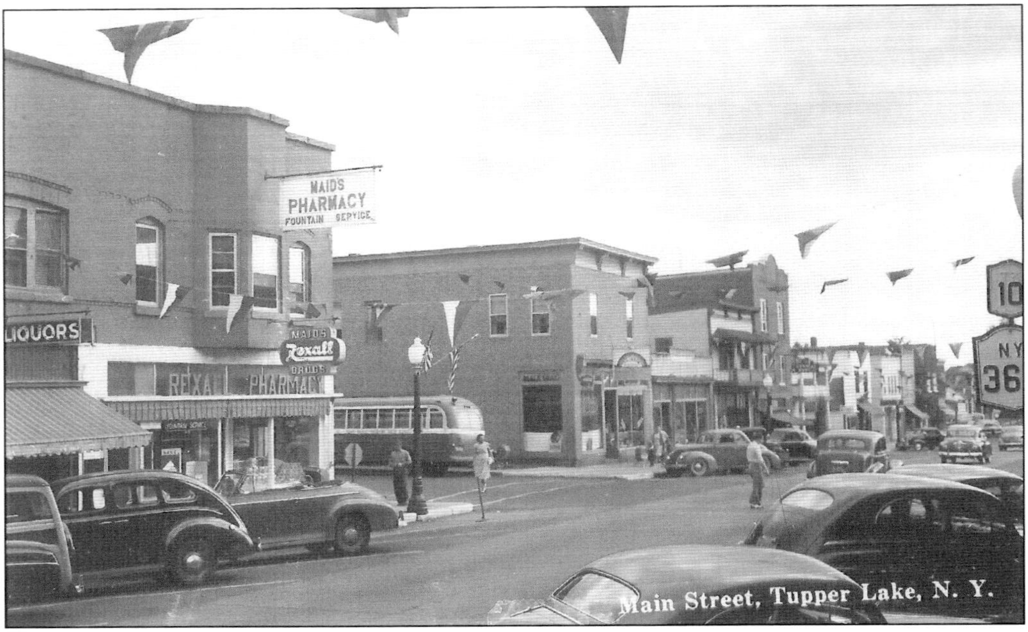

Park Street looks spiffy in this 1950s picture with diagonal parking, a paved street, and concrete sidewalks. Tupper Lake had come a long way from its pioneer days. (Author's collection.)

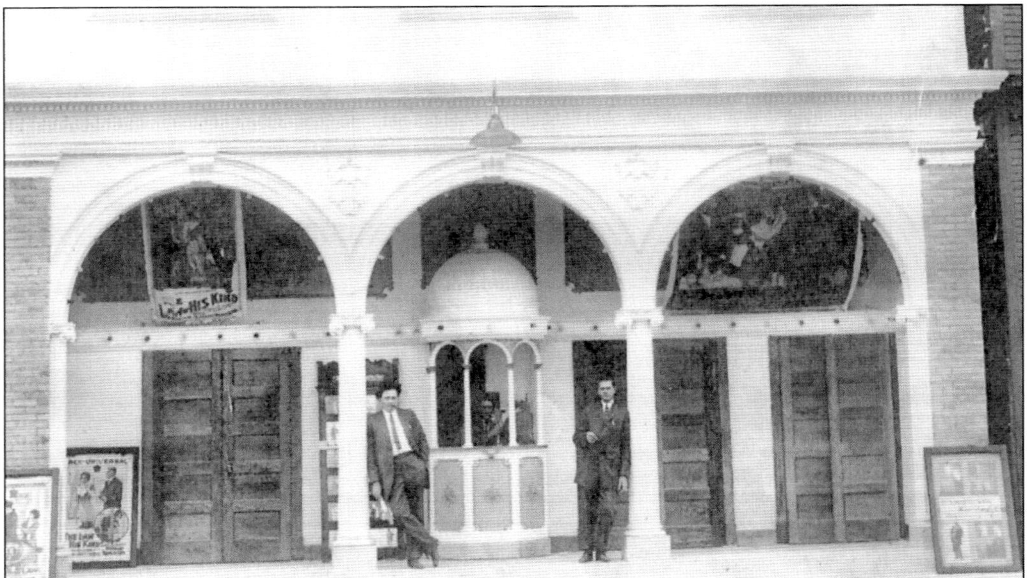

The Palace Theater opened in 1914 and has been Tupper Lake's main movie house ever since. On each side, substantial firewalls were constructed, which protected the structure from two major fires—one in 1957 and another in 1966, which left the adjoining buildings, for the full length of the block, ruined. (Goff Nelson Library Collection.)

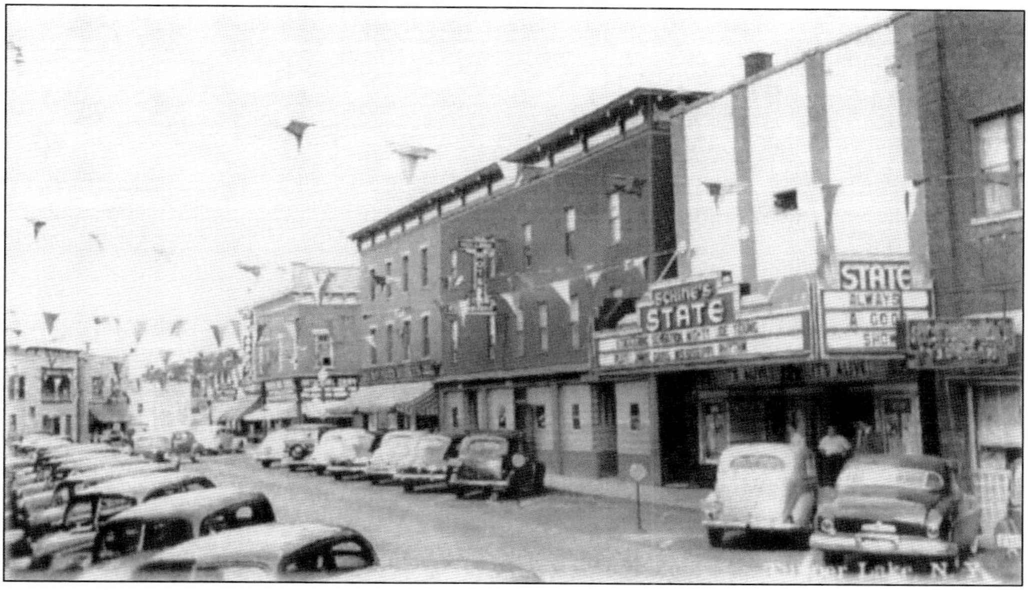

In 1935, the Schine theater chain took control of the old Palace and modernized it. They added sound, remodeled the facade, and renamed it the State Theater. It closed in 1975, but in 1982, a nonprofit group called Project Pride was organized with the goal of reopening the State, which was achieved two years later. (Author's collection.)

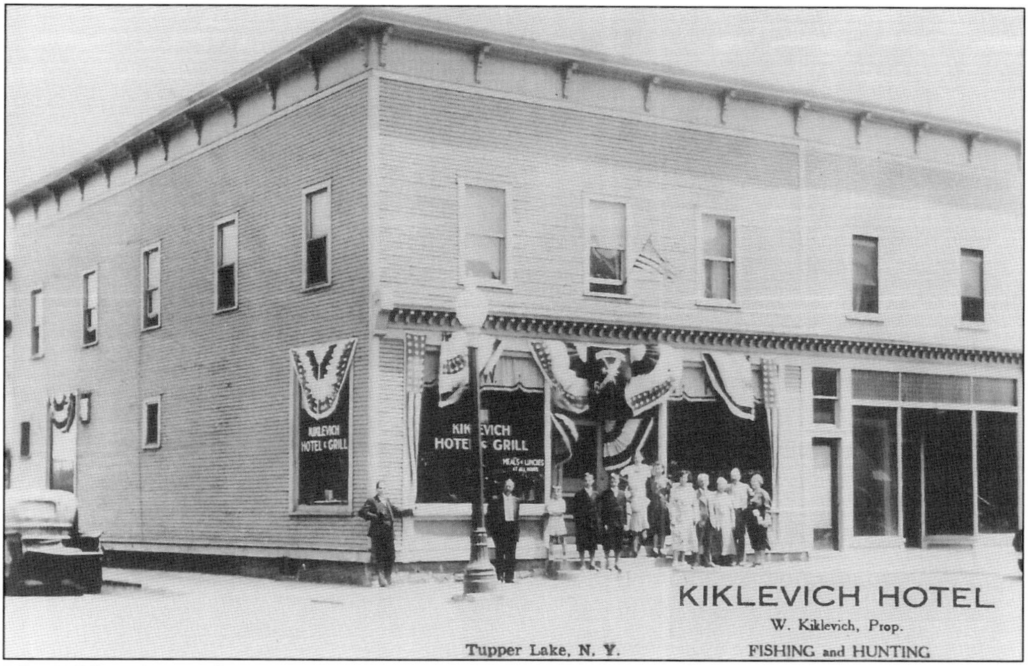

The Kiklevich Hotel at 38 Main Street was a popular eatery run by Walter Kiklevich and his wife, Veronica. He was born in Minsk, Russia, and came to America in 1907. He made his home in Tupper Lake for more than 45 years, operating the hotel until he retired in 1957. (Author's collection.)

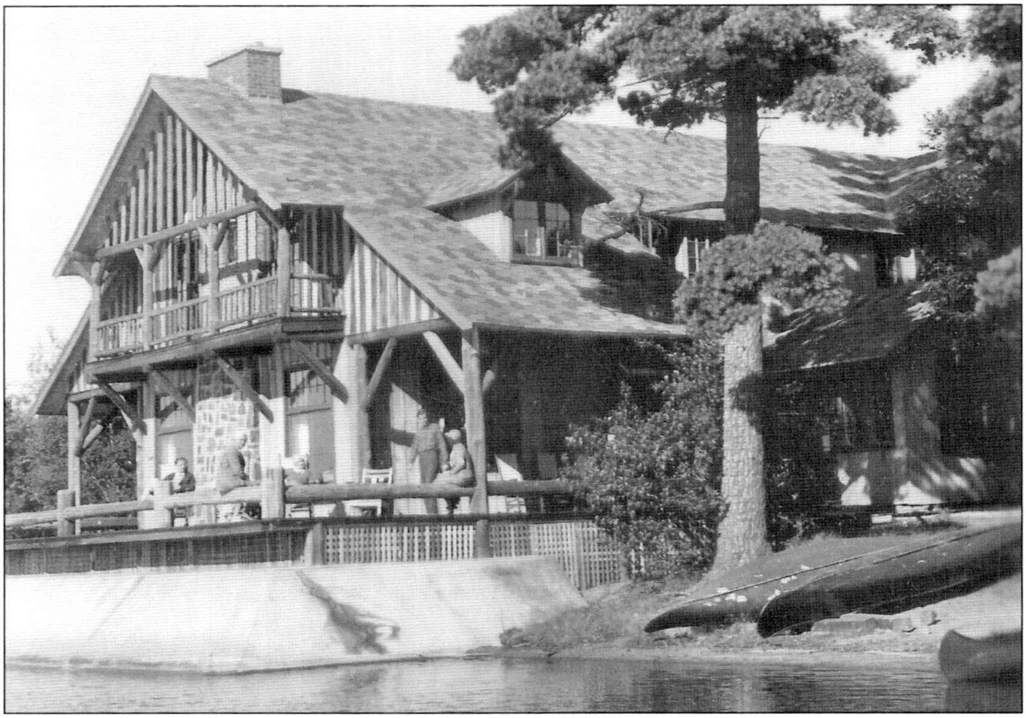

This is the clubhouse on nearby Big Wolf Lake. In 1912, a devastating fire consumed the forest surrounding the lake, so upsetting the owner, the druggist Mr. Haas, that he never returned, selling the property to Ferris Meigs, president of the Santa Clara Lumber Company, who created the Big Wolf Association and subdivided the lakefront property. (Author's collection.)

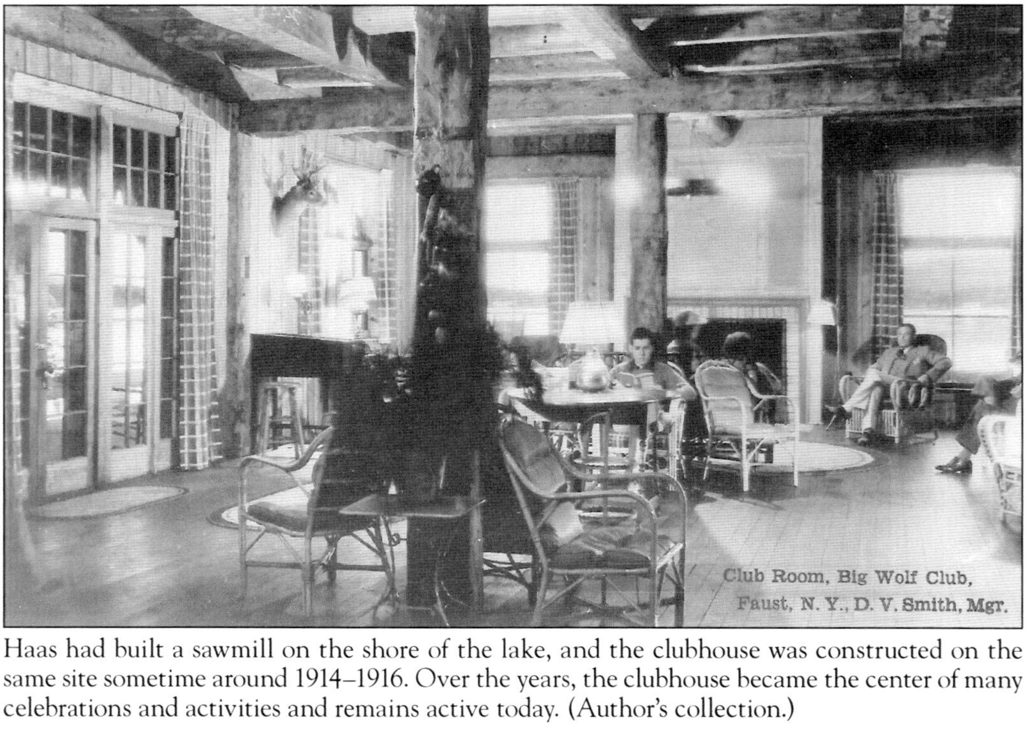

Haas had built a sawmill on the shore of the lake, and the clubhouse was constructed on the same site sometime around 1914–1916. Over the years, the clubhouse became the center of many celebrations and activities and remains active today. (Author's collection.)

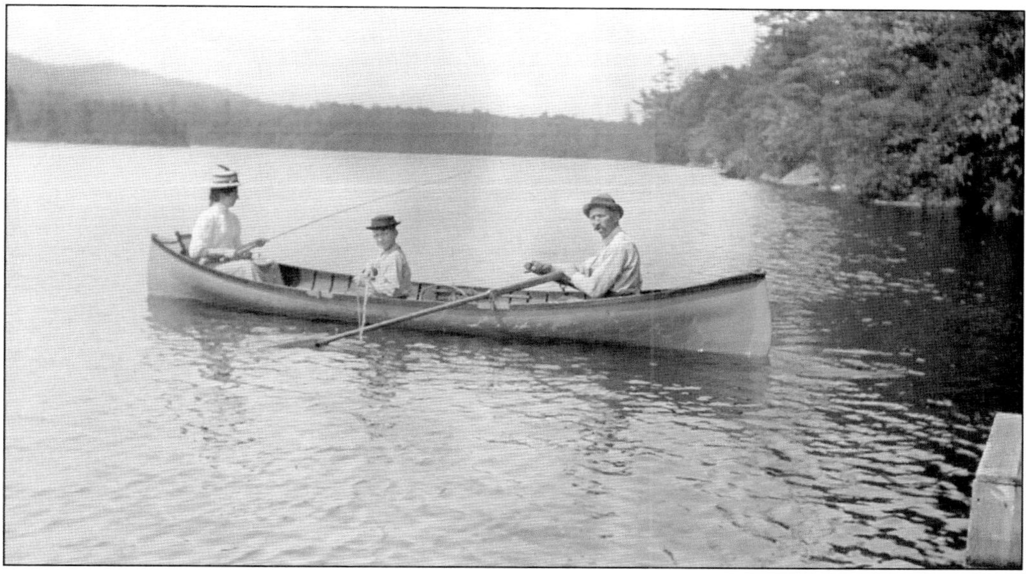

Fred Moody takes the family for an outing in his Adirondack guide boat. Fred was the son of Simeon Moody, the pioneer settler who first cleared the site for a farm on Stetson Road around 1857, later called the Pioneer Place Barry Farm. Fred Moody was the overseer of the Read Park and stables complex. (Author's collection.)

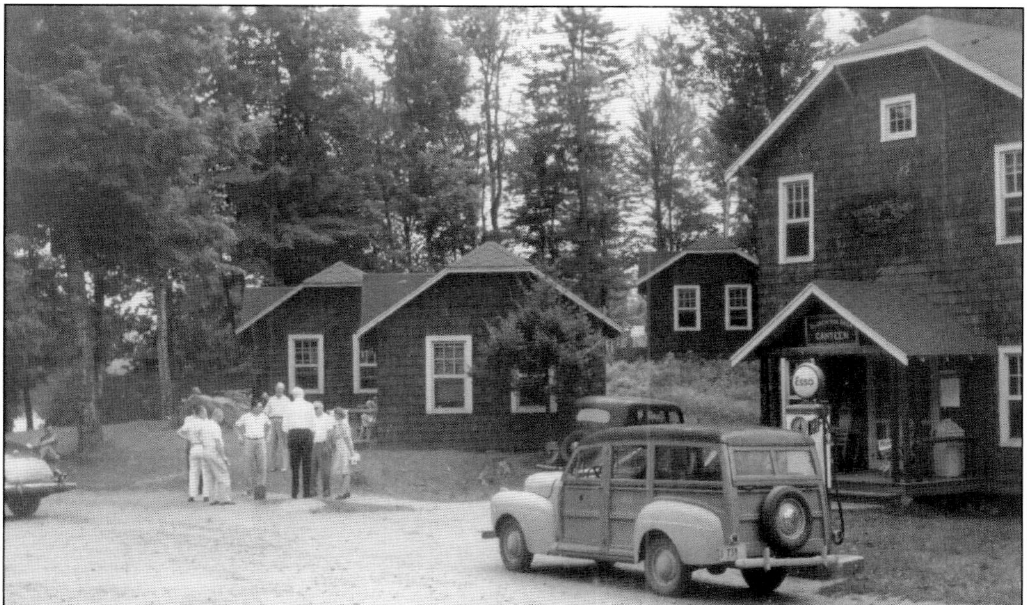

For more than 60 years, the Legion Camp provided economic prosperity for Tupper Lakers and recuperation for veterans. In the late 1970s, the property, including the cottages and their antique furnishings, went on the auction block. (Author's collection.)

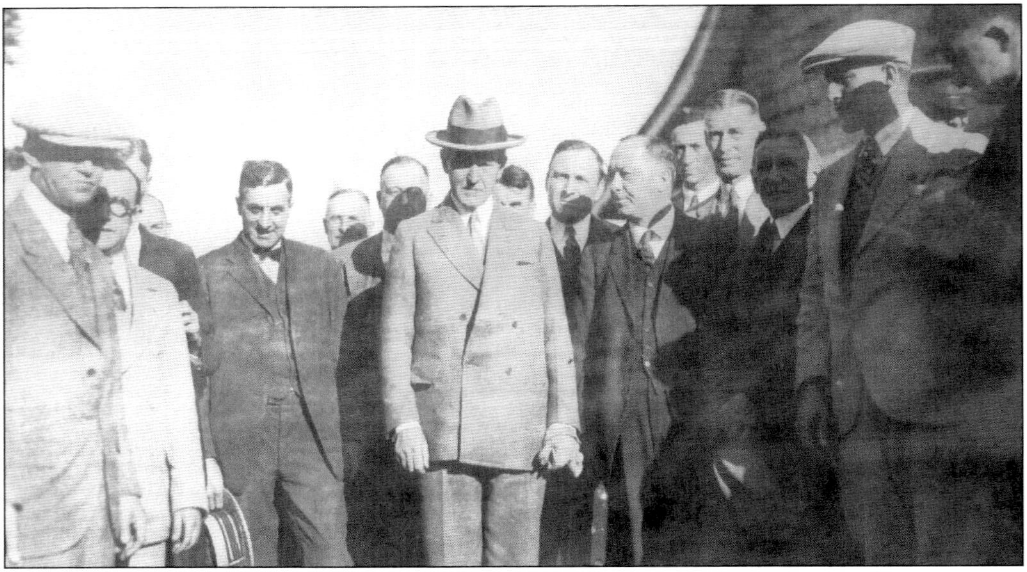

Pres. Calvin Coolidge, who was vacationing at White Pine Camp, accepted the invitation from the American Legion to visit the Legion Mountain Camp on Big Tupper. He arrived about 3:00 p.m. in a closed limousine, with a state police motorcycle escort and secret servicemen riding ahead and behind him. The cortege moved through Tupper's streets, with the whole town out to catch a glimpse of the president. (Goff Nelson Library Collection.)

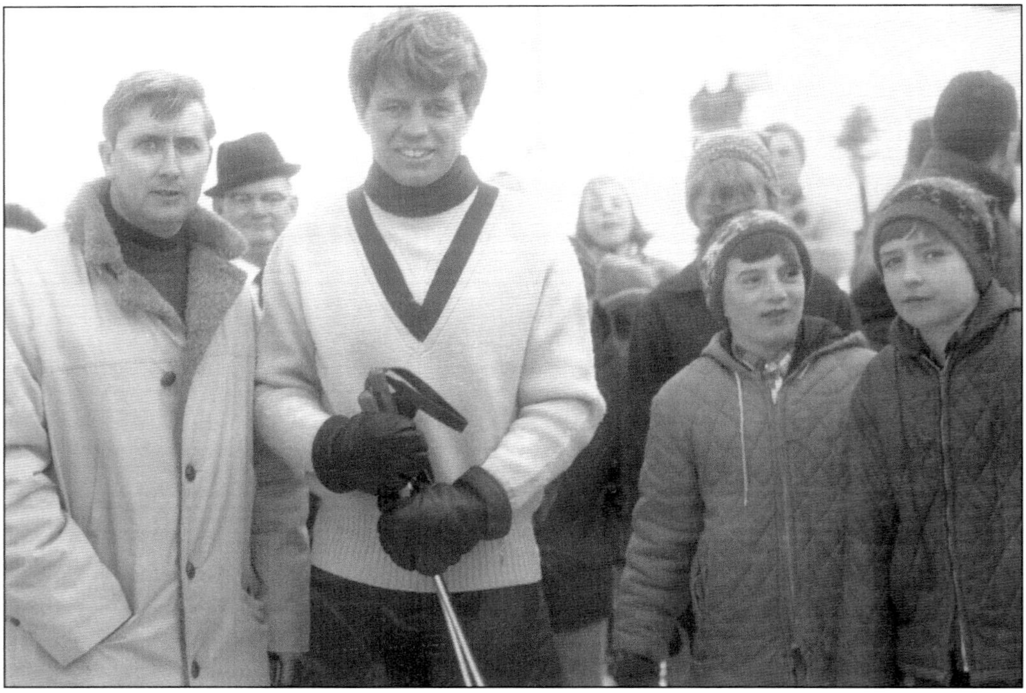

Tupper Lake figured prominently in the news during the losing battle to save Sunmount Veterans Hospital, when several nationally known figures came to town. Sen. Robert Kennedy arrived, accompanied by two top staffers from the *New York Daily News*, Philip Santora, a Pulitzer prize-winning journalist, and photographer John Duprey, for an inspection tour of the hospital. He also took some time for skiing and a photograph shoot at Big Tupper. (Goff Nelson Library Collection.)

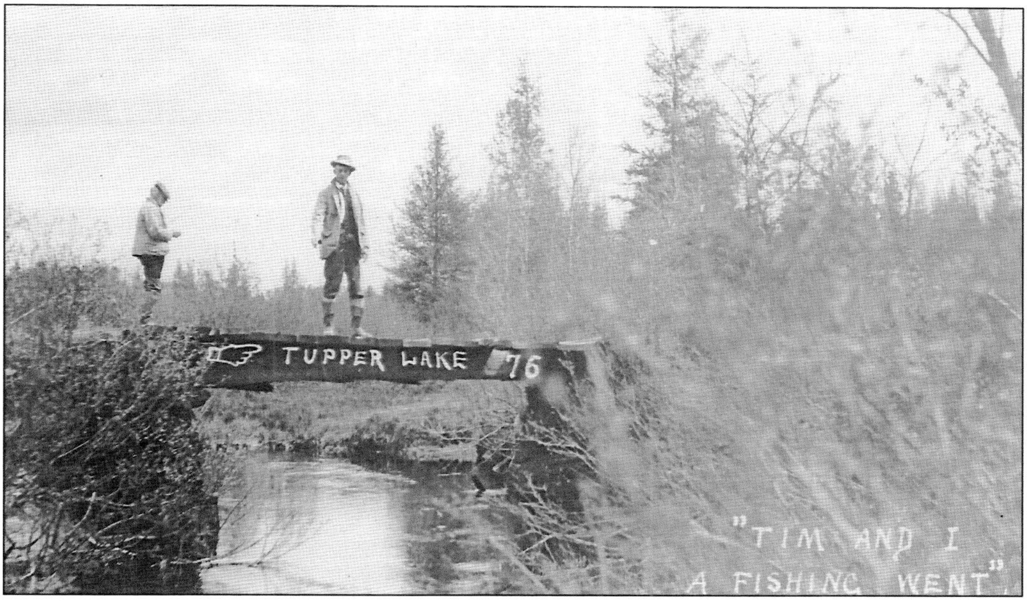

Local fishing has always been a draw for tourism and a relaxing repast for locals. Many early postcards were produced promoting area fishing. (Author's collection.)

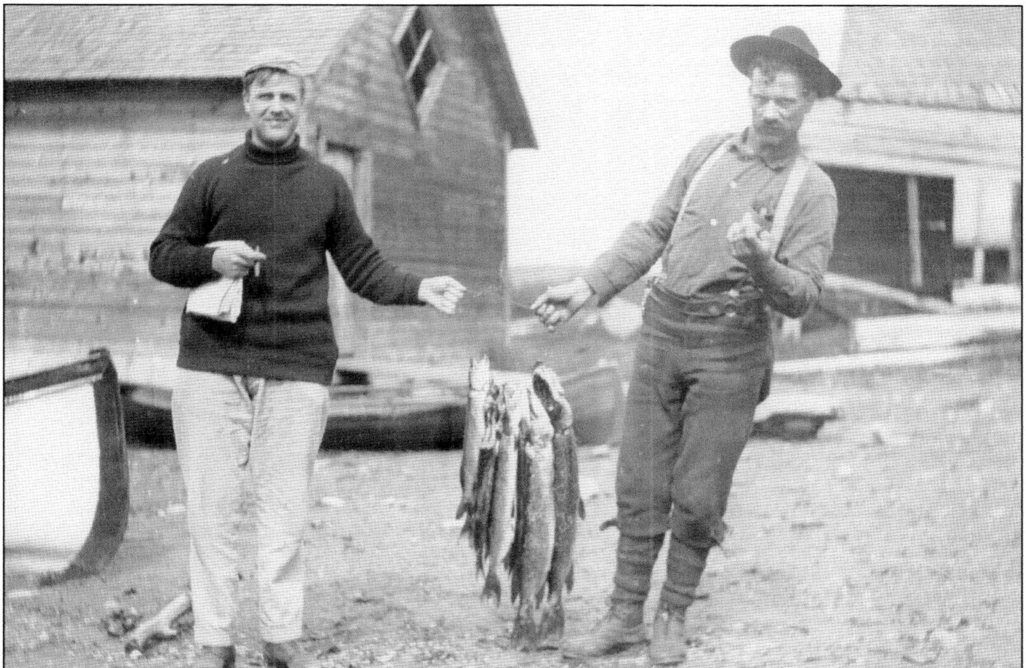
Some hefty northern pike was produced from Raquette Pond, a resource that provided tasty fare for those willing to laze away the day on the lake. (Goff Nelson Library Collection.)

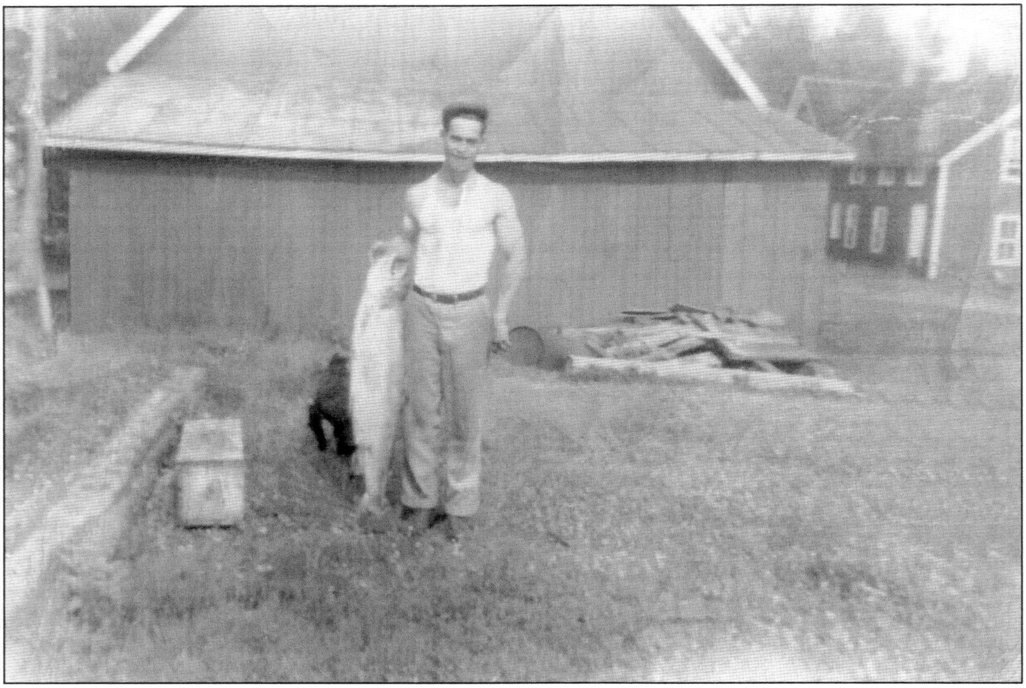

Local fisherman Morris Sequin poses with a lake trout that was supposedly caught in Gull Pond. The fish was never weighed and the true location of the catch may never be known because in Tupper Lake one never really divulges their special fishing spot. (Sally Kopp.)

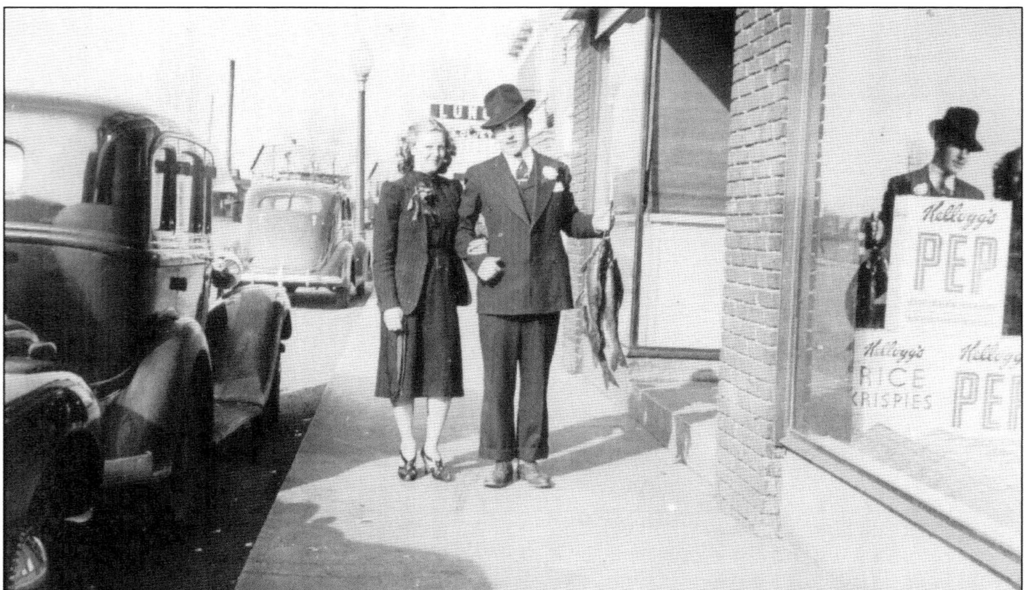

Genevieve and Wallace Burnett pose proudly in downtown Faust, holding what appears to be a fine catch of walleye. (Author's collection.)

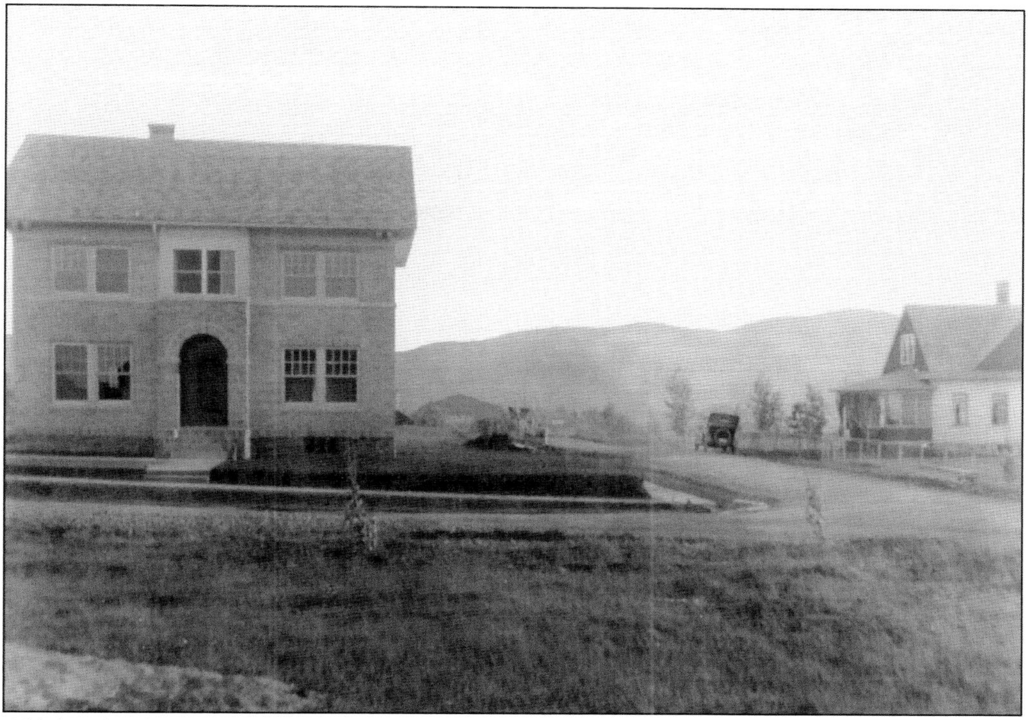

Old farmland was sold off for building lots as workers began to settle the village. This house, which stands today on the corner of Freeman and Lindsey Streets, had a spectacular view when it was first built. Today, the roads are lined with homes and landscaped trees, blocking the view. (Author's collection.)

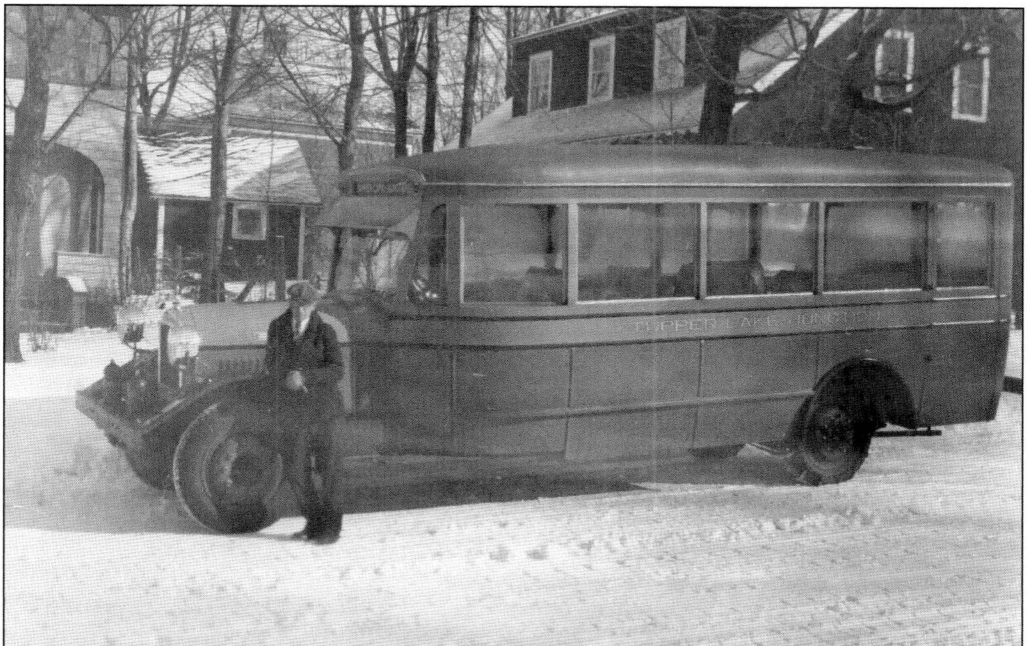

The Tupper Lake Junction school bus was used for many years to carry students back and forth from Faust to the uptown schools. (Author's collection.)

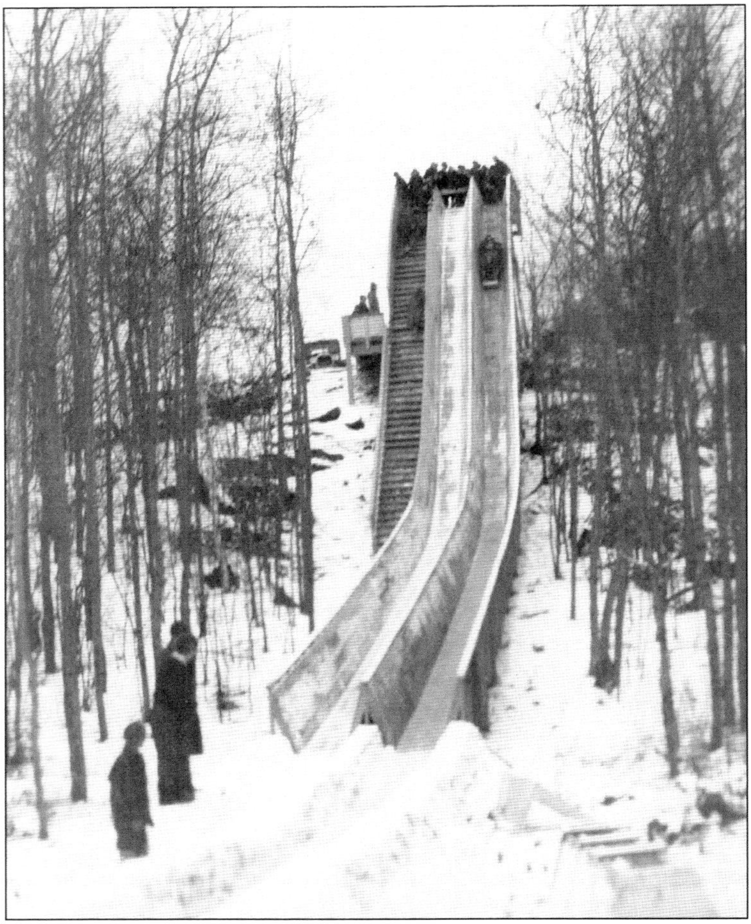

The toboggan slide built at the cliff edge of the Rock Ridge quarry was a popular place for village children during the winter months. The slide did not end until it was well into frozen Moody Marsh. (Goff Nelson Library Collection.)

Although the winters were long and cold, Tupper Lakers never passed up an opportunity to enjoy the great outdoors. Jock the Barber (with the mustache) plays cards with his friends on Floodwood Pond. (Author's collection.)

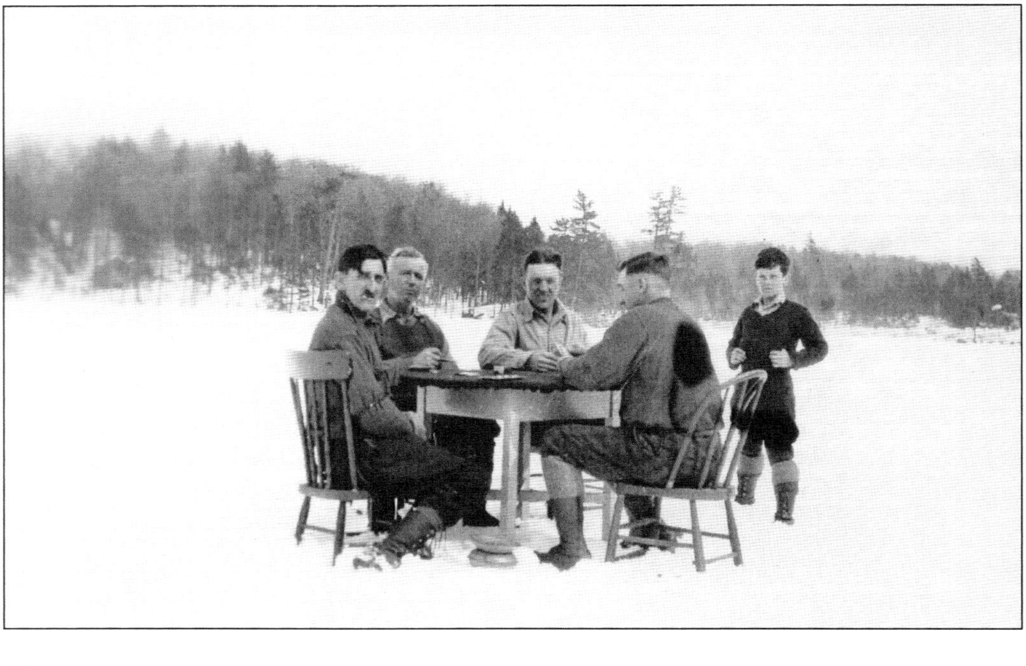

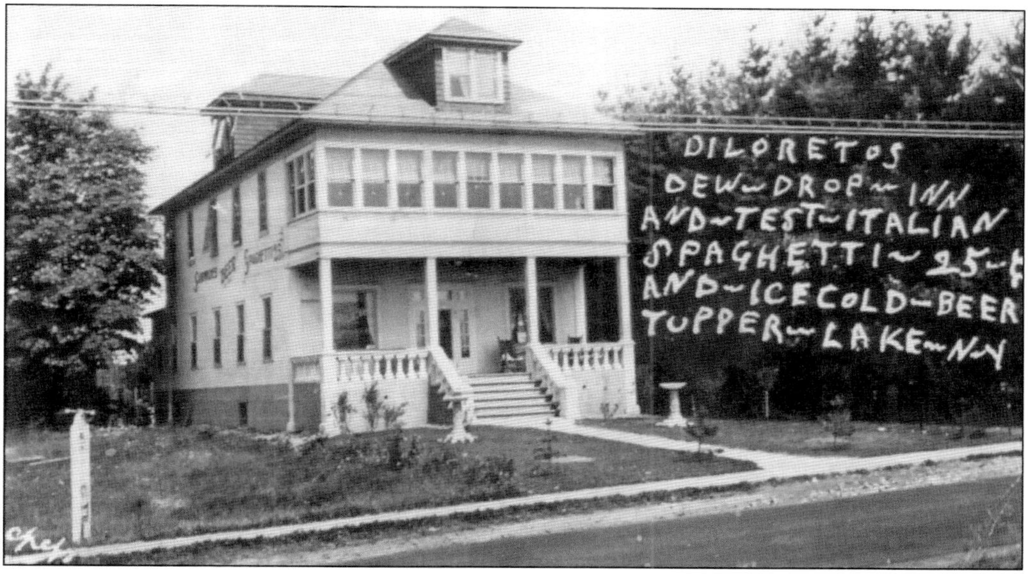

Dominic DiLoreto, a mason by trade, erected the Hotel DiLoreto at 349 Park Street in 1925. The building now houses Larkin Apartments. (Author's collection.)

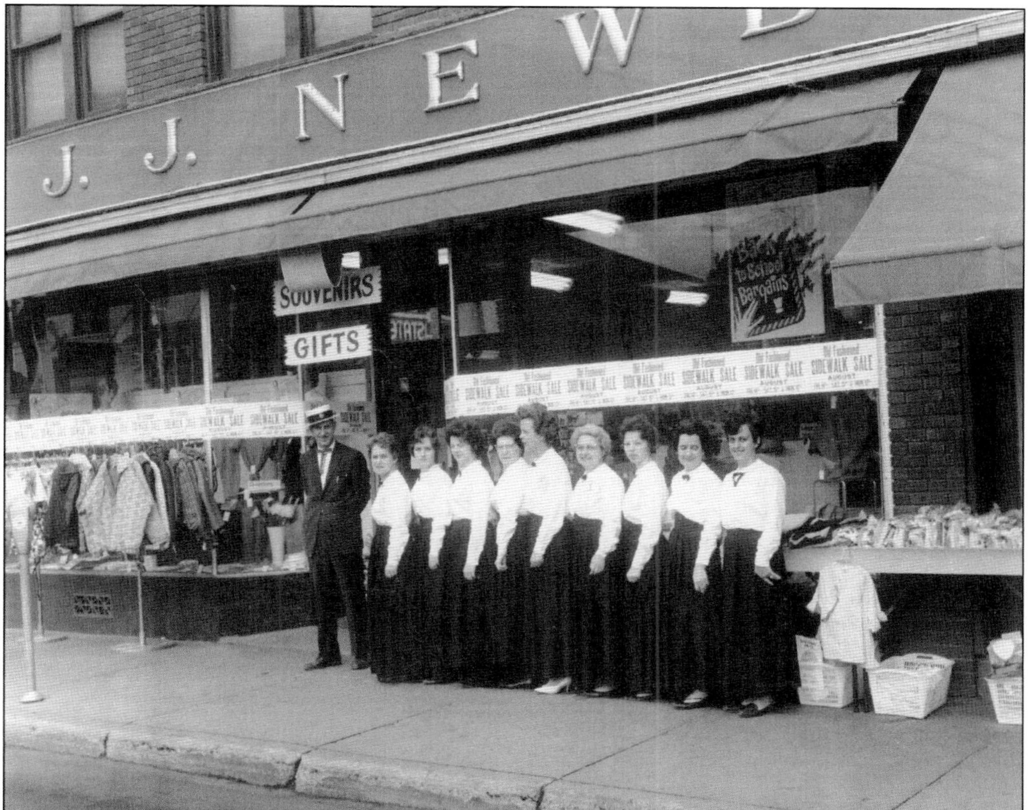

Ambrose Marquise, manager of the local J.C. Penney store, poses with his troupe of girls. J.C. Penney stores were the dollar stores of that time and residents rued the day that the store closed its doors. (Goff Nelson Library Collection.)

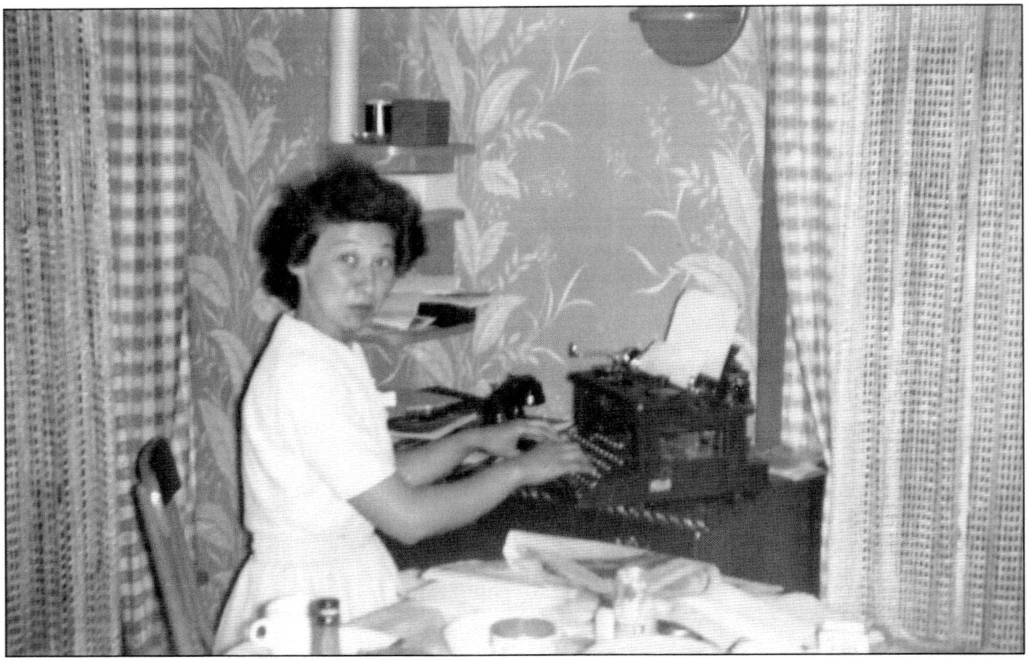

Kathleen Bigalow, star reporter and photographer for the *Tupper Lake Free Press*, poses at the typewriter early in her career. From the 1950s to 2000, her photographs documented the modern era in Tupper Lake. After she turned 80, she started a retail store called the Sorting Gap, reminiscent of Tupper Lake's logging heritage. (Author's collection.)

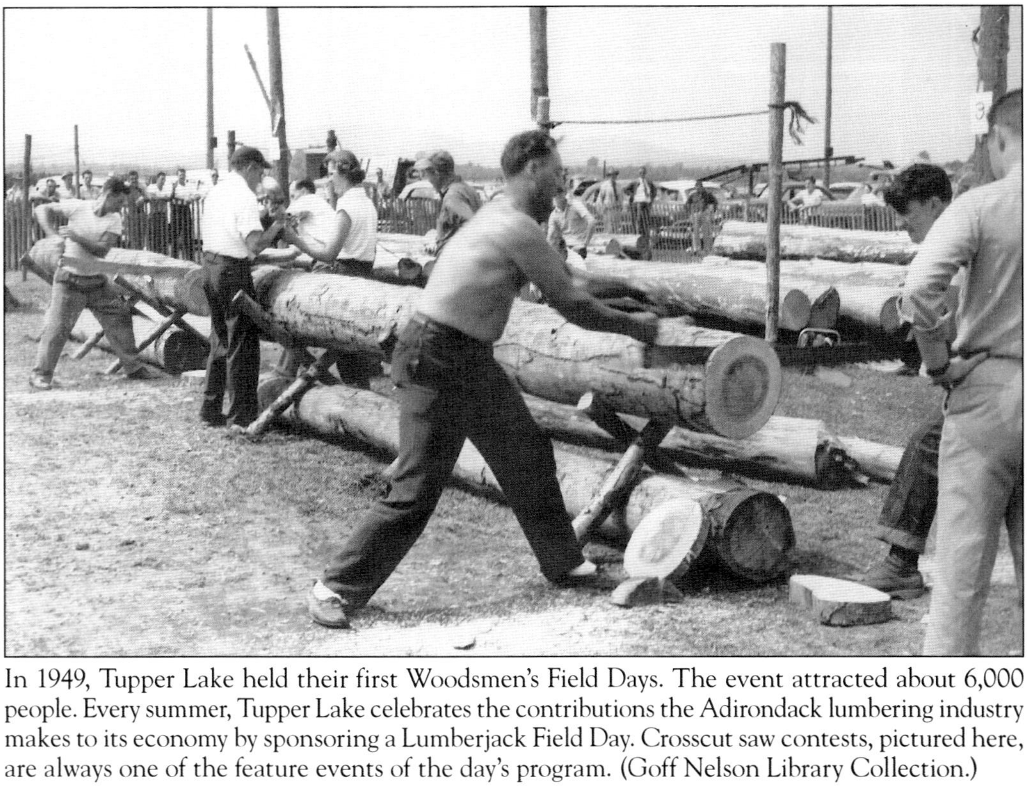

In 1949, Tupper Lake held their first Woodsmen's Field Days. The event attracted about 6,000 people. Every summer, Tupper Lake celebrates the contributions the Adirondack lumbering industry makes to its economy by sponsoring a Lumberjack Field Day. Crosscut saw contests, pictured here, are always one of the feature events of the day's program. (Goff Nelson Library Collection.)

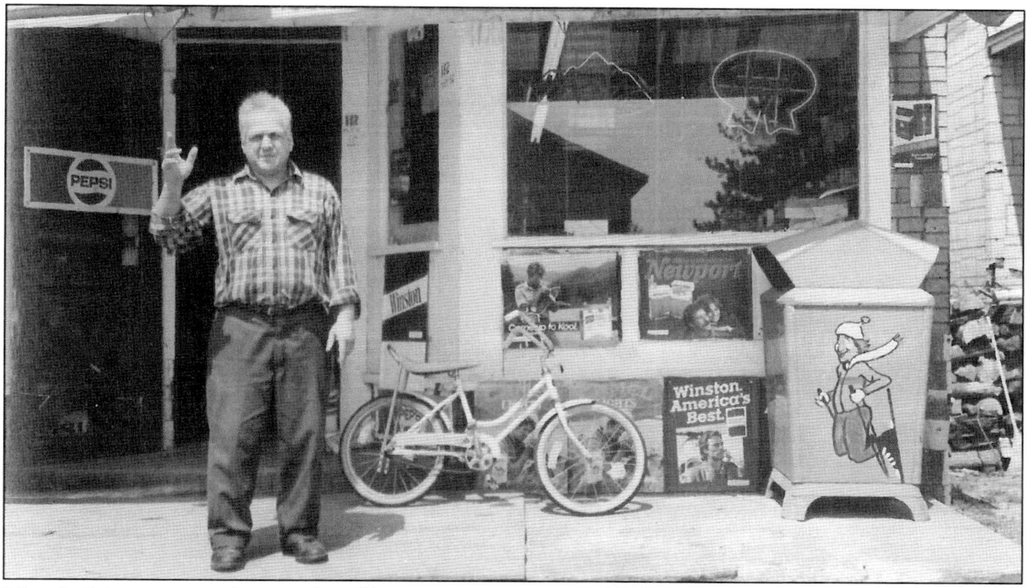

Mandy Maroun stands outside of his grocery store, established in Tupper Lake's early years by his father, Charlie (Said) Maroun, on the corner of Main and Prospect Streets opposite the Holy Name Church. (Goff Nelson Library Collection.)

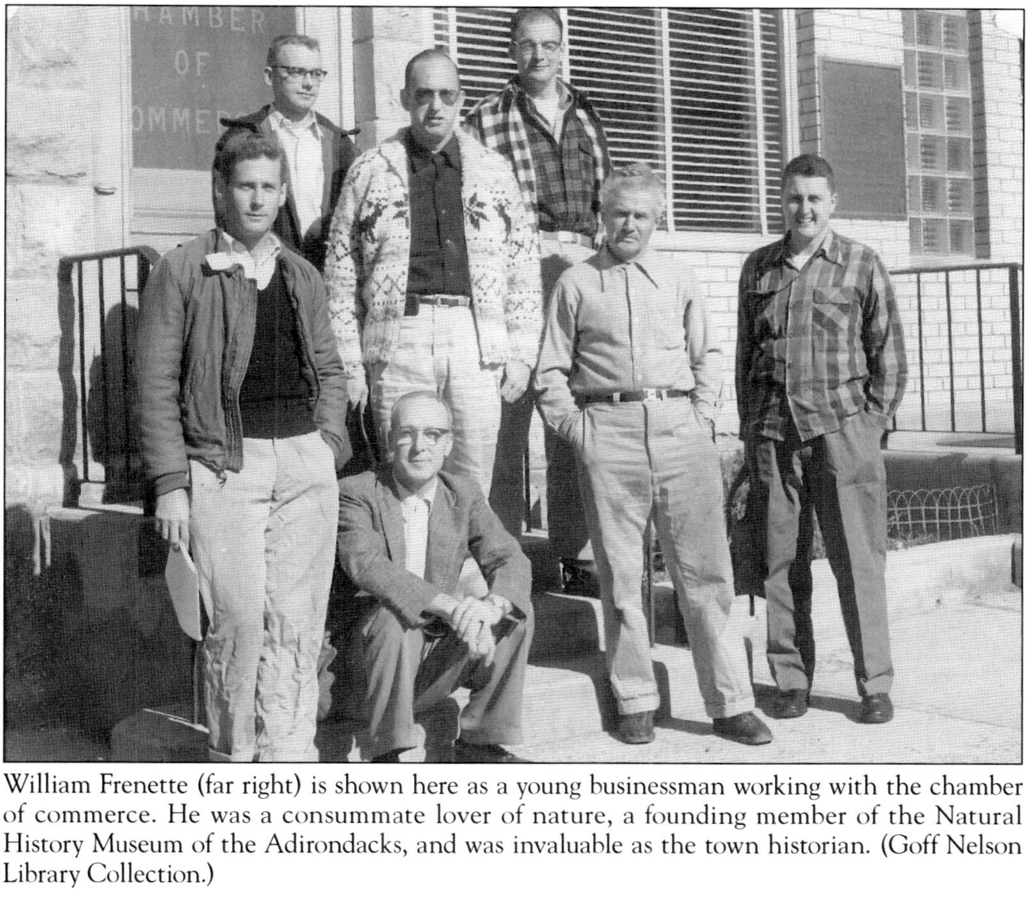

William Frenette (far right) is shown here as a young businessman working with the chamber of commerce. He was a consummate lover of nature, a founding member of the Natural History Museum of the Adirondacks, and was invaluable as the town historian. (Goff Nelson Library Collection.)

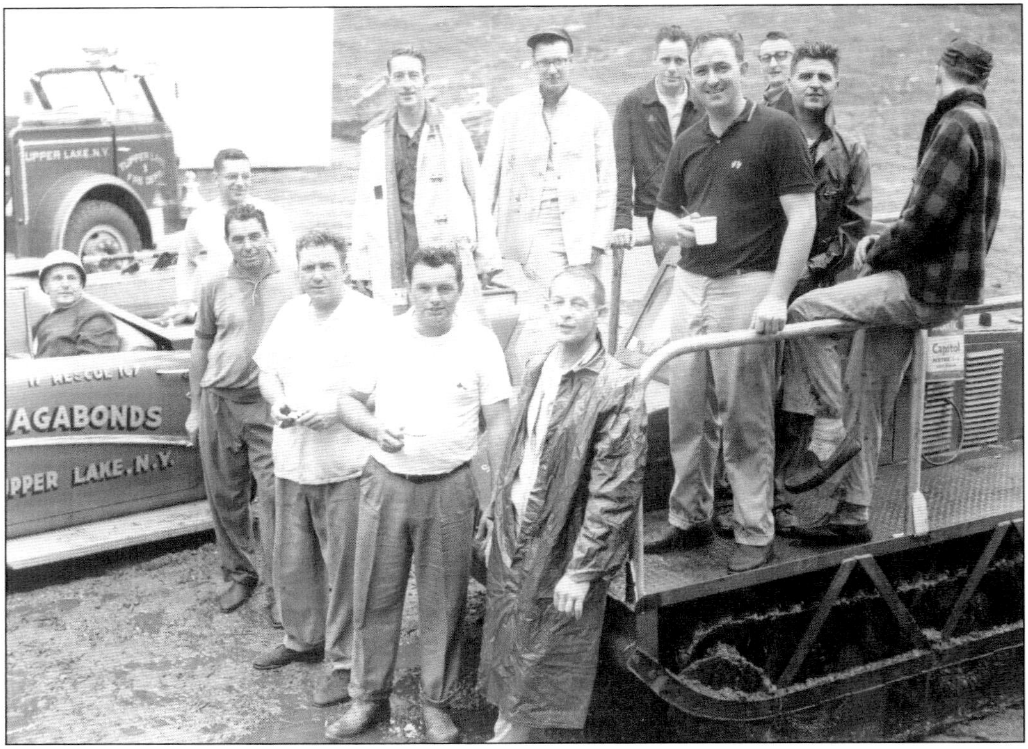

The Tupper Lake Fire Department regularly assists with people stuck on chairlifts at Big Tupper. Members include Mike Sabin (in race car) and, from left to right, (standing in foreground) Dick Sabin, Raymond Fuller, Lawrence Fuller, Dick Savard, and Jim Brown; (on tractor) Roy Brown, "Rinky" Vaillancourt, Joe Desbrais, Frank McCauley, Jim Frenette, Don Sabin, and unidentified. (Goff Nelson Library Collection.)

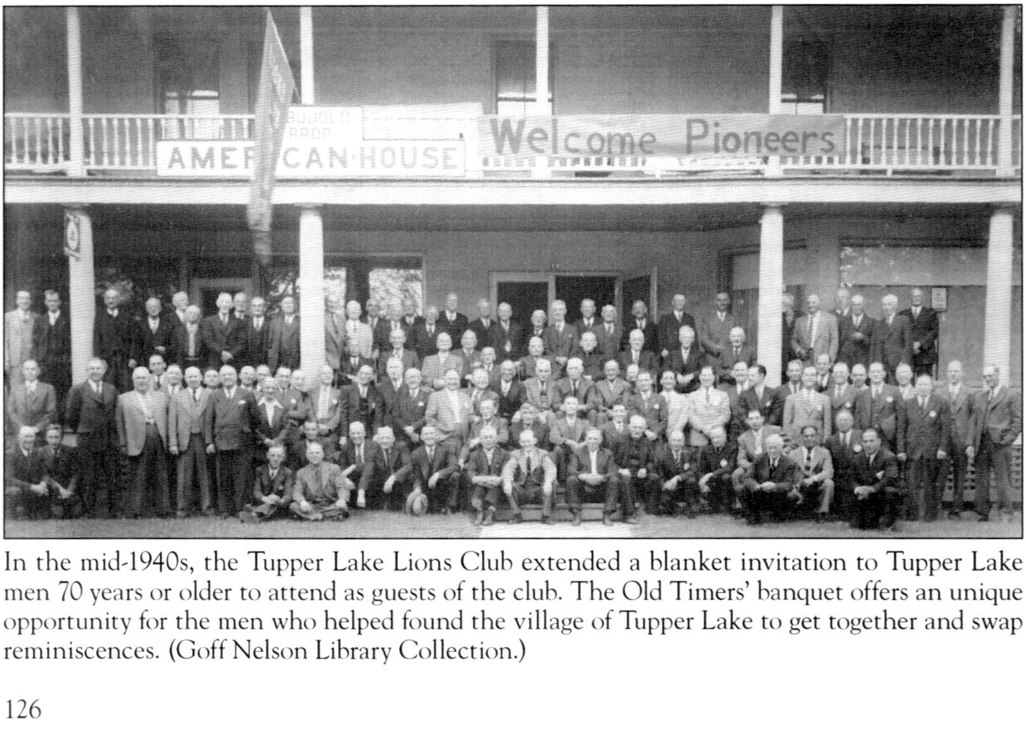

In the mid-1940s, the Tupper Lake Lions Club extended a blanket invitation to Tupper Lake men 70 years or older to attend as guests of the club. The Old Timers' banquet offers an unique opportunity for the men who helped found the village of Tupper Lake to get together and swap reminiscences. (Goff Nelson Library Collection.)

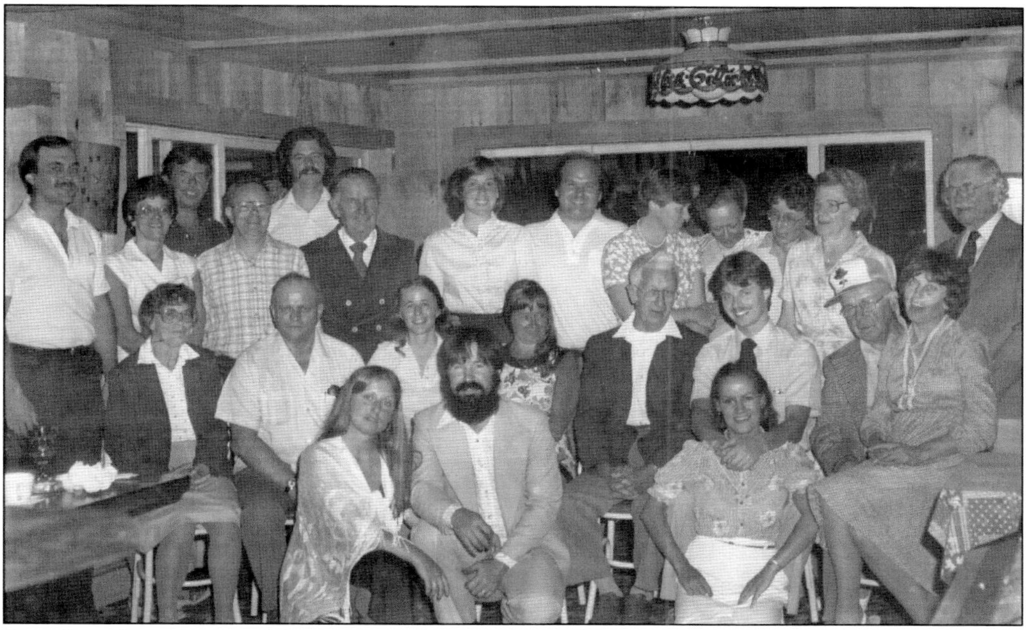

Friends and employees of the *Tupper Lake Free Press* celebrate Louis Simmons's 50th anniversary as editor. Simmons is in the second row, fifth from the left. On his left is the present editor, Dan McClelland. (Goff Nelson Library Collection.)

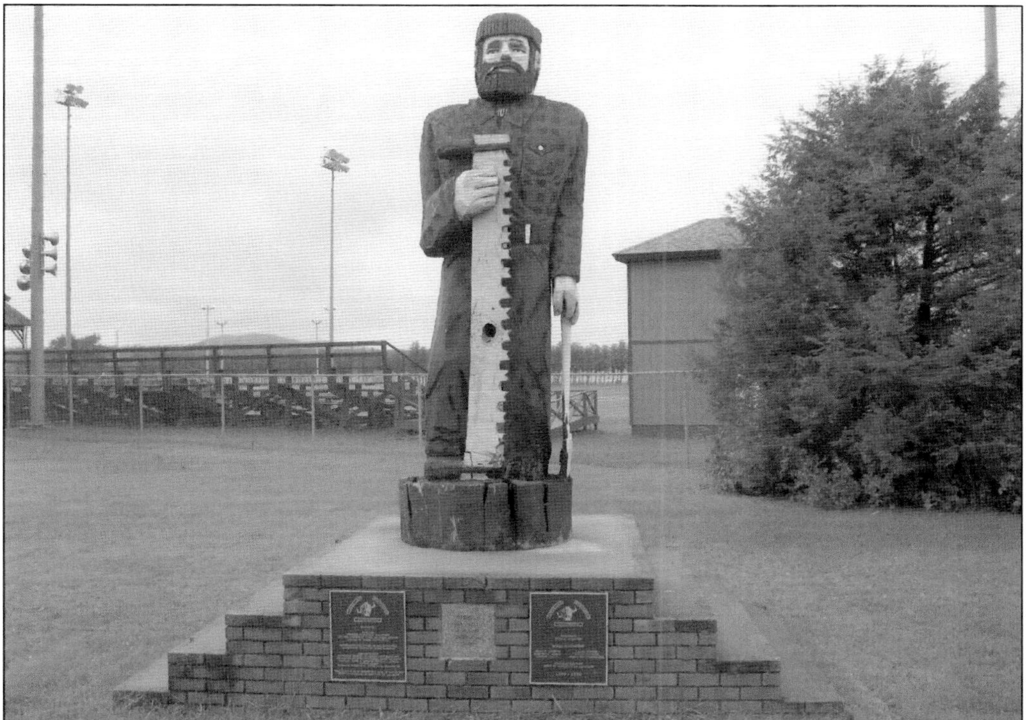

This chainsaw carving of a lumberjack stands at the Tupper Lake municipal park in proud memory of the village's past. The municipal park is located on the site of the original mill built by John Hurd, whose vision and foresight shaped Tupper Lake. (Author's collection.)